Revised
Exploring English 7

Dr K. Padmini Shankar

The publishers would like to thank the following for their suggestions and inputs:

English Department
Nowgong Mission High School
Nagaon, Assam

Sister (Dr) Molly Kaniampadickal
St Mary's Higher Secondary School
Guwahati, Assam

English Department
Little Flower Higher Secondary School
Dibrugarh, Assam

English Department
St Joseph's Convent Higher Secondary School
Tezpur, Assam

Balwinder Deol
Head of the Department, English
Mount St Mary's School, New Delhi

Portia Benazir
Head of the Department, English
Howard Public School, Hyderabad

Collins

Revised
Exploring English 7

Dr K. Padmini Shankar

Published by Collins India
A division of HarperCollins*Publishers* India Private Limited
HarperCollins *Publishers*
A-75, Sector 57, Noida, Uttar Pradesh 201301, India
1 London Bridge Street, London, SE1 9GF, United Kingdom
2 Bloor Street East, Toronto, Ontario M4W 1A8, Canada
Lvl 13, 201 Elizabeth Street (PO Box A565, NSW, 1235),
Sydney NSW 2000, Australia
195 Broadway, New York, NY 10007, USA

Browse the complete Collins catalogue at
www.collins.in

First edition 2015
Latest revised edition 2018

Reprint: 10 9

ISBN: 978-93-5277-140-0

Typesetting and page layout by Q2A Media Services Private Limited, Recto Graphics

Cover layout by Rahul Dhiman

Printed and bound in India by Thomson Press India Ltd

ACKNOWLEDGEMENTS

The authors and publishers wish to thank and acknowledge the following for granting us permission to use copyright material:

Sachin Leaves India in Tears by permission of The Times of India Group © BCCL. All rights reserved *The Festival of Eid* abridged and adapted from Khushwant Singh's translation of Munshi Premchand's *Eidgah;* IANS for *Music Maestro A. R. Rahman,* The Jewish Chronicle Online for *Palestinian and Israeli Children are Batting for Peace*; Ann Jungman for *Matti's Miracle* from *Collins Big Cat: Matti's Miracle* (HarperCollins Publishers); Subhadra Sengupta for *The Pataliputra* Mystery, Valmik Thapar for *Kaziranga, Grassland of the Giants,* Ruskin Bond for *Harold: Our Hornbill* from *An Island of Trees: Nature Stories and Poems*; *The Louse and the Mosquito* by Vikram Seth, copyright © Vikram Seth, 1990; *Professor Shonku and the Spook* by Satyajit Ray from the original *Professor Shonku o Bhoot*.

The publishers have applied for permission for the following:

Floating school in Bangladesh from *Bangladesh: Innovative solutions to improve education for the disadvantaged* by Manos Antoninis from World Education Blog (https://gemreportunesco.wordpress.com/2014/04/08/bangladesh-innovative-solutions-to-improve-education-for-the-disadvantaged/); *Cardboard Bookbags Unfold Into Desks For Schoolchildren* by Leah Gonzalez (from http://www.psfk.com/2014/05/cardboard-backpack-desk.html); *E-learning* from the War Child website (http://www.warchildholland.org/project/e-learning)

Acknowledgements for these will be made in the future editions of the book.

Every effort has been made to trace copyright holders and to obtain their permission for the use of copyright material. The authors and publishers will gladly receive any information enabling them to rectify any error or omission in subsequent editions.

Illustrations

Unit 3: *Matti's Miracle,* Michael Foreman and Priyankar Gupta. All other illustrations Q2A Media Services Private Limited, Danish Zaidi.

Photographs

p12: Associated Sports Photography/Alamy; p13: © POOL/Reuters/Corbis, Michael Steele; p15: MANAN VATSYAYANA; p17: Harjeet Singh Narang; p23: fcafotodigital; p32: hpkalyani; p34,35,36: s_bukley/Shutterstock.com; p58: mooinblack/Shutterstock.com; p59: Ryan Rodrick Beiler/Shutterstock.com; p73: maxicam; p80: Shutterstock.com: Paskee, Dona_Bozzi, Sadik Gulec, Sam DCruz; p84: SAJJAD HUSSAIN, s_bukley/Shutterstock.com, Everett Collection/Shutterstock.com, Reuters/CORBIS, © Indiapicture/Alamy; p85: Featureflash/Shutterstock.com; p90: Bettmann/CORBIS, Eye Ubiquitous/Alamy, Tim Graham/Alamy; p99: Hulton-Deutsch Collection/CORBIS, Karan Kapoor/CORBIS, Neveshkin Nikolay/Shutterstock.com, imagedb.com/Shutterstock.com; p107: ilbusca, lenny777, ksana-gribakina, elena_bulgakova; p108: neelsky/Shutterstock.com; p109: David Evison/Shutterstock.com; p144: Smokhov; p151: sorbetto

KEY TO ICONS

The **book** icon indicates the beginning of each reading passage.

The **audio** icon indicates a listening activity.

VBQ The **VBQ** tab indicates value-based questions.

PREFACE

Revised Exploring English is a multi-skill course in English, designed for children and young people growing up in a world of global communications. It aims to develop their cognitive abilities, train them to think critically and communicate effectively in a wide variety of contexts. It adheres to the latest National Curriculum Framework. The series has been revised and updated based on detailed user feedback.

Built around salient themes, the units in the book comprise carefully selected reading texts authored by Indian and global writers. They cater to a variety of student interests and needs, motivate engagement and promote critical thinking. Through the reading of the texts, learners are expected to develop as thinking individuals who are keenly aware of the world around them – linguistically competent, cognitively able, and morally responsible.

The eight-level series includes coursebooks, workbooks and literature readers for levels 3 to 8. Each level is also accompanied by a comprehensive Teacher's Resource Book and digital resources for the teacher in the form of an interactive DVD.

Coursebooks 6–8

Each unit in Books 6–8 includes a non-fiction prose passage, a fictional text and a poem. A unit comprises the following components:

- Warm-up: includes tasks which stimulate the learner's interest in the theme of the unit.
- Reading 1: a factual piece that introduces the topic and motivates students to explore further. The information-rich texts cover a variety of contemporary writing genres, including reviews, authentic reports, journalistic articles, autobiographical pieces and travelogues. The contextual glossary helps learners with difficult or literary words.
- Comprehension 1: comprises factual questions that encourage close reading as well as scanning for specific details, and ensure a thorough understanding of the information in the text.
- Comprehension 2: comprises inferential, evaluative and value-based questions that develop higher order thinking skills by encouraging learners to analyse the facts of the story and to draw parallels between events in the text and their own experiences.
- Vocabulary check: includes activities which ensure that learners understand key words in the text.
- Language skills: covers areas such as pronunciation, spelling and punctuation that give learners the edge in making their speech more fluent and their writing more accurate. Components such as dictionary work also encourage learner autonomy.
- Reading 2: a fictional piece, such as a short story or an extract from a novel. These include both classic and contemporary texts. It is also followed by Comprehension 1 and Comprehension 2.
- Vocabulary: the tasks here check the learner's understanding of useful vocabulary in the story, and provide extension exercises based on the theme of the unit.
- Grammar: includes a short application-based explanation of concepts, illustrated through contextual examples, and followed by tasks which provide extensive practice. The exercises are graded, ensuring that the learner moves from simpler tasks to more practical applications.
- Listening: related to the theme of the unit and presented in authentic contexts, it includes activities which provide practice in listening for both specific and general meaning, as well as in identifying vocabulary and grammar topics already taught in the unit.
- Speaking: includes individual, pair and group work for practising spoken English related to the theme of the unit. Prompts and useful phrases give learners a springboard for the tasks, providing practice in English that they will be able to use in real-life situations.

- Writing: includes guided and free writing tasks derived from the reading text, which encourage creativity while enabling learners to create a meaningful and fluent piece of text.
- Poems: these have been carefully chosen to appeal to learners, with questions that range from the factual to the interpretative. It is followed by an activity loosely related to the theme of the poem.

Projects: include creative and research-based activities which encourage teamwork.

Life skills: built around values and skills, it consists of tasks that equip learners to deal with real-life situations as balanced individuals.

Workbooks

The Workbooks are designed to complement the Coursebooks through the careful mapping of grammar and vocabulary, with additional practice to review and reinforce concepts. The grammar sections include a short reminder of the grammar point covered in the Coursebook. Further practice in comprehension, vocabulary, language skills and writing is also provided.

Literature Readers

The Literature Readers teach critical appreciation of literature through short stories, folktales and fairytales, extracts from quality literature and classic novels, and poems from various eras and regions. A range of text-types is covered, with learners' attention being drawn to the genre of each piece. Literary devices are also highlighted, with a glossary of literary terms at the end of each book.

Teacher's Resource Books

The Teacher's Resource Books contain model lesson plans, photocopiable worksheets covering all the pedagogical aspects included in the Coursebooks, answer keys to all exercises, along with extra analytical activity sheets.

Digital resources

The Collins DigiSuite DVD comprises:

1. **Enhanced e-book:** includes the coursebook in digital format with additional features like audio, animated poems, pronunciation help and interactive exercises.
2. **Test generator:** an easy-to-use tool to help teachers create tests with a few clicks.
3. **Teacher resources:** includes lesson plans, answer keys, listening texts, additional worksheets, further project ideas, and extra support with assessment.

We hope that the course will foster a love for reading in young learners and provide teachers with language acquisition tools that can be used to effectively impart communication skills and equip young minds with an awareness about the world.

Dr K. Padmini Shankar, Series Editor

KEY FEATURES

In this unit, I will ... lists the learning objectives for the unit.

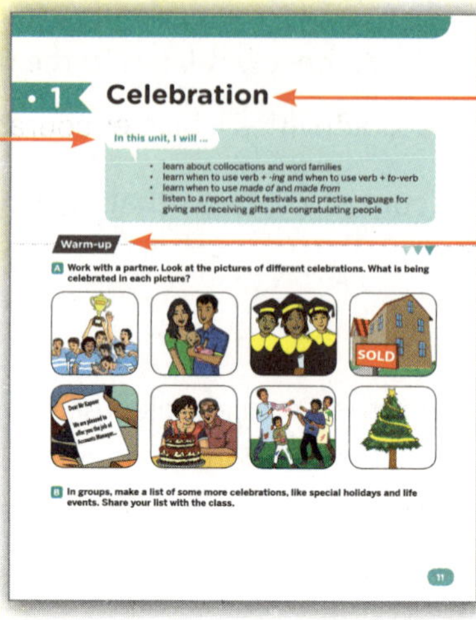

Each unit is built around a **theme**.

Warm-up has activities related to the theme of the unit.

Each unit covers texts belonging to a rich variety of genres, by Indian and international authors. **Reading 1** includes a non-fiction prose text. **Reading 2** includes a fictional prose text.

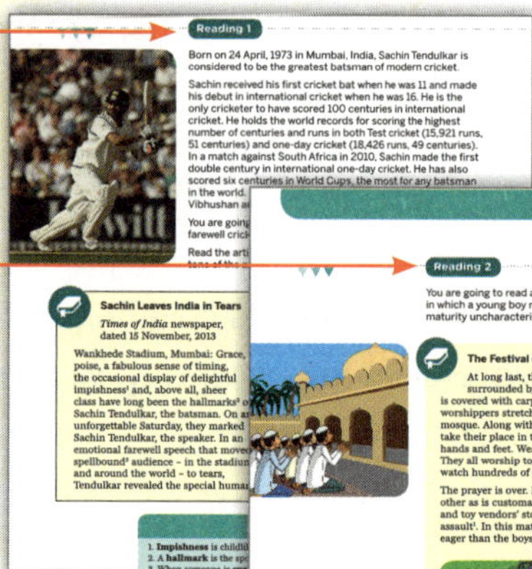

Both Reading sections are followed by exercises. **Comprehension 1** checks factual understanding through gap-filling, multiple choice, reference to context as well as 'wh-' questions.

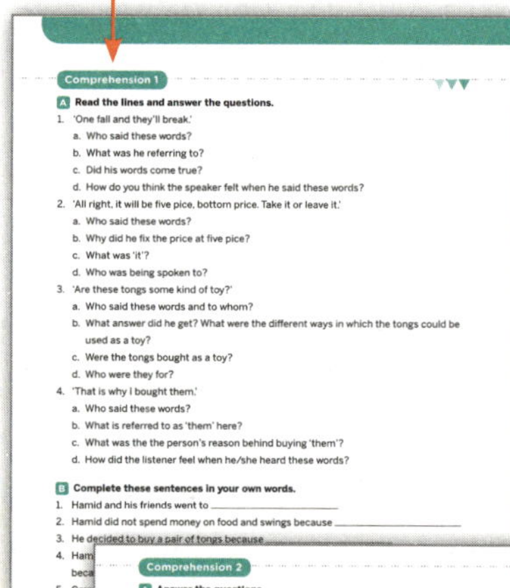

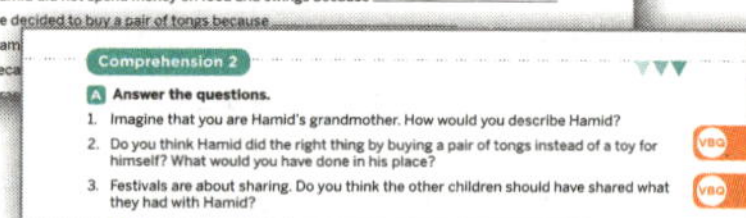

Wordfile lists difficult words and phrases and gives meanings along with their usage.

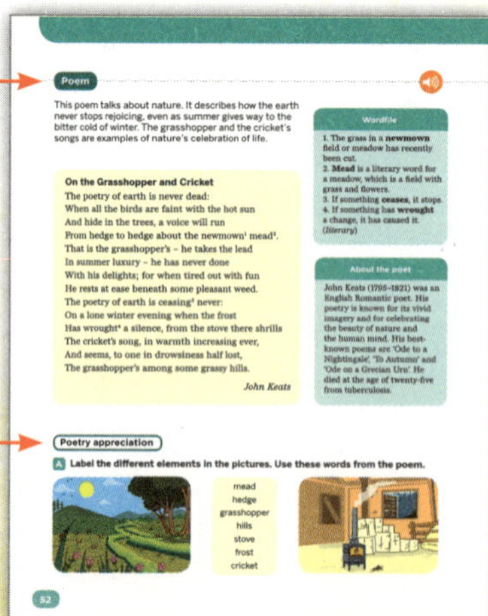

Each unit also includes a **Poem** followed by **Poetry appreciation** and an **Activity** related to the poem.

Comprehension 2 checks analytical, evaluative, inferential and interpretative skills. It also includes value-based questions, indicated by an icon.

Vocabulary check and **Vocabulary** enrich the learner's language.

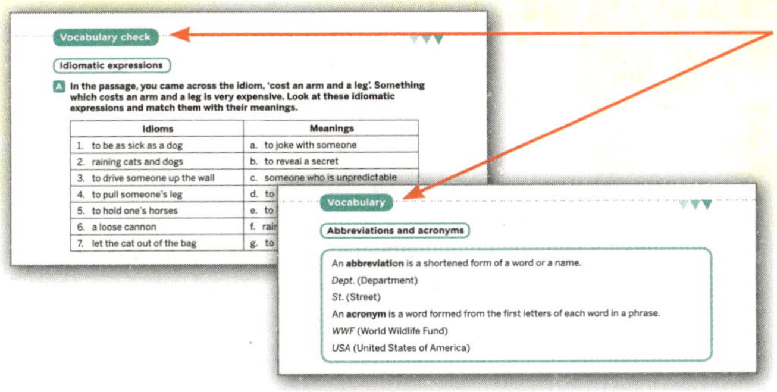

Language skills encourages the use of dictionaries and focuses on phonics and spelling.

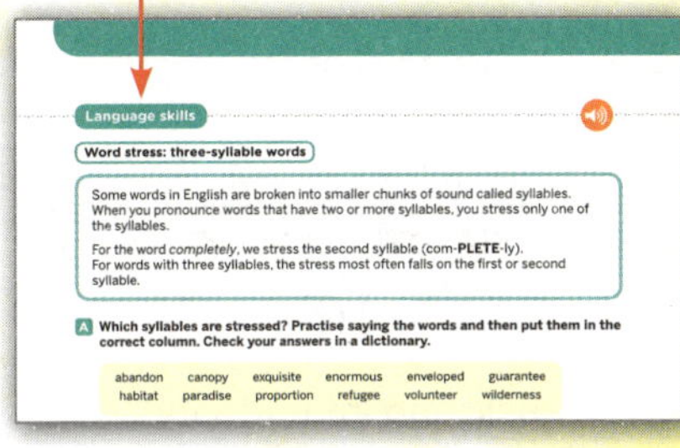

Grammar builds language proficiency through communicative and usage-based tasks.

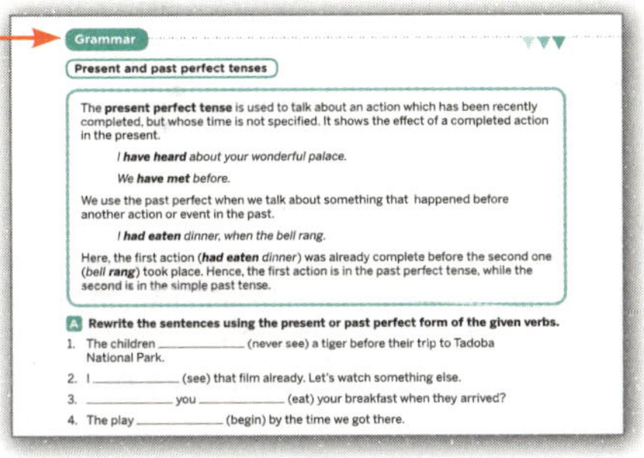

Writing tasks help the students develop their imaginative and critical thinking abilities and challenge them to explore new ways of expressing themselves effectively and creatively.

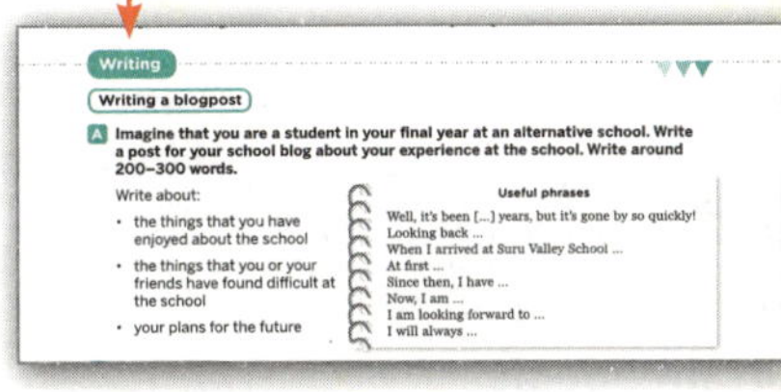

Listening and **Speaking** exercises focus on honing oral and aural skills through listening comprehension, group discussions and role plays.

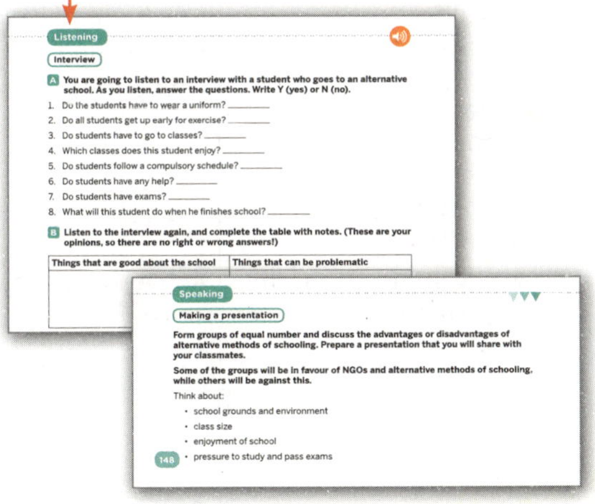

Project and **Life skills** pages encourage group work and aid in formative assessment. They help students imbibe values and attitudes required to overcome challenges in real life.

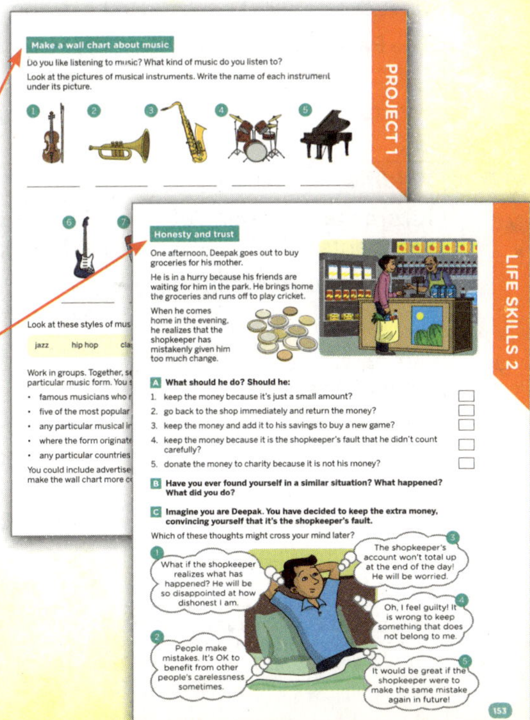

CONTENTS MAP

Unit	Title	Reading Comprehension	Vocabulary	Grammar
1	**Celebration** Sachin Leaves India in Tears The Festival of Eid *Other's Successes*	Factual, inferential, extrapolative, value-based Factual, inferential, extrapolative, value-based Poetry appreciation, metaphor	Collocations: adjectives to describe a person; *made of* and *made from*: substances	Verb + *-ing* form (gerund, present participle) or verb + *to* (infinitive)
2	**Music and Musicians** Music Maestro A. R. Rahman Music and Immortality *On the Grasshopper and Cricket*	Factual, extrapolative, value-based Factual, inferential, extrapolative, value-based Poetry appreciation, personification	Word definitions; words related to awards and fame; classifying words; analogies	Clauses: main and subordinate
3	**War and Peace** Palestinian and Israeli Children are Batting for Peace Matti's Miracle *In Flanders Fields*	Factual, extrapolative, value-based Factual, inferential, value-based Poetry appreciation, alliteration	Words related to sport; forming antonyms by adding prefixes; abbreviations and acronyms; ailments and their related organs; words related to war	Transitive and intransitive verbs
	Project 1: Making a wall chart about music			
	Life skills 1: Peer pressure			
4	**Important People** Steve Jobs: Do What You Love The Pataliputra Mystery *Invictus*	Factual, inferential, extrapolative, value-based Factual, inferential, value-based Poetry appreciation	Adjectives with degrees of meaning; verb-noun collocation; synonyms and antonyms to describe important and successful people; crossword	*I wish* ... and *If only* ... Present and past perfect tenses
5	**Wildlife** Kaziranga, Grassland of the Giants Harold: Our Hornbill *The Louse and the Mosquito*	Factual, inferential, extrapolative, value-based Factual, inferential, extrapolative, value-based Poetry appreciation	Using suffixes to form adjectives	Active and passive voice
6	**Think Differently** A Helping Hand for Children in Need Professor Shonku and the Spook *You Can be Whatever You Want to be!*	Factual, inferential, extrapolative, value-based Factual, inferential, extrapolative, value-based Poetry appreciation	Idiomatic expressions; oxymoron; one word substitution; error-correction	*Will* and the future perfect tense Simple, compound and complex sentences
	Project 2: Preparing a scrapbook on birds			
	Life skills 2: Truth and honesty			

Language skills	Listening	Speaking	Writing	Activity
Dictionary work: creating nouns with suffixes	Listening to a radio report about festivals and answering questions and gap filling	Role play: congratulating someone and giving thanks	Writing a descriptive account of a celebration	Making a presentation on a recent sporting event
Punctuation: commas	Listening to pieces of music, noting reactions to them and discussing questions related to them	Narrating a personal experience Planning an event by making suggestions, expressing agreement or disagreement	Writing a report for the school magazine about a musical performance	Writing an ode
Spelling commonly confused words; Dictionary work: a word with two meanings	Listening to a text and checking whether it is correct	Group work: acting out a scene from the story	Writing an informal letter	Discussing problems faced by refugees Group work: creating a plan of action to help refugee children
Pronunciation: unscrambling words; sentence stress	Listening to a play and answering questions Listening to a passage and gap filling	Group work: acting out a scene from the play	Writing a formal letter expressing regret, apologizing and asking for forgiveness	Making a poster
Pronunciation: stress on three-syllable words	Listening to a passage and stating true or false and gap filling	Doing a classroom survey and conducting a group discussion on it	Writing a narrative account	Writing a narrative poem
Dictionary work: words with the prefix *bio-*	Listening to an interview and answering questions and taking notes	Conducting a group discussion on a given topic followed by a presentation	Writing a blogpost about school life Writing a diary entry	Writing about one's dream

CONTENTS

1 Celebration

In this unit, I will ...

- learn about collocations and word families
- learn when to use verb + *-ing* and when to use verb + *to* + verb
- learn when to use *made of* and *made from*
- listen to a report about festivals and practise language for giving and receiving gifts and congratulating people

Warm-up

A **Work with a partner. Look at the pictures of different celebrations. What is being celebrated in each picture?**

B **In groups, make a list of some more celebrations, like special holidays and life events. Share your list with the class.**

Reading 1

Born on 24 April, 1973 in Mumbai, India, Sachin Tendulkar is considered to be the greatest batsman of modern cricket.

Sachin received his first cricket bat when he was 11 and made his debut in international cricket when he was 16. He is the only cricketer to have scored 100 centuries in international cricket. He holds the world records for scoring the highest number of centuries and runs in both Test cricket (15,921 runs, 51 centuries) and one-day cricket (18,426 runs, 49 centuries). In a match against South Africa in 2010, Sachin made the first double century in international one-day cricket. He has also scored six centuries in World Cups, the most for any batsman in the world. Sachin has also received the Padma Shri, Padma Vibhushan and the Bharat Ratna awards.

You are going to read an article about Sachin Tendulkar's farewell cricket match.

Read the article. What words would you use to describe the tone of the article?

Sachin Leaves India in Tears

Times of India newspaper, dated 15 November, 2013

Wankhede Stadium, Mumbai: Grace, poise, a fabulous sense of timing, the occasional display of delightful impishness[1] and, above all, sheer class have long been the hallmarks[2] of Sachin Tendulkar, the batsman. On an unforgettable Saturday, they marked Sachin Tendulkar, the speaker. In an emotional farewell speech that moved a spellbound[3] audience – in the stadium and around the world – to tears, Tendulkar revealed the special human beneath the legendary cricketer, and made adoring fans fall in love with him all over again.

India had won the match by an innings and 126 runs, and the 2–0 series triumph took them to No. 2 in the ICC test rankings, but all that was reduced to a mere footnote[4]. Pragyan Ojha picked up the man of the match award for his 10-wicket haul – and was lustily cheered for dedicating his award to Sachin. The loudest applause through the awards ceremony was reserved for Ravi Shastri, for handing over the mike to Sachin and saying, 'It's all yours.'

Wordfile

1. **Impishness** is childlike playfulness.
2. A **hallmark** is the special quality or ability of a particular person.
3. When someone is **spellbound**, their attention is held as if by magic.
4. An event that is described as a **footnote** is considered minor or unimportant.

Sachin: the first and youngest ever sportsman to get the Bharat Ratna

Sachin Tendulkar on Saturday became the first sportsman to be conferred the Bharat Ratna. At 40, he is by far the youngest person to get India's highest civilian honour, overtaking Rajiv Gandhi, who was given the award posthumously[5], at 46. CNR Rao, 79, a world-renowned authority on solid state and materials chemistry and chairman of the PM's science advisory council, has also been chosen for the award, which has been conferred on only 43 persons since it was instituted in 1954. It was last given four years ago, to Hindustani music doyen[6] Bhimsen Joshi. Speculation has it that Rahul Gandhi, who came to Wankhede to watch Sachin's last innings on Friday, was so moved by the upsurge[7] of emotion that he made a strong pitch for an immediate announcement.

Sachin had carried along a list to ensure he didn't forget anyone, but he referred to it only occasionally. Mostly, he spoke extempore[8] and straight from the heart. He began in a choked voice, pleading with the delirious crowd that had stayed on its feet through the presentation ceremony to settle down and let him speak. As the audience quietened somewhat, he composed himself and said, 'My life, between 22 yards for 24 years, it is hard to believe that this wonderful journey has come to an end.'

He thanked his father, 'The most important person in my life, and I have missed him a lot since 1999, when he passed away. He gave me freedom at the age of 11, and told me, "Chase your dreams, but do not take shortcuts. The path might be difficult but don't give up." He told me to be a nice human being, which I will try my best to always do. Every time I have done something special and showed my bat, it was for my father.'

Wordfile

5. When something is done **posthumously**, it is done after the person's death.
6. The **doyen** of a group or profession is the most respected person in it.
7. An **upsurge** is a rapid rise.
8. When someone speaks **extempore**, they speak with no preparation.

The boyish streak in him surfaced as he spoke of his delight that his coach, Ramakant Achrekar, had finally come to watch him play in a stadium. 'In the last 29 years, Sir has never ever said, "Well played" to me because he thought I would get complacent[9] and stop working hard. Maybe he can push his luck[10] now and say, "Well done" on my career, because there are no more matches, Sir, in my life.'

He repeated the message that he had given to the Indian team when skipper MS Dhoni presented him with the special cap for his 200th test. 'All of us are so, so fortunate and proud to be a part of the Indian cricket team ... I know you will continue to serve the nation in the right spirit and right values.' At a time when a probe[11] is underway into charges of fixing, the simple statement spoke volumes.

As he neared the end of his 20-minute speech, he said, 'I know it is getting a bit too long.' The crowd roared back 'noooooooooooo'. They could quite happily have heard him go on for hours. But Sachin wrapped it up briskly. 'I want to thank all the people here who have flown in from various parts of the world, and have supported me endlessly. Time has flown by rather quickly, but the memories you have left with me will always be with me forever and ever, especially "Sachiiin, Sachin," which will reverberate[12] in my ears till I stop breathing.'

The crowd promptly launched into a full-throated performance of 'Sachiiin, Sachin', even as Tendulkar's voice broke on 'Goodbye'. There was a brief conference on the field, possibly about whether or not he should do a lap of honour[13]. But for the crowd, there was no question about it. They weren't going to budge till he went around the stadium once.

And so, Tendulkar took a tricolour in his hands and began his round. Halfway through, he was hoisted on the shoulders of Captain MS Dhoni and Vice Captain Virat Kohli. Kohli was barely a year old when Sachin made his debut.

Dhoni, on whom the mantle[14] of the team's senior statesman now falls, made his test debut in 2005, by which time Sachin had been playing for almost 16 years.

As the procession slowly wound its way around the field, the crowd roared hoarsely, but full-throatedly, clapped, thumped chairs and boards, stomped feet and smiled through flowing tears.

Vikas Singh

Wordfile

9. When someone is **complacent**, they are satisfied, and do not want to change things.
10. To **push your luck** means to take a risk.
11. A **probe** is an investigation into illegal activity.
12. When a sound **reverberates** in your ears, you hear it in your mind again and again.
13. A **lap of honour** is a round that an athlete or team takes around a stadium because of their achievement.
14. When someone takes on the **mantle** of something, they take on an important duty.

Did you know?

Cricket, which some say originated in the 13th century, is the second most popular sport in the world, second only to football, and is played in more than 130 countries. The first recorded match was played in 1646 and the official laws (not rules) of cricket were created in 1744 in London, England.

Comprehension 1

A Answer the questions.

1. What is the article about?
2. When did the event take place?
3. Before Sachin Tendulkar, who was the youngest person to receive the Bharat Ratna?
4. State two pieces of advice Sachin's father gave him.
5. According to Sachin, why did his coach never say to him, 'Well played'?

B Circle the correct sense (meaning): a or b.

1. '... a fabulous sense of timing, ... and, above all, sheer class ...'
   In this line, 'class' means ...
   a. impressive ability or skill. b. a period of time for teaching.
2. '... an emotional farewell speech that moved a spellbound audience ...'
   In this line, 'moved' means ...
   a. changed from one place to another. b. made someone feel strong emotions.
3. '... he made a strong pitch for an immediate announcement.'
   In this line, 'pitch' means ...
   a. a sports field. b. words said to persuade someone.

C Read the statements below and mark them as true (T) or false (F).

1. Sachin read his speech to the crowd. ________
2. Only 43 people have been awarded the Bharat Ratna. ________
3. For his 200th test, Sachin was presented with a special bat. ________
4. The crowd thought Sachin's speech was too long. ________
5. After Sachin's speech, the crowd sang a song. ________

Comprehension 2

1. 'Sachin remains the most popular batsman in the world of Indian cricket.' Prove this statement by giving examples from the report.
2. Sachin Tendulkar wanted to share the moment of joy with everyone – his teammates, children and supporters. Do you think happiness is doubled when shared? VBQ

VBQ 3. Sachin thanks his father and his coach in his farewell speech. Discuss the importance of showing gratitude to those who stand by us through good and bad times.

Vocabulary Check

Collocations

A **collocation** refers to a combination of two or more words that are used together frequently.

*He began in a **choked voice** ...*

*Sachin is a **legendary cricketer**.*

A Fill in the blanks using adjectives from the box that collocate with the nouns in the sentences.

heavy	regular	maiden	strong	severe

1. India had a ______________ team in 2011.
2. ______________ exercise keeps us fit.
3. The players were under ______________ pressure.
4. The bowler was famous for bowling ______________ overs.
5. There was ______________ traffic outside the stadium.

B Complete the sentences with the words used to describe people.

emotional	ecstatic	delirious	overwhelmed	keen	affectionate

1. The ______________ crowds roared with joy when the player scored the winning goal.
2. The footballer felt very ______________ while receiving the 'Man of the Match' award.
3. Ramesh is a ______________ sportsman who practises several hours a day.
4. He takes good care of his pets. He is very ______________ towards them.
5. When the team won the match, the ______________ players hugged each other.
6. The hunter was ______________ with fear at the sudden sight of a tiger two feet away.

Language skills

Word families: Creating nouns

We can create nouns by adding suffixes to some adjectives and verbs.

We can create nouns from some adjectives using **-ness** or **-ity**.

happy → *happi**ness***   *possible* → *possibil**ity***

We can create nouns from some verbs using **-tion/-sion** or **-ment**.

celebrate → *celebra**tion***   *decide* → *deci**sion***   *enjoy* → *enjoy**ment***

Note that some of the adjectives and verbs require spelling changes.

A **Create nouns from these adjectives and verbs using suffixes. Put them in the correct columns according to the suffixes used. Use your dictionary. Add one more noun of your own to each column.**

Adjectives		Verbs	
capable	responsible	adore	possess
complex	sad	appoint	replace
nervous	simple	arrange	dedicate
ready	weak	astonish	excite

Nouns			
-ness	***-ity***	***-tion/-sion***	***-ment***

B **Now, fill in the blanks using the correct nouns from exercise A.**

1. The ________________ of the problem puzzled scientists for many years.
2. I have made an ________________ with my doctor for next week.
3. The ________________ Kunal showed towards his work earned him the respect of his colleagues.
4. The ______________ of receiving the guests at the airport was given to Kavya.
5. Mahatma Gandhi lived a life of great ________________.
6. Ramya always makes her travel ________________ at the last minute.

Reading 2

You are going to read an excerpt from *The Festival of Eid* in which a young boy named Hamid shows sensitivity and maturity uncharacteristic for his age.

The Festival of Eid

At long last, the *Eidgah* comes into view. It is surrounded by palm trees and its cemented floor is covered with carpets. There are row upon row of worshippers stretching well beyond the courtyard of the mosque. Along with others, people from Hamid's village take their place in the back rows, after washing their hands and feet. Wealth and status do not matter here. They all worship together and it is a beautiful sight to watch hundreds of people praying together.

The prayer is over. People meet and embrace each other as is customary. Then they descend on the sweet and toy vendors' stores like an army moving to an assault[1]. In this matter, the grown-up villager is no less eager than the boys.

Look, here is a swing! Pay one pice[2] and enjoy riding up to the heavens and then plummeting[3] down to the earth. And here is a roundabout strung with wooden elephants, horses and camels! Pay one pice and have twenty-five rounds of fun. Hamid's friends, Mehmood, Mohsin and Noorey and other boys mount the horses and camels. Hamid

Wordfile

1. An **assault** is an attack or raid by the military on an enemy position.
2. A **pice** is an old Indian coin which was worth 1/64 of a rupee.
3. When something **plummets**, it falls straight down at a high speed.

watches them from a distance. All he has are five pice. He can't afford to part with a third of his treasure for a few rounds of fun.

His friends dismount and run across to the rows of toy shops. Mehmood buys a soldier in khaki uniform and red turban, with a rifle on his shoulder, ready for action. Mohsin buys a smiling water carrier, ready to sprinkle water on dusty roads. Noorey acquires a lawyer. How impressive he looks, attired in a black gown, with a gold watch-chain and a fat book in his hand.

All these toys cost two pice each, too expensive for Hamid. 'They are made of clay,' he tells his friends. 'One fall and they'll break.' But his eyes look at them greedily and he wishes he could hold them in his hand for just a moment or two. But young boys are not givers, particularly when they have something new.

After the toys, it is sweets. Someone buys sesame-seed candy, others *gulab-jamun* or *halwa*. They smack their lips with relish. Only Hamid is left out. He looks at the others with hungry eyes.

After the sweet vendors, there are a few hardware stores and shops of real and artificial jewellery.

There is nothing to attract the boys' attention. So they go ahead – all of them except Hamid, who stops to see a pile of tongs. It occurs to him that his granny does not have a pair of tongs. Each time she bakes *chapatis*, the iron plate burns her hands. If he were to buy her a pair

of tongs, she would be very pleased. She would never burn her fingers; it would be a useful thing to have in the house. What use are toys? They are a waste of money. You can have some fun with them, but only for a very short period of time. Then you forget all about them.

Hamid asks the shopkeeper, 'How much is the pair of tongs?'

'Six pice,' he replies.

Hamid's heart sinks. He only had five pice! The shopkeeper looks at Hamid's crestfallen[4] face and says, 'All right, it will be five pice, bottom price. Take it or leave it.'

Hamid gratefully takes the pair of tongs from the shopkeeper. He carries it on his shoulder as if it were a gun. And struts[5] up proudly to show it to his friends.

Mohsin laughs and says, 'Arc you crazy? What will you do with the tongs?' Hamid flings it on the ground and replies, 'Try throwing your water carrier on the ground. Every bone in his body will break.'

Mahmood says, 'Are these tongs some kind of toy?'

'Why not?' retorts Hamid. 'Place them across your shoulders and it is a gun; wield them in your hands and it is like the tongs carried by singing mendicants[6] – they can make the same clanging as a pair of cymbals. One smack and they will reduce all your toys to dust. But none of them can harm my lion-hearted warrior.'

The children now realize that Hamid's tongs are undoubtedly far superior to their toys. Their toys will break but Hamid's tongs will remain as they are for years.

The boys are now anxious to handle the tongs. In exchange, they offer their toys to Hamid for examination. 'What beautiful toys they are! I was only pulling your leg,' says Hamid. 'How can a pair of tongs compare with such lifelike toys?' But the boys are not convinced.

It is eleven o'clock. Those who had gone to the *Eidgah* have just returned. The village is once again agog[7] with excitement. Mohsin's younger sister runs to him and grabs the water carrier from his hand. As she jumps with joy, the toy slips from her grasp, falls and breaks into pieces. Brother and sister come to blows[8]. Both howl and both get rebuked by their angry mother. Noorey fixes a seat for

Wordfile

4. Someone who is **crestfallen** feels disappointed.
5. When someone **struts**, they stand up very straight and walk in a proud way that suggests they think they are better than other people.
6. A **mendicant** is a person, usually of a religious group, who lives by asking others for food or money.
7. When people are **agog**, they are very curious or eager to hear or see something.
8. When two people **come to blows**, they start hitting each other.
9. When you **gobble** food, you eat it very quickly and noisily.

his lawyer, sits him on it and fans him with a bamboo leaf. Is it a gust of wind or a blow from the fan that throws the lawyer to the ground? That is the end of him. Mehmood's soldier survives, but manages to break a leg while guarding the village. Mehmood breaks his other leg so that the poor man can at least sit and do his duty in comfort!

Now let's hear what happened to our friend Hamid. As soon as she hears his voice, Granny Ameena runs out of the house, picks him up and kisses him. Suddenly she notices the tongs in his hand, 'Where did you find these tongs?'

'I bought them.'

'How much did you pay for them?'

'Five pice.'

Granny Ameena is angry. What a peculiar child! He remained thirsty and hungry the whole morning and all he could find to buy was a pair of tongs! She scolds him for his foolishness.

Hamid replies in an injured tone, 'You burn your fingers every day on the iron plate. That is why I bought them.'

The old woman's temper suddenly changes to love. What a selfless child! What concern for others! What a big heart! How he must have suffered seeing the boys buying toys and gobbling[9] sweets! Even at the fair, he thought of his old grandmother! Granny Ameena's heart is too full for words.

She breaks down and weeps. It is strange. Hamid, the little boy, has become Hamid the adult. And Ameena, the old woman, has become Ameena, the child. Tears fall unceasingly from her eyes, and she blesses Hamid a thousand times! Little Hamid! How can he understand the storm of emotions in Ameena's heart?

Munshi Premchand

About the author

Munshi Premchand (1880–1936) was one of the most celebrated Indian writers of the early 20th century. His short stories and books were not only depictions of the reality of life in the village, but also works of social criticism at a time of the struggle for freedom in India. He contributed greatly to the freedom movement that led to India's independence.

Comprehension 1

A Read the lines and answer the questions.

1. 'One fall and they'll break.'
   a. Who said these words?
   b. What was he referring to?
   c. Did his words come true?
   d. How do you think the speaker felt when he said these words?
2. 'All right, it will be five pice, bottom price. Take it or leave it.'
   a. Who said these words?
   b. Why did he fix the price at five pice?
   c. What was 'it'?
   d. Who was being spoken to?
3. 'Are these tongs some kind of toy?'
   a. Who said these words and to whom?
   b. What answer did he get? What were the different ways in which the tongs could be used as a toy?
   c. Were the tongs bought as a toy?
   d. Who were they for?
4. 'That is why I bought them.'
   a. Who said these words?
   b. What is referred to as 'them' here?
   c. What was the the person's reason behind buying 'them'?
   d. How did the listener feel when he/she heard these words?

B Complete these sentences in your own words.

1. Hamid and his friends went to ____________________
2. Hamid did not spend money on food and swings because ____________________
3. He decided to buy a pair of tongs because ____________________
4. Hamid's friends were convinced that the pair of tongs was better than their toys because ____________________
5. Granny Ameena cried because ____________________

Comprehension 2

A Answer the questions.

1. Imagine that you are Hamid's grandmother. How would you describe Hamid?
2. Do you think Hamid did the right thing by buying a pair of tongs instead of a toy for himself? What would you have done in his place? VBQ
3. Festivals are about sharing. Do you think the other children should have shared what they had with Hamid? VBQ

B Imagine these situations.

1. You are Hamid. What are your thoughts and feelings about the day you spent at Eidgah?
2. You have a small amount of money. How will you spend it?

Vocabulary

Made of **or** ***made from*****?**

We can say something is **made of** a kind of material.

The toys are ***made of*** *clay.*

The tongs are ***made of*** *metal.*

We use **made from** when the material is changed into a different form.

Curd is ***made from*** *milk.*

Paper is ***made from*** *wood.*

A Read the sentences and circle the correct options.

1. My t-shirt is made (of/from) cotton.
2. Tofu is made (of/from) soybeans.
3. Candles are made (of/from) wax.
4. *Gulab jamun* is made (of/from) milk.
5. These tyres are made (of/from) rubber.
6. Kheer is made (of/from) rice.
7. Glass is made (of/from) sand.
8. Chocolate is made (of/from) cocoa beans.

B **Complete each sentence with *of* or *from* and the correct word from the box.**

clay	wool	flour	leather	milk	plastic	trees	wood

1. My granny's favourite chair is made ____________
2. The sweater is made ____________
3. *Chapatis* are made ____________
4. My transparent ruler is made ____________
5. Butter is made ____________
6. My shoes are made ____________
7. Paper is made ____________
8. This vase is made ____________

C **Find seven celebration words and write them down. Use your dictionary for help.**

aaafparadejdhgshreceptionjkndaunfetesjhdajhgahd

jamboreesjkhfghousewarmingsndbfsnmsdffeastjfhiuwsfrwhegala

Grammar

Infinitives, gerunds and participles

When we talk about two actions that are done together by the same person, we can place the second verb directly after the first verb.

*Mohsin **enjoyed riding** the roundabout.*

*The toy soldier **manages to break** a leg.*

1. Some verbs are always followed by an **-ing** form.

*He **finished eating** his gulab jamun.*

*Would you **mind opening** the window?*

Here are some common verbs that are usually followed by the **-ing** form.

admit	**avoid**	**consider**	**delay**	**deny**	**describe**	**dislike**	**enjoy**
finish	**imagine**	**keep**	**mention**	**mind**	**miss**	**practise**	**suggest**

Two types of verbs take the **-ing form**. These are **gerunds** and **present participles**.

Gerunds usually act as nouns in a sentence. Just like nouns, gerunds can act as the subject or a direct object in a sentence.

***Swimming** is a good form of exercise. (gerund as the subject of a sentence)*

*Stella likes **cycling**. (gerund as direct object)*

Participles are of two kinds: present and past participle. Present participles end with **-ing**, while past participles end with **-ed**, **-d**, **-t**, **-en**, **-n**. They usually perform the function of an adjective.

*The **talking** parrot surprised him. (present participle)*

*The cries of the **excited** children filled the circus. (past participle)*

2. Other verbs are always followed by a **to + verb** form. This verb form is known as an **infinitive**. Infinitives can act as nouns, adjectives or adverbs.

*It's **beginning to rain**.*
*I don't **want to eat** any more rice.*
*He **seems to be** tired after the walk.*

Here are some common verbs that are usually followed by an infinitive.

afford agree appear ask attempt choose decide deserve expect happen hesitate hope intend refuse tend

3. Some verbs can be followed by either a gerund or an infinitive.

Liking and not liking: **like love prefer hate**

Remembering and forgetting: **remember forget**

Starting and stopping: **start stop begin continue**

For some of these, there is a change in meaning.

remember

*I **remembered to buy** a toy for my brother*. (I did not forget to do it.)
*I **remember buying** a toy, but I don't know what happened to it*. (I remember that I bought a toy.)

stop

*She **stopped to buy** a bottle of water at the shop*. (She had a purpose for stopping.)
*She **stopped buying** coffee because it was too expensive*. (She does not buy it any more.)

try

*He **tried to quiet** the crowd*. (He made an effort to quiet the crowd.)
***Try drinking** a glass of water to stop the coughing*. (See if it has an effect.)

A Read the sentences and circle the correct words. Sometimes, both options are correct.

1. Be nice, and try to avoid (to upset/upsetting) anyone, please.
2. If you need anything, don't hesitate (to call/calling) me.
3. I hate (to waste/wasting) my time doing nothing.
4. On weekends, I tend (to spend/spending) a lot of time outdoors.
5. Do not attempt (to remove/removing) the lid while it is hot.
6. Since I broke my leg, I miss (to walk/walking) to school.
7. After two days, we can begin (to see/seeing) the plants growing.
8. I tried (to make/making) sure he was comfortable.

B **Complete the sentences with the correct form of the verbs.**

fast (= not eat) | go | lock | meet | play | stay | win | buy

1. Can you imagine ______________ for a month?
2. Oops! I think I forgot ______________ the door.
3. He suggests ______________ next week.
4. Someday I'll be able to afford ______________ you an expensive car.
5. I suggested ______________ for a walk because I think you need some exercise.
6. They don't deserve ______________ the championship.
7. Kulsum chose ______________ at home while we went to the party.
8. Does anyone want ______________ table tennis?

Listening

Festivals around the world

A **Listen to the radio report about festivals around the world and answer these questions.**

1. At which festival do people ...
   a. travel far and wide to be with family? ______________
   b. give each other red packets? ______________
   c. commemorate the power of faith and courage? ______________
   d. eat pumpkin pie? ______________
   e. light candles for each day? ______________
   f. purify themselves with water? ______________

2. When are the following festivals celebrated?
   a. Chinese New Year: ______________
   b. Sekrenyi: ______________
   c. Hanukkah: ______________
   d. Thanksgiving: ______________

B **Listen again. Complete the sentences with information from the report.**

1. Chinese New Year is sometimes called ________ ________ ________.
2. At the stroke of midnight on Chinese New Year, ________ are set off to drive away ________ ________.
3. For the Sekrenyi Festival, men wash away their ills and ________ by splashing water on their chests, ________ and ________.
4. The seventh day of the Sekrenyi Festival is marked by a day of ________ for the young men.
5. The Jewish holiday Hanukkah is also known as the ________ ________ ________.
6. Thanksgiving first took place in ________, but did not become an official holiday until ________.
7. The first Thanksgiving dinner was held by Native Americans and ________.

Speaking

Congratulations and thanks

During celebrations, you often want to congratulate people, thank them and present them with gifts. Here are some useful phrases.

Congratulating people	Giving gifts	Saying thank you
Well done! You've done a great job! You did really well! Congratulations, you did it! Congratulations to ... • all of you! • the bride and groom! • the birthday girl/boy! I would like to congratulate you on ...	Guess what I bought you! I got you something. I hope you like it. Look what I have for you! Here's a little gift for you. Enjoy! I thought you might like this for ... Happy Birthday! Happy Anniversary! It's only something small, but I hope you like it. Please accept this gift from me/ all of us. We'd like to give you this gift and say how proud we are of you/ happy we are for you.	Thank you so much! That's very kind of you! Oh, you shouldn't have! This is exactly what I needed. Now, I can ... Oh thank you, it's lovely/beautiful! I'd like to thank you all for ... • organizing this celebration • your support • the beautiful presents • your generosity

Here is a conversation in which one speaker thanks the other for bringing him/her a birthday gift.

Speaker A: Hello! I am so glad you could come.

Speaker B: Hello! Happy birthday to you! I brought you a present.

Speaker A: Thank you!

Speaker B: I thought you might like a pair of roller skates.

Speaker A: Wow! That is just what I wanted. Thank you very much!

Work with a partner. Take turns role-playing the situations.

Birthday party

Student A: Today is your 13th birthday and your parents have invited all your friends for a party. Greet the guests and thank them for coming and for their gifts.

Student B: Your friend has turned 16. You are at his/her birthday party. Congratulate him/her and present him/her with a gift.

Wedding anniversary

Student A: You are a happy grandparent as it is your 40th wedding anniversary and your grandchildren are giving you a surprise party. Greet the guests and thank them for coming and for their gifts.

Student B: You are at a party celebrating your grandparents' 40th wedding anniversary. Congratulate your grandmother/grandfather and present him/her with a gift.

Writing

Write about a celebration that you have attended, either in your honour or for someone else. You can use these points in your description:

- Where was the celebration?
- What food did you eat?
- What gifts did you receive or give?
- Was it a formal or an informal party?

Use the words you have learned in the unit as much as you can.

Useful phrases

I was a bit nervous because ...
There was so much food that ...
I enjoyed eating as many sweets as I could.
I had hoped to get a new ...
I really don't like going to big parties.
I had intended to just say a quick thank you, but ...
When we got there, we realized we'd forgotten to bring the gift.

Plan

1. Say when and where the party was and who it was for.
2. Describe what you saw as you walked into the party, e.g. food, decorations.
3. Describe the events of the party and your thoughts and feelings about what happened.

You can make notes here.

Poem

Read this poem about the way we should deal with success and failure.

Other's Successes

Can you go to another who wins in the fight
And give him a handshake that's true?
Do you find yourself feeling a sense of delight
In the good work another may do?
Or deep in your heart are there envy and hate,
When you see someone getting ahead?
Do you sneer[1] at his luck and rail at your fate?
If you do all your courage has fled.
If you haven't learned to rejoice in the deed
Of your brothers and give them a cheer,
You haven't discovered the pathways that lead
To genuine happiness here.
If you cannot say to a brother, 'I'm glad
You have conquered,' and give him your hand,
Your life must be gloomy and woefully sad[2],
You're building your mansion on sand.
Did you secretly gloat[3] when another had failed,
Did you sneer at the efforts he made?
Did it inwardly please you to see him assailed[4],
Did you chuckle[5] to see him outplayed?
If this is the part you have chosen to play,
If you are as selfish as this,
Though he falls in the thick and the heat of the fray[6],
Your failure is greater than his.

Edgar Albert Guest

Wordfile

1. If you **sneer at** someone or something, you express your contempt for them by the expression on your face or by what you say.
2. When you are **woefully sad**, you are extremely sad.
3. A person **gloats** when he is proud of his success and looks down upon other people.
4. Here, **assailed** means defeated or upset.
5. When you **chuckle**, you laugh quietly.
6. A **fray** is a fight or a competition.

About the poet

Edgar Albert Guest (1881–1959) was an American poet and journalist. Often called the 'People's Poet', he also hosted a weekly radio show, and was part of a television series called *A Guest in Your Home*. Most of his poems present an optimistic view of life. Guest considered himself 'a newspaper man who wrote verses.'

Poetry appreciation

A Answer the questions.

1. What are some of the negative reactions to someone else's success which the poet mentions?
2. How does a true winner react to another's success?
3. The poet says, 'You're building your mansion on sand.' This is a metaphor. In a metaphor, a person or thing is compared to an unrelated person or thing by stating that they are similar in a particular way. What do you think a mansion stands for in the given line? What does the line mean?
4. How does the poet describe a selfish person?
5. Do you congratulate your opponent if he/she wins a game or competition against you? Give reasons for your answer. VBQ
6. What is the message of the poem? Do you agree with it? VBQ

B Match the words in column A with their definitions in column B.

Column A	Column B
1. delight	a. a competition or fight
2. rejoice	b. to feel happy about someone else's failure
3. genuine	c. to feel or show great joy
4. gloat	d. a feeling of great pleasure
5. mansion	e. real
6. fray	f. a large, impressive house

Activity

You know that it is important to achieve success in all that we do, but even more important is to do so fairly.

In sporting events, fair play is given as much importance as a good performance. In every major tournament, awards are given to teams which play the game fairly and in the spirit of sportsmanship.

Choose any recent sporting event. It can be the cricket World Cup, the Commonwealth Games, or the FIFA World Cup. Then, do some research on the following:

- the team which has been given the fair play award in the tournament.
- examples when the team played fairly, even if it resulted in the team losing the match.

Make a presentation about the team. You can include photos and newspaper cuttings to make it more interesting. Also mention what lesson you learnt from the team.

• 2 Music and Musicians

In this unit, I will ...

- learn about analogies and where to use the comma
- learn about main and subordinate clauses
- listen to some music and discuss it
- plan an event using language for making suggestions
- write a report for my school magazine

Warm-up

A Match the names of these musicians with the instruments they play.

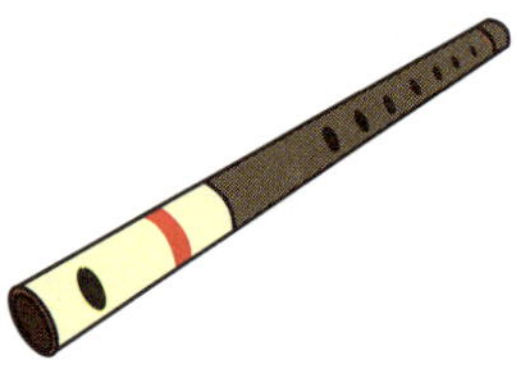

Ravi Shankar	santoor
Zakir Hussain	flute
Jyotsna Srikanth	violin
Hariprasad Chaurasia	sarod
Shiv Kumar Sharma	shehnai
Amjad Ali Khan	tabla
Bismillah Khan	sitar

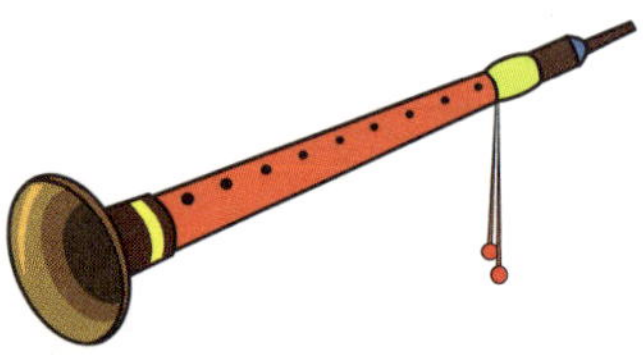

B Discuss these questions with your classmates.

Have you heard any of these musicians? If so, do you like them?

Who are your favourite musicians?

Can you play a musical instrument? If so, which one?

If you can't play a musical instrument, which one do you like to listen to most?

Reading 1

A. R. Rahman is a famous Indian musician. He began composing music for films in the 1990s with the Tamil film *Roja*. Since then, he has composed music for many Indian and international films, and has become one of the world's most notable and prolific music composers.

Do you know any songs composed by A. R. Rahman? Discuss with a partner.

A. R. Rahman has also won numerous awards, including two Oscars in 2009.

Read an interview with A. R. Rahman.

Music Maestro A. R. Rahman

A. R. Rahman does not need an introduction. His name itself speaks of his musical accolades[1]. *Time Magazine* has honoured him with the title 'Mozart[2] of Madras' and several Tamil critics have coined the nickname 'Isai Puyal' (meaning 'Music Storm') for him. He was voted one of the 100 most influential people by *Time Magazine*. He made history by winning two Oscars in 2009 for the music of *Slumdog Millionaire*. A. R., as he prefers to be called, is also one of the top-selling recording artists in the world.

Interviewer: Welcome A. R. Tell us something about your journey from Kodambakkam to Hollywood.

Rahman: Hello. My journey has been unpredictable. When I was a child, I never thought that I could perform properly. I became famous at the age of 11 because I used to appear in a children's show every Sunday. I used to play film songs that made me quite popular. Fame was not an unusual thing even then. But I acquired more confidence with age and time. It is great to meet one's favourite stars like Oliver Stone and visit places in America, like Los Angeles. So, it is really a big trip from here to there.

Interviewer: Are you enjoying it?

Rahman: Yes, in a way.

Did you know?

A. R. Rahman is the first Indian to win two Oscars. The first Indian to win an Oscar was Bhanu Athaiya. She won an Oscar in 1983 for Best Costume Design for the film *Gandhi*.

Wordfile

1. An **accolade** is something that people do or say to show how much they admire someone.
2. Wolfgang Amadeus **Mozart** was one of the most influential composers of all time.

Interviewer: Do you consider yourself to be lucky?

Rahman: Well, I think it is a very complex question. Luck can happen once but then we need to sustain it. For that we need to have a state of mind and a way of life. Because I feel that there is definitely destiny[3] and divinity[4], which is based on the love and prayers of your well-wishers.

Interviewer: Is it true that one of the forces that has shaped your life is your mother?

Rahman: When I was quite young, my father died. My mother suffered a lot to help me build my career. When I made my studio, she invested money in it and bought me equipment. She always stood by me as a wall of protection. Whatever decisions she took were guided by the fact that I should remain in the field of music because I wasn't too clear at that point in time whether I wanted to be a musician. I was more interested in scientific things and electronics. I am grateful to her for guiding me and helping me realize my potential.

Interviewer: With success in probably every musical composition, how have you timed your tasks?

Rahman: I started doing very limited films. When a composer would do 30 films in a year, I would take up only four or five films. It was enough for me. I live with a song, sometimes for a week, sometimes for six months, trying to fix what is wrong with it. Because, I believe, that if I don't like it people will not like it either. I have gone by that rule, and so far it has worked for me. God has been kind to me. Music is like a baby in a mother's womb for nine months. You just cannot expose it till the time is right. That is the reason I work in a very isolated way.

Interviewer: Tell us something about the important people in your life.

Rahman: Apart from my family, very few people could understand what I wanted to do. Sridhar was one of them. He was my sound engineer, but I looked upon him as another composer. We worked 14–18 hours a day. His death has left a great vacuum in my life. I believe that sometimes friends are closer than your own family.

Did you know?

A street in a town called Markham near Toronto in Canada has been named after A. R. Rahman. Now its residents live on Allah-Rakha Rahman Street.

Wordfile

3. **Destiny** is what will happen to somebody in the future, especially things that they cannot change or avoid.
4. **Divinity** is the state of being a god or a goddess.

Interviewer: What was your reaction on being nominated and then on winning the Oscars?

Rahman: I was surprised because we entered two songs for the Oscars and then won an Oscar for both. It is a big deal!

Interviewer: Where did you get the idea of getting different sounds about Jai Ho? Where did you come up with the idea of getting Spanish, Hindi and English for the song?

The cast and crew of *Slumdog Millionaire*

Rahman: Well, I think it was almost like a celebration. I do not know, it was just that I wanted to do a crazy song. I wanted to write an original song. Sometimes you get this instinct[5] and you just go with it.

Interviewer: How has winning Oscars changed your life?

Rahman: Yes, winning the Oscars has changed my life. Now I can't even attend places of prayer without being recognized. Even when I am at malls in the US, children freeze in recognition when they see me. But I try to concentrate on my music. I am not the kind of person who can pull himself away from music, do other things, and then go back to music. It has been a full roller coaster ride for me from New York to Dubai ... to Calicut ..., Pune, Mumbai, Delhi, Chennai ... I visit two cities every day. Everywhere they want to congratulate me and I can't say no. I have also been conferred[6] with an honorary doctorate by the Aligarh Muslim University.

Interviewer: What is the approach of the West towards the Asians after you lifted the Oscars?

Rahman: The impact of *Slumdog Millionaire* was tremendous. It really helped change the perception[7] of the West towards the Third World Countries. Earlier, when talented Asian musicians approached Western companies, they encountered difficulties, but now things have changed. The West is ready to listen to us.

Interviewer: It was such a pleasure talking to you. All the best.

Rahman: Thank you.

Wordfile

5. **Instinct** is the natural tendency that a person or animal has to behave or react in a particular way.
6. If someone **confers** an honour on you, they give it to you.
7. Your **perception** of something is the way you think about it.

Comprehension 1

A **Tick [✓] the correct statement.**

1. A. R. Rahman was not famous when he was a child. Now he is famous and confident. [ ]
2. A. R. Rahman was famous when he was a child but was not very confident. He became more confident as he got older. [ ]
3. A. R. Rahman was famous when he was a child and was very confident. He became less confident as he got older. [ ]

B **A. R. Rahman's mother helped him a lot. Which of the following did she do? Choose three answers.**

1. She gave him money to study electronics. [ ]
2. She gave him money for his studio. [ ]
3. She bought him equipment. [ ]
4. She encouraged him to become a scientist. [ ]
5. She encouraged him to become a musician. [ ]

C **Who are the most important people in A. R. Rahman's life? Choose one answer.**

1. Only his old sound engineer, Sridhar.
2. Famous people in Hollywood , such as Oliver Stone.
3. His family and friends, especially his old sound engineer, Sridhar.

D **Winning the Oscars has changed A. R. Rahman's life. Describe three things that have changed.**

E **How has the approach of the West towards Asians changed since A. R. Rahman won the Oscars? Choose one answer.**

1. The West is more willing to listen to Asian musicians.
2. The West is unwilling to listen to Asian musicians.
3. Asian musicians no longer want to approach Western companies.

Comprehension 2

1. Would you like to be a celebrity? Why/why not?
2. Do you know of a musician, dancer or painter, or any other famous person who struggled to reach the top? Is it only luck that is required to become successful? What kind of commitment and attitude are required from someone who would like to excel? VBQ

Vocabulary check

Word definitions

A Complete the definitions with words from the interview.

1. When something is u__________, it is difficult to know what is going to happen.
2. To s__________ something means to continue or maintain it for a long time.
3. If you i__________ money, you give it in the hope that the value will increase.
4. When you e__________ something, you show it to other people.
5. If you are i__________ you are separated from other people.
6. If someone leaves a v__________ in your life, you miss them because they are no longer there.
7. An i__________ is a feeling that is not based on facts.
8. When something is t__________, it is very impressive.

B There are several words in the interview relating to awards and fame. Complete the sentences with these words.

honoured recognition star enter title congratulate vote nominated

1. I'd like to __________ you on winning this award.
2. That's such a great poem! Why don't you __________ the competition?
3. The film was __________ with four International Indian Film Academy Awards.
4. The film is excellent. It's been __________ for five Academy Awards.
5. After 20 years, he has won an award. Finally, he has the __________ he deserves.
6. The soundtrack is so good that I think the composer is the real __________ of the film.
7. Last year, the lead actor received the honorary __________ of Doctor of Arts from a French university.
8. Do you think my song is the best in the competition? If so, then please __________ for it!

Language skills

Punctuation: the comma (,)

A comma marks a slight pause between different parts of a sentence.

We use a comma:

1. in lists:

   It has been a full roller coaster ride for me from New York to Dubai, then Pune, Mumbai, Delhi and Chennai.

   Note that we do not usually put a comma before 'and' at the end of a list.

2. in direct speech:

   a. just after the reporting verb, when the reporting verb comes before the speaker's words:

      Rahman ***said,*** *'I started doing very limited films.'*

   b. just after the speaker's words, when the reporting verb comes after the speaker's words:

      'I started doing very limited films,' ***said*** *Rahman.*

3. to separate clauses:

   When I was a child, I never thought that I could perform properly.

   Apart from my family, very few people could understand what I wanted to do.

4. after a sentence starter:

   Well, *I think it is a very complex question.*

   However, *things soon changed.*

5. to separate a part of a sentence that could be removed without affecting the sense:

   His latest book, **Room at the Top,** *came out last month.*

Add the missing commas in these sentences.

1. If you are unable to complete your work on time please let me know.
2. Mahatma Gandhi said 'Be the change that you wish to see in the world.'
3. After we had finished studying for the exam we decided to go out for a walk.
4. I rang the bell knocked on the door and called her name but no one came.
5. I do not exercise regularly but I know that it's very important to do so.
6. 'We build too many walls and not enough bridges' said Newton.

Reading 2

Mian Tansen is one of the most important musicians in India's history. He was a brilliant composer, musician and singer in the sixteenth century, in the court of the Mughul Emperor Akbar. He was a great influence on Indian classical music, and composed several *ragas* which you can still hear today.

You are going to read about Mian Tansen's life. Before you read, look at the words on the right from the passage. How do you think these words relate to his life as a singer? Discuss with a partner.

Now, read the passage. As you read, note how the words relate to Tansen's life as a singer and a musician.

lion	squirrels
clouds	rain
jewels	fire

Music and Immortality

There is a tomb in Gwalior, which is shaded by the branches of a tamarind tree. It is said that a singer can enhance his or her music skills by just eating one leaf from that tree. This is the tomb of India's greatest musician, Mian Tansen, whose music was so enriching[1] that it still nourishes the soil where his ashes were buried almost six hundred years ago.

Tansen was born to Mukund Mishra and his wife after they had gone to the great Sufi saint and musician, Hazrat Mohammad Ghaus, begging for a child. Mukund Mishra was a poet and a lover of music so when a son was born to him, Mukund hoped that he would become a musician and named him Tansen – the master of *taan*, or musical notes.

Tansen, however, showed no interest in music while growing up. Instead, he liked to spend his time in the forest chasing animals and imitating their sounds. One day, while he was sitting on a tree, chirping like sparrows, he saw a group of travellers crossing the forest. As the travellers drew near, Tansen took a deep breath and let out a loud roar. The people, thinking that a lion was nearby, ran for their lives; but when they heard a young boy laughing at their terror, they realized they had been fooled.

An old man among the travellers gestured to Tansen to come down from the tree.

Wordfile

1. Something that is **enriching** improves the quality of something else.

'Come down,' the old man said gently. 'I'm not angry with you. I want to talk to you about that roar. It was very convincing. You have great talent.'

Tansen descended from the tree.

'I am Guru Haridas,' the old man said. 'Who are your parents? I would like to meet them.'

Guru Haridas was a renowned[2] saint and music teacher. When Tansen took him to his house, his parents recognized Guru Haridas instantly.

'Mukund Mishra, I have come to talk to you about your son,' said the guru. 'He has great talent. I would like to take him with me to my *ashram* and train him as my *shishya* (disciple).'

At Guru Haridas's *ashram*, Tansen began learning the traditions of Indian classical music. He perfected his skills under Guru Haridas and, now, when he sang, nature responded. When he sang *Raga Todi* to evoke the animal spirits, squirrels, deer and rabbits came scampering into the *ashram*. When he sang *Megh Malhar*, clouds began to form in the sky.

Tansen trained with his guru for ten years. When he was about twenty, his father died. Just before he passed away, Mukund Mishra told his son to go and see Pir Baba Mohammad Ghaus in Gwalior.

The old Pir was happy to see the boy and to learn that he had received training in music from the great Guru Haridas. 'But now your training in the *ashram* is over,' he told Tansen. 'It is time for you to train in the real world.'

Taking leave from his guru, Tansen began to live with Mohammad Ghaus. He spent the next three years perfecting his skills under Ghaus' guidance. During this time, Pir Baba arranged for him to sing in Gwalior's court and also to hear other musicians there.

Soon, the word of Tansen's talent spread. He was asked to be King Ramachandra's court musician and soon after he was asked to join Emperor Akbar's court.

In Agra, Tansen was given a warm welcome. Akbar introduced him to his court officials and musicians. The following morning, Tansen received a message from the

Wordfile

2. A **renowned** person is well known and respected.

Emperor, requesting that he perform at a celebration that evening.

Tansen knew that this performance would be a test of all his years of training.

The royal *darbar* (court) was crowded that evening. When Tansen arrived, Emperor Akbar stepped down from his throne and led him to an *asan* (seat) in the centre. Soon the doors of the courtroom were closed and the lights were dimmed.

Tansen began his *alaap* (introduction to the raga). The listeners felt that they had transcended[3] the boundaries of earth and had entered some ethereal[4] place.

There was a hushed silence in the court after he stopped singing. And then, the applause began. It grew and grew. When he looked towards the Emperor, he saw him standing too, clapping.

'Mian Tansen,' said the Emperor, 'You are a true jewel. From today, you can become one of our *navratna* - our most precious nine jewels.'

Tansen's fame spread throughout the country. Kings and princes from all over came to hear him sing. Tansen became such a favourite of the Mughal Emperor that the other musicians grew jealous and sought ways to discredit him. But Tansen always managed to defeat them in every contest. One day, they proposed to the Emperor that Tansen should sing the *Deepak Raga*. This raga, if sung by a true master, invokes[5] fire, and can not only light lamps, but also ultimately burn the singer.

Tansen accepted the challenge.

That night Emperor Akbar went to Tansen's house and begged him to reconsider. But Tansen was adamant[6]. 'I beg your forgiveness for disobeying you, but I must accept this challenge. I cannot let my guru and my goddess be insulted by refusing to perform one of the most beautiful *ragas* of our tradition.'

'But is there any way to counter the power of the *raga*?'

'Yes,' Tansen replied. 'If a singer, capable of summoning the elements, can sing *Raga Megh*, I can be saved.'

'But who will sing *Raga Megh*?' said the Emperor.

Wordfile

3. When you **transcend** something, you go beyond it.
4. Something that is **ethereal** has a delicate, supernatural beauty.
5. When something **invokes** another thing, it produces it or makes it happen.
6. If you are **adamant**, you are determined not to change your mind.

'There is someone who can accomplish this feat. Her name is Rupa. She was a student with me at my guru's *ashram*. She has complete knowledge of this raga. I would like to train her for fifteen days,' said Tansen.

Tansen brought Rupa to Agra and began to train her. On the sixteenth day, the court was prepared for the big event. Large, unlit lamps were placed around Tansen's *asan*, a big bowl of cold water was put on the table, and a pile of dry wood was stacked in the courtyard.

Rupa herself sat facing Tansen, frightened.

Finally, Akbar gave the signal for the music to begin and Tansen began his *alaap* (opening notes). As note built upon note, the people in the court began to feel an unnatural warmth. When Tansen transitioned into the body of the *jod* (the song), the heat became unbearable and everyone began to sweat. As Tansen reached the climax of the first *taan*, the dry wood in the courtyard burst into flames. One by one, the unlit lamps became brilliant with light. Soon, the water in the large bowl began to boil. By this time the courtiers were all groaning from the unbearable heat, but the man whose voice sang like the flames of a fire hypnotized them. Even as they listened, they saw Tansen's face turn ashen. The heat generated by the *raga* was consuming him from inside.

'Rupa,' the Emperor called. 'Sing. Sing *Megh*.'

But Rupa, transfixed[7] by the power of Tansen's voice, couldn't even move her lips.

Tansen's wife's wails burst into her trance, and she broke into the *alaap* of *Megh*. However, her voice faltered and had no effect on Tansen's body, which had begun to sag. But he continued to sing until finally, he collapsed on the floor.

A cry of despair broke out of everyone's throat.

By now, Rupa's voice had begun to gain power. She closed her eyes. Her voice began to soar to the skies and clouds began to gather. People watched in awe, cooled by the sudden change in temperature. Then the clouds burst and rain poured down from the heavens, dousing the burning pile of wood in an instant. Two courtiers carried Tansen outside, directly under the cooling rain. As Rupa concluded *Megh*, Tansen opened his eyes.

The great musician, Mian Tansen, lived that day, and he will live for ever, immortalized[8] by his music.

Wordfile

7. If you are **transfixed** by something, you cannot move because you are so amazed.
8. If someone is **immortalized**, they are famous and people will remember them for a long time, even after death.

Comprehension 1

A Read the questions and tick [✓] the best answers.

1. What did Tansen like to do when he was a child?
   a. He liked to stay at home and to sing. ☐
   b. He liked to be in the forest, imitating the calls of animals. ☐
   c. He liked to play with lions. ☐
2. What did Tansen study at Guru Haridas' ashram?
   a. He learned about music. ☐
   b. He studied the weather. ☐
   c. He learned about nature and animals. ☐
3. Where did he go when he left Guru Haridas' ashram?
   a. He went back to his parents' house. ☐
   b. He went to Emperor Akbar's court in Agra. ☐
   c. He went to live with Pir Baba Mohammad Ghaus. ☐
4. Tansen became famous at court. How did other musicians feel?
   a. They were jealous. ☐
   b. They were impressed. ☐
   c. They were surprised. ☐

B Complete the table.

Event	Effect
1. Tansen roared like a lion.	He scared a group of travellers away. An old man (Guru Haridas) heard him and recognized his talent.
2. Tansen sang at Guru Haridas' ashram.	
3. Tansen sang for Emperor Akbar for the first time.	
4. Tansen sang the *Deepak Raga* at court.	
5. Rupa sang the *Raga Megh* at court.	

C Answer the questions.

1. What do you know about Tansen's childhood?
2. Which people helped and supported Tansen? How?
3. What effect did Tansen's singing have on people and nature?
4. How is Tansen immortal?

Comprehension 2

1. Imagine that you were at the court when the singing competition took place. Describe what you saw.
2. Both Tansen and A. R. Rahman have or had people in their lives who supported and encouraged them. Why do you think it is important for people to have such support in their careers? Complete the mind map with your ideas. VBQ

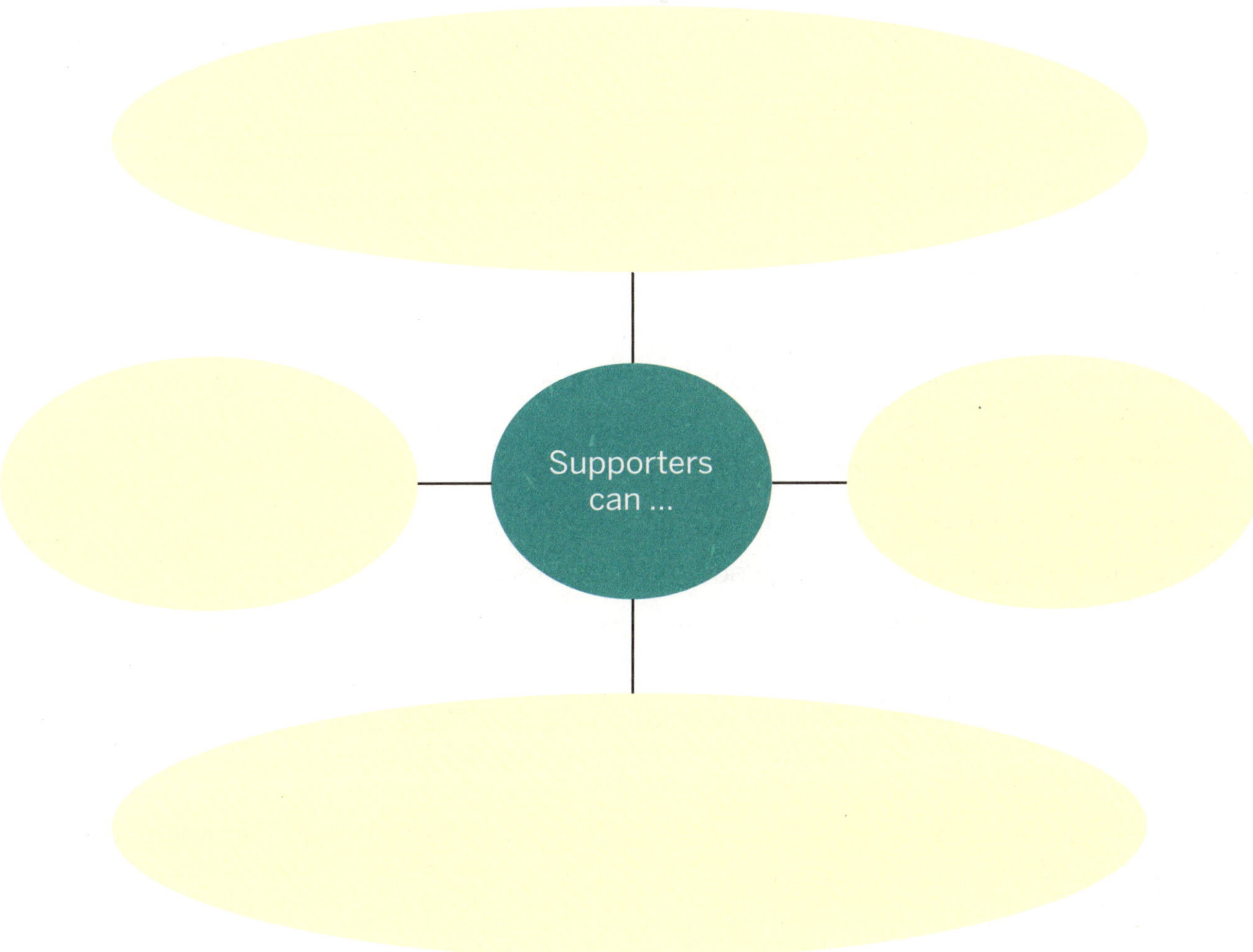

Vocabulary

Words from the text

A **Look at these words. They are from the texts about A. R. Rahman and Tansen. Put the words in the correct columns.**

recording artist	notes	sound engineer	critic	soundtrack	lyrics
classical music	studio	composer	song	singer	court

People	Places	Musical styles	Other
musician			

B **Work with a partner. Add more words to each column.**

Analogies

An **analogy** is a comparison of two things that are related in some way. Analogies can be made when the two things are:

1. synonyms (happiness—joy)
2. antonyms (happiness—sadness)
3. the first thing is a part of the second (page—book)
4. the first thing is a tool used by, or for, the second (scissors—hairdresser or scissors—haircut)

When we work on solving analogy problems, we use the following wording:

__________ *is to* __________ *as* __________ *is to* __________.

Happy *is to* ***sad*** *as* ***big*** *is to* __________. (Here, the answer is **small**, because both pairs of words are antonyms.)

C **Find the relationship between the words. Then complete the analogies.**

1. Strum is to guitar as beat is to tabla.
2. __________ is to piano as string is to sitar.
3. __________ is to melody as word is to story.
4. Choreographer is to dance as __________ is to music.
5. Brush is to painter as anvil is to __________.
6. Painting is to artist as __________ is to singer.
7. Actor is to __________ as musician is to concert.
8. Violinist is to violin as __________ is to piano.

Grammar

Main and subordinate clauses

A ***clause*** is a group of words that has a subject and a verb. It can be a complete sentence.

I took my dog to the park.

It can also be a part of a sentence.

He did not pick up the phone ***because he was very busy****.*

The second sentence has two clauses:

1. He did not receive the phone (main clause)
2. because he was very busy (subordinate clause)

A **main clause** is one that expresses a complete thought and has a subject and a verb. It can stand independently within or as a sentence. The sentence, 'I took my dog to the park.' is also a main clause.

A **subordinate clause** is one that cannot stand alone. Like a main clause, a subordinate clause also has a subject and a verb.

But it differs from a main clause in that it expresses an incomplete idea and usually begins with a relative pronoun (*who*, *whom*, *which*, etc) or a subordinating conjunction (*because*, *before*, etc). Look at two more examples. The words in bold are subordinate clauses.

When the dog barked, *the children ran away.*

This is the man ***who fell down at the supermarket.***

A **Write down whether the words in italics form a main clause or a subordinate clause.**

1. *The man* who was wearing a red shirt *walked into the hospital.*
2. Mary had a little lamb *whose fleece was white as snow.*
3. Before you leave, *you must check your belongings.*
4. *We are free to do what we want* until school reopens.
5. *If you cannot run fast,* you should not participate in this event.
6. We met at the supermarket, *where we were both buying groceries.*
7. The frog thinks *that it is a nightingale.*
8. Where is the book *that I gave you yesterday?*

B **Underline the main clauses and circle the subordinate clauses in these sentences.**

1. I want to reach home before it gets dark.
2. She missed the bus, which left five minutes before time.
3. Although they protested, the rules were not changed.
4. The crowd cheered when Tansen sang.
5. This is the gentleman who helped us with our luggage.
6. I was absent because I was sick.
7. If you do not eat well, you will fall ill.
8. We waited for him, though we were not sure that he would come.

Listening

Music and me

Tansen's music had an effect on both people and nature. Animals were attracted to the *ashram;* people felt that they had moved beyond the earth to a beautiful place; they felt transfixed.

Music affects people in many different ways. It can take you to other places; it can make you feel many different emotions: a song might make you feel great, or maybe sometimes it will make you feel upset.

Discuss with your friends how music makes you feel different emotions. Record your ideas in your notebook.

A **Listen to five pieces of music. As you listen, note down how each piece makes you feel.**

1. ______________________________
2. ______________________________
3. ______________________________
4. ______________________________
5. ______________________________

B **Discuss these questions with your classmates.**

- Did you have different reactions to these pieces of music or did you feel the same?
- Which pieces of music made you feel good and why?
- Which pieces of music did you not like and why?

Speaking

Narrating a personal experience

A **When you narrate a personal experience to people, you describe it from your own point of view. A personal experience is expressed in the first person, using the pronouns 'I' and 'we'.**

Imagine that you attended a live performance by A. R Rahman. Talk to your friends about the experience. You should include these points:

- a description of the performance
- your experience of interacting with A. R Rahman and members of his team
- the high points of the performance
- why it was memorable for you

Planning an event

B **Imagine that your school is organizing a special assembly. The headmistress, teachers and students from your school will attend. The headmistress is inviting local VIPs and also journalists from your local newspaper. She has asked you and your classmates to organize musical performances for the assembly.**

In groups of four or five, discuss these questions and make notes. When you are ready, share your plans with the rest of your class.

- How many people will perform at the assembly?

- Who will perform? You can choose people from your school or outside.
- What will each performer do? Will they sing or play music?
- For how long will each person perform?

Useful phrases

Making suggestions

I think we should ...

What about ...?/How about ...?

We could ...

Agreeing and disagreeing

Great!

Yes, that's a good idea.

Yes, let's do that!

I'm not so sure about that.

Hmm, maybe, but ...

I don't think we should do that.

Writing

Think about a time when you watched a musical performance. If you have never watched a musical performance, imagine a performance by your favourite musician.

Write a report about the performance for your school magazine.

Your report should contain:

A headline: This is a short phrase or clause that describes your report.

Introduction: This should capture the most important aspect of the event. It should be catchy and capture the attention of the reader.

The main section: This will include all the details of the music event. You can also include a few lines spoken by important persons or audience members about the event.

Conclusion: This is the section where you conclude your report by stating the main points in brief and giving any other additional information in short.

Here are some ideas to help you.

- What was the event? When was it held and where?
- How was the atmosphere before the performance? Who was the audience? How did they feel?
- Who was performing? What did they perform? How long did it last?
- How would you describe the performance? How did it make you feel?
- How did the audience react during the performance?
- How did the event end?

Useful phrases

Last week/summer/year, I went to see ... at ... in ...
Before the show/concert, the atmosphere was electric/expectant.
The audience was full of anticipation.
The orchestra played ...
... sang two of my favourite songs.
The show lasted ... hours.
The audience clapped and cheered.
The orchestra stood up and bowed.
I went home tired but happy.

Show your report to your classmates.

Do they have any advice on how you can improve your report?

Checking a classmate's work

Clarify: ask for clarification if anything isn't clear.
Value: value your classmate's work; be supportive.
Suggest: make helpful suggestions where you can.

Poem

This poem talks about nature. It describes how the earth never stops rejoicing, even as summer gives way to the bitter cold of winter. The grasshopper and the cricket's songs are examples of nature's celebration of life.

On the Grasshopper and Cricket

The poetry of earth is never dead:
When all the birds are faint with the hot sun
And hide in the trees, a voice will run
From hedge to hedge about the newmown[1] mead[2].
That is the grasshopper's – he takes the lead
In summer luxury – he has never done
With his delights; for when tired out with fun
He rests at ease beneath some pleasant weed.
The poetry of earth is ceasing[3] never:
On a lone winter evening when the frost
Has wrought[4] a silence, from the stove there shrills
The cricket's song, in warmth increasing ever,
And seems, to one in drowsiness half lost,
The grasshopper's among some grassy hills.

John Keats

Wordfile

1. The grass in a **newmown** field or meadow has recently been cut.
2. **Mead** is a literary word for a meadow, which is a field with grass and flowers.
3. If something **ceases**, it stops.
4. If something has **wrought** a change, it has caused it. (*literary*)

About the poet

John Keats (1795–1821) was an English Romantic poet. His poetry is known for its vivid imagery and for celebrating the beauty of nature and the human mind. His best-known poems are 'Ode to a Nightingale', 'To Autumn' and 'Ode on a Grecian Urn'. He died at the age of twenty-five from tuberculosis.

Poetry appreciation

A **Label the different elements in the pictures. Use these words from the poem.**

mead
hedge
grasshopper
hills
stove
frost
cricket

B Answer the questions.

1. 'The cricket's song, in warmth increasing ever,
   And seems, to one in drowsiness half lost,
   The grasshopper's among some grassy hills.'
   a. When and where does a cricket sing?
   b. What does the song of the cricket remind one of?
   c. Explain the phrase, 'in warmth increasing ever'.
2. 'The poetry of earth is never dead:' Do you agree? Give your reasons.
3. Keats describes a grasshopper and a cricket in his poem. According to the poem, how are the grasshopper and the cricket similar? How are they different?
4. Write down the rhyme scheme of the poem.
5. The poet has used personification in the poem.
   Personification is a literary device in which animals and non-living things are imagined as human beings with thoughts, actions and emotions. Pick out a few lines from the poem that personify the earth and its creatures.
6. In the poem, Keats writes about summer and winter in England. Think about your own experience of summer and winter. In your notebook, write the answers to these questions:
   a. What is the weather like?
   b. How does the weather affect animals and people? How do they feel? What do they do?
   c. What sounds can you hear in each season?

Activity

Keats' poem 'On the Grasshopper and Cricket' is called an **ode**. An ode is a poem to celebrate and praise a specific person, place or object.

Write an ode of your own.

Use these points while writing the ode.

- Think of a person, a place or an object that you like very much. It could be something in nature, a piece of music, a singer or musician, or anything else.
- In your notebook, write down some adjectives and phrases that describe how you feel about that person, place or object.
- Write a short verse about that 'something' in your notebook (6–10 lines).
- Find or draw a picture to illustrate your ode.
- Read your ode to your classmates and teacher. If your ode is about a person you know, give them a copy of your ode to read.

3 War and Peace

In this unit, I will ...

- study a dictionary entry for a word with two meanings
- learn some abbreviations and acronyms, and to form antonyms using prefixes
- learn about transitive and intransitive verbs and phrasal verbs
- correct incorrect English and act out a scene with some given expressions

Warm-up

Look at these symbols of peace. What are they and what do they mean? What else do you know about the symbols? Do you think world peace is possible? Discuss with your classmates.

1

2

3

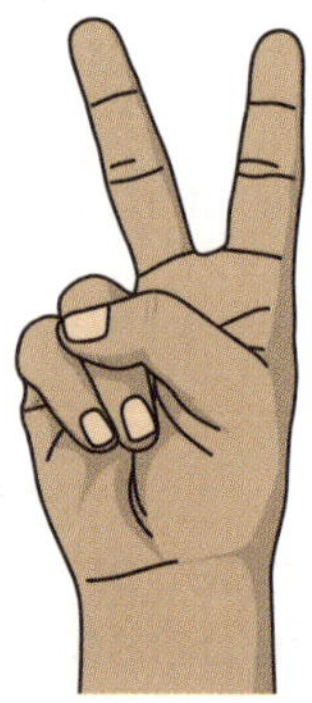

4

5

6

7

Reading 1

Here is another symbol for peace. It has three words for 'peace' written on it: *shalom* in Hebrew; *salaam* in Arabic; and *peace* in English. What do you think this symbol represents? Discuss with a partner.

This symbol represents peace in the Middle East. It asks for an end to the long conflict between Jewish people living in Israel and Arab Palestinians living in the West Bank and the Gaza Strip. Children in these countries have grown up with the conflict, and although they are neighbours, it is often difficult for Israelis and Palestinians to become friends. In 2015, there was an increase of violence between the two sides. Many lives were lost in the conflict, thousands of people were displaced and homes destroyed.

It is surprising that cricket has been the harbinger of peace and harmony in the troubled region. A novel concept, Cricket 4 Peace, was initiated a few years ago to bring together Israeli and Palestinian children from disadvantaged communities.

But has the project been successful in its endeavour of inculcating the old virtues of peace and harmony? Let us read about a Palestinian boy, Shehadeh Salamin, who won an international prize.

Palestinian and Israeli Children are Batting for Peace

A Palestinian boy who plucked up the courage[1] to play cricket with Israelis has won an international prize from Israel's biggest cricketing organization.

Three months ago, sixteen-year-old Shehadeh Salamin from the West Bank entered an International Cricket Council Europe competition entitled 'How has cricket made a difference to your life?'

He wrote about how his sporting contact with Jewish youngsters has given him a 'new lease of life'[2], and as a result has won a rollout cricket pitch for the Israel Cricket Association (ICA).

Mr Salamin wrote in his story: 'All my life, I dreamt of being a famous Palestinian footballer ... until our village was introduced to cricket. The game rapidly became our flagship sport, with most kids preferring cricket over soccer.'

Wordfile

1. If you **pluck up the courage** to do something frightening, you make an effort to be brave enough to do it.
2. If somebody has been given **a new lease of life**, they are more lively and active than they were in the past.

The local youngsters decided to play with Israeli youngsters in Beersheva, even though Mr Salamin admits that he had 'concerns', but the Israeli coach's 'words broke the barrier of fear in me'. He wrote that cricket made him more confident.

He concluded: 'Today I dream of a cricket club in Palestine and of becoming the first Palestinian cricketer to play in an international league. I'm sure that with those Israeli and Palestinian children who participated with me, we can also realize the dream of peace together.'

The ICA's Cricket for Peace programme has signed up 120 children, half of them Israeli and half Palestinian, who play cricket together in Beersheva or Dimona once a month.

The Peres Centre for Peace oversees the complex logistics involved in getting permits for the youngsters to pass through Israeli checkpoints[3].

The accolade has special significance, given that in most of the 37 country members of the International Cricket Council Europe, cricket is far more widespread and well resourced than in Israel.

The International Cricket Council Europe's development manager for Europe, Nick Pink, said that the ICA has 'deservedly received worldwide recognition for the way they have used cricket as a vehicle to break down global barriers in and around Israel'.

Herschel Gutman, cricket development officer for the ICA, said that the friendships that the youngsters build on the pitch continue between matches. 'The players are connecting all the time with each other on Facebook, as are the coaches – it is building relationships and creating connections.'

For the ICA's chairman of 19 years, Stanley Perlman, the award was recognition of a long-standing vision. 'This was a dream of mine, to have Palestinian kids playing with Israeli kids,' he said. 'It's a wonderful feeling to have world recognition for something that has been so hard to do.' The future of the Cricket for Peace programme is not certain, despite the award. It costs £30,000 a year to run, and only half of its costs for 2013 have been secured.

Nathan Jeffay, March 28, 2013

Did you know?

A **rollout cricket pitch** is like a carpet for playing cricket. It is portable so you can take it to different places to play – even on concrete! They were developed in South Africa and can be up to 30 metres in length.

Wordfile

3. A **checkpoint** is a place where traffic and people have to be stopped and checked.

Comprehension 1

A Read these statements about the Cricket 4 Peace programme and mark them as true (T) or false (F).

1. The programme has 120 children. ________
2. Most of the children are from Israel, and a small number are Palestinian. ________
3. The children play cricket together once a month in Israel. ________
4. The players and the coaches don't have a very good relationship. ________
5. The programme does not have all the money it needs for its future. ________

B Shehedah Salamin plays cricket with the Cricket 4 Peace programme. Complete this paragraph about Shehedah.

Shehedah is [1]__________ years old and he is from [2]________________. He wanted to be a [3]__________ but then he discovered a new sport, [4]__________. He decided to play with children from [5]__________. He liked the Israeli coach and he became more [6]__________. Now he would like to play in his own country, and he would like to be the first Palestinian to play in [7]________________. He recently entered a competition and he won a [8]________________.

C Shehedah wrote about the question: 'How has cricket made a difference to your life?' Which of the following is true? Choose three answers.

1. He now feels more lively and active.
2. It has helped him to achieve his dream of becoming a footballer.
3. He was afraid to play with Israeli children but the coach helped him to overcome his fear.
4. He believes that all the children on the programme will help to bring about peace.
5. He hated Israeli children and still doesn't like playing with them.

D Shehedah says that he 'plucked up the courage to play cricket with Israelis'. This illustrates the fear that he had about playing with Israeli children. Find a sentence in the passage which shows the fear that the young Palestinians felt.

E What is the role of the Peres Centre for Peace in the programme? Choose the best answer.

1. It checks the permits of all the children on the programme. ☐
2. It helps children to get permits to enter Israel. ☐
3. It promotes cricket in the region. ☐

Comprehension 2

Nick Pink says the ICA has 'received worldwide recognition for the way they have used cricket as a vehicle to break down global barriers in and around Israel'.

This means that the ICA has used cricket as a way to get Israelis and Palestinians to connect with each other.

VBQ 1. Do you think something like cricket can break down barriers? Do you think it can bring peace to countries that are in conflict? Discuss with a partner.

VBQ 2. Apart from sports, what other things can be used to bring people together, to create and sustain a bond?

Vocabulary check

Sports

A There are lots of words related to sports in the article you have just read. Complete the sentences about sports using these words. Use your dictionary to help you.

pitch footballer club coach soccer league

1. My team is bottom of the __________ at the moment.
2. Did you know that football is called __________ in American English?
3. Rakesh goes to football training every day after school. He wants to be a professional __________ when he is older.
4. The __________ was too wet for the teams to play today.
5. The team members are really improving their skills with the new __________. She is excellent.
6. I've just joined a hockey __________.

Forming antonyms by adding prefixes

B Use the prefixes *dis-*, *in-*, *il-*, *ir-*, *im-* or *un-* to form the antonyms of these words.

1. polite __________
2. regular __________
3. accurate __________
4. legal __________
5. comfort __________
6. sure __________
7. balanced __________
8. available __________
9. necessary __________
10. order __________
11. logical __________
12. tamed __________

Language skills

Using a dictionary

A Read the dictionary entry for the word 'barrier' and answer the questions.

barrier /bæriə/ (barriers)

1. N-COUNT A barrier is a fence or wall that prevents people or things from moving from one area to another. *The crowds stood behind barriers at the side of the road.*
2. N-COUNT A barrier is something such as a law or policy that makes it difficult or impossible for something to happen. *Taxes are the most obvious barrier to free trade.*

Word Partnership

Use *barrier* with:

v. **break down a** barrier, **cross a** barrier (1)

n. barrier **islands/reef, police** barrier (1)

prep. barrier **between** (1) (2)

adj. **psychological** barrier, **racial** barrier (2)

1. The word *barrier* can be used as how many different parts of speech? ________________
2. How many meanings does it have? ________________
3. Read these two sentences from the passage. Which meaning does the word *barrier* have in these sentences, (1) or (2)? ________________
   a. The Israeli coach's words broke the barrier of fear in me.
   b. They have used cricket as a vehicle to break down global barriers in and around Israel.
4. Write an example sentence for each meaning. Use the phrases in the Word Partnership box to help you.

   ____

   ____

B Circle the correct spelling.

1. newmonia pneumonia neumonia
2. acommodate accomodate accommodate
3. attendance attendence atendence
4. mischievous mischeivous mischievious
5. occasion occassion ocassion
6. weird wierd weired

Reading 2

The Second World War began in 1939. In the period before the war, life became very difficult for Jewish people in Germany. They lost their jobs and businesses; they were not allowed to go to public schools, cinemas or theatres; and they were not allowed to live in certain places. Many were killed. During this time, around 10,000 Jewish children went to live in the United Kingdom. They lived with local families during the war.

This is the story of Matthias Pincus, known as Matti in the story. Matti is one of the many German Jewish children who are being sent to England by their parents because Germany has become unsafe for Jews. This story is set in 1938, the year just before the Second World War began.

Read this story to find out how Matti copes with being separated from his parents and moving to a new country.

Matti's Miracle

Matti is on a train to England with other children and a group leader.

The train arrives at the station. There are groups of people waiting on the platform. The little group gets off the train and waits at the platform.

All the children are gradually taken away by families. Soon only Matti is left.

They see a woman rushing towards them.

They arrive at a little station and are received by Mr Williams.

Mr and Mrs Williams take Matti home with them. Back at home, Mrs Williams shows Matti his room.

Matti quickly tears open the letter.

Dear Matti,

Just a few lines so you know that we are always thinking of you and hope to join you very soon. Pappi has applied for visas for us to come to England and we trust they'll arrive quickly.

Please try to be happy in England and not to worry about us. I'm sure that your family in England will be nice to you, so be brave, my darling.

All my love always,

Mutti

Matti sits down at the table and grabs a pen.

Dear Mutti and Pappi,

I have arrived. I'm living in a little thatched cottage, just like the ones you see in the pictures of England. My room is small but very light, and there are football pictures up on the wall! Uncle Jack is a chauffeur and drives a very big car for a rich lady. Aunt Lily and Uncle Jack are both very nice.

I miss you so much and want to cry all the time but I know that I'm one of the lucky ones and try not to. The worst thing is not being able to understand everything they say. But I'm glad you taught me some English and I know I'll get better at speaking it when I go to an English school.

I love you Mutti and Pappi. Come here soon!

Matti

Mr and Mrs Williams send Matti to school and he gradually settles down in his new school and home.

One day while returning from school, Matti unknowingly ventures into someone's private property.

Matti is terrified. The last time he has seen guns was when his father was arrested. He runs back home in fright.

But it turns out that the lady was none other than Lady Dorincourt.

To his astonishment, Lady Dorincourt responds in German!

A few days after Lady Dorincourt's visit, Mrs Williams finds Matti crying.

So that evening, Matti goes to the big house clutching an apple strudel[6].

Lady Dorincourt, who lives alone in the big house, welcomes him warmly.

Lady Dorincourt rings the bell, and an old lady staggers in.

Over the next few days, Matti visits the big house often and keeps Lady Dorincourt company.

Matti leaves that afternoon feeling more excited than he has in ages.

But things change when he meets Lady Dorincourt the next time.

Matti returns home in the depths of despair. The weeks go by and he starts having problems in school, and at home. He can't concentrate on his lessons and he hardly eats a thing or says a word. As each day passes, the situation is becoming worse and worse in Germany.

One evening, the phone rings. Lady Dorincourt has suffered a stroke[7] and is in hospital. Matti and Mrs Williams decide to visit her there.

Matti shyly gives Lady Dorincourt a warm hug.

Ann Jungman

Wordfile

1. **Sussex** is an area in the south of England.
2. **Lady** is a title used in front of the names of some women from the upper classes.
3. A **poacher** is someone who illegally catches animals, fish or birds on someone else's property.
4. The **Gestapo** were the secret police in Germany from 1933 to 1945. They imprisoned many Jews illegally and treated them cruelly.
5. A **refugee** is a person who has been forced to leave their country because there is a war there, or because of their political or religious beliefs.
6. **Apple strudel** is a type of apple cake, often eaten in Germany.
7. When someone has a **stroke**, a blood vessel in their brain bursts, which may kill them or cause one side of their body to be paralysed.
8. Something which is **ghastly** is unpleasant or frightening.

Comprehension 1

A Number the sentences in the order of events in the story.

1. Matti receives a letter from home with some news. The police in Germany have attacked his father. ________
2. Lady Dorincourt goes to hospital. She can only go home if she has someone to provide food and medical advice. ________
3. Matti goes to live in a village with Mr and Mrs Williams. ________
4. Matti takes a cake to Lady Dorincourt and asks her if his parents could work for her as servants. ________
5. Mrs Williams persuades Lady Dorincourt to arrange for Matti's parents to come and work for her. ________
6. One day, Matti goes into the woods and finds that they belong to Lady Dorincourt. ________
7. Matti arrives in England with other children from Germany. ________
8. Lady Dorincourt says that it is not possible to bring Matti's parents over from Germany at the moment. ________

B Answer the questions.

1. How do the children feel when they arrive in England?
2. Matti speaks a little English. How did he learn it?
3. What is Mr Williams' job, and who does he work for?
4. Why is it difficult to bring Matti's parents to England as refugees?
5. What do Matti's parents do for a living?
6. Why doesn't Lady Dorincourt agree to sign the forms at first?
7. Why does she agree to sign the forms in the end?

Comprehension 2

1. At the end of the story, Lady Dorincourt agrees to sign the forms to bring Matti's parents over to England. Matti says: 'It won't be easy for them at first.'

   Why do you think it might be difficult for Matti's parents at first? Share your responses with a partner.

2. How does Matti cope with being separated from his parents and moving to a new country? Find examples in the story which illustrate your answer.

   Think about:

   - how he feels
   - the language
   - his new home and school
   - his host parents

VBQ 3. What, according to you, are the acts of kindness in the story?

VBQ 4. Imagine you are Matti. How would you have persuaded Lady Dorincourt to bring your parents from Germany? What did Matti do wrong? How would you avoid making the same mistake?

Vocabulary

Abbreviations and acronyms

An **abbreviation** is a shortened form of a word or a name.

Dept. (Department)

St. (Street)

An **acronym** is a word formed from the first letters of each word in a phrase.

WWF (World Wildlife Fund)

USA (United States of America)

A Find the full forms of these abbreviations and acronyms.

1. UNICEF ____________________
2. VIP ____________________
3. Capt. ____________________
4. Gen. ____________________
5. CID ____________________
6. NASA ____________________
7. WHO ____________________
8. POW ____________________
9. UFO ____________________
10. Lt. ____________________
11. SARS ____________________
12. AWOL ____________________

Inside the body

B **In the story 'Matti's Miracle', Lady Dorincourt has a stroke, and has to go to hospital. A stroke occurs when blood cannot reach the brain.**

Write the name of the part of the body that each of these illnesses involves. Write 'brain', 'blood', 'lungs' or 'heart'.

1. asthma attack ___________
2. clot ___________
3. haemorrhage ___________
4. bronchitis ___________
5. migraine ___________
6. tuberculosis ___________
7. cardiac arrest ___________
8. glaucoma ___________
9. peptic ulcer ___________
10. arthritis ___________

War words

C **Circle the odd one out.**

1. rebel soldier guard professor
2. regiment squadron union battalion
3. scalpel ammunition weapon missile
4. assault invasion lecture ambush
5. battle seminar clash fight

Grammar

Transitive and intransitive verbs

Read these sentences from the story 'Matti's Miracle'.

The little group ***waits*** *on the platform.*
The train ***arrives*** *at the station.*
I should ***apologize****.*
They ***live*** *in a Sussex village.*

The verbs *waits*, *arrives*, *apologize* and *live* are **intransitive** verbs.

This means that they are not followed by an object. (An object is a noun or a pronoun which receives the action of a verb.)

Now read these sentences from the story.

Mrs and Mr Williams ***send*** *Matti to school.*
I will ***take*** *some German cake to her.*
I ***borrowed*** *the car for today.*
It would ***solve*** *everything.*

The verbs *send*, *take*, *borrow* and *solve* are **transitive** verbs. That means that they are followed by an object.

The nouns *Matti*, *cake*, *car* and *everything* are the objects in the sentences above.

A Read these sentences from the story. Are the verbs in bold transitive or intransitive? Write *T* or *I*.

1. We'll **miss** our train home. ______
2. Matti unknowingly **ventures** into someone's private property. ______
3. So that evening, Matti **goes** to the big house. ______
4. Can you **make** some tea? ______
5. Mrs Williams **finds** Matti **crying**. ______ ______
6. I've already **acquired** a new family and a splendid grandson. ______
7. The doctor **prescribed** complete bed rest for Lady Dorincourt. ______
8. The teacher **solved** all the problems. ______

You know that a phrasal verb is a verb that is made up of a main verb and a preposition like **up**, **out** or **down**.

Phrasal verbs can also be **intransitive** or **transitive**. When a phrasal verb is **intransitive**, the parts of the verb are not separated.

The bus ***broke down****.*

Now look at this **transitive** phrasal verb which has the direct object 'my father'.

They ***beat up*** *my father.*

When a phrasal verb is **transitive**, it is sometimes possible to separate the parts of the verb. This is nearly always done when the object is a pronoun.

They ***beat*** *him* ***up****.*

B **Read the sentences. Are the highlighted phrasal verbs transitive or intransitive? Write *T* or *I*.**

1. We all **sat down** to have our dinner. ______
2. Roy gradually **settled down** in his new school. ______
3. We **put off** our picnic for two weeks. ______
4. After a series of bad incidents, things finally started **looking up**. ______
5. Would you please **look up** a word in the dictionary? ______
6. The technicians **set up** our new home theatre. ______

C **Read these sentences with transitive phrasal verbs. Change the object to a pronoun and rewrite each sentence so that the phrasal verb is separated.**

1. Families gradually take away the children.

   Families gradually take them away.

2. Matti quickly tears open the letter.

   ______

3. Will you fill in the forms?

   ______

4. Atul gave up eating mangoes many years ago.

   ______

5. Our teacher turned down our request for an outing.

   ______

6. Could you please switch on the radio?

   ______

Study tip

Some phrasal verbs can be separated, and some cannot.

*They can **look after** me.* (We can't say 'They can look me after.')

She put out the light. (We can also say 'She put the light out.')

When you come across a new phrasal verb, write an example sentence in your notebook to show whether the verb is separable or non-separable.

Listening

Matti's English

A **Matti is learning English during his stay in England. Listen to six things he says. Does he use English correctly? Write 'correct' or 'incorrect' in your notebook.**

B **Listen to Matti again. This time, write the correct versions in your notebook. Then discuss your answers with a partner.**

Speaking

Act out a scene

A **Look at these things that people say in the story. Who says them, and what is the situation?**

1. How do you do?
2. What's up?
3. Fancy that!
4. Pleased to meet you.
5. What a relief!
6. I never heard the like!
7. Bless you, dear.
8. The cheek of it!
9. Poor dear!

B **Work in pairs and act out one or more of the following scenes. You can use some of the expressions from exercise A.**

Scene 1

Student A: You are Matti. You are at the station waiting for Mrs Williams. Greet her.

Student B: You are Mrs Williams. You have arrived late at the station to meet Matti. Greet Matti, apologize for being late and explain why. Comment on Matti's English.

Scene 2

Student A: You are Matti. You are very upset because you have had bad news from home about your father. Explain to Mrs Williams.

Student B: You are Mrs Williams. You want to know what has happened. Try to comfort Matti.

Scene 3

Student A: You are Lady Dorincourt. You are ill in hospital. You don't want to stay there and you try to persuade the doctor to let you go home.

Student B: You are the doctor. You tell Lady Dorincourt that she needs to have help at home. You try to persuade her to stay in hospital.

Writing

Imagine that you are Matti. Lady Dorincourt has agreed to fill in the forms so that your parents can come to England.

Write a letter to your parents to tell them what has happened.

Begin your letter using the given phrases, and use the suggestions to help you write the paragraphs.

Dear Pappi and Mutti,

I am writing to you with some very good news.
[Tell your parents that they can come to England.]

Let me tell you how this has happened. One day, I went into some woods and I met …
[Briefly tell the story of Lady Dorincourt, mentioning how at first she refused to fill in the forms.]

As you can imagine, I was feeling very upset. Then suddenly …
[Briefly tell the story of Lady Dorincourt's illness and how she agreed to fill in the forms.]

Now I am feeling …
[Briefly say how you are feeling and what you will do when your parents arrive.]

All my love always,
Matti

Poem

'Flanders Fields' is a common name for the vast grassy areas in Belgium where thousands of young men died during the First World War. Red poppies grew in the fields over the graves of the fallen soldiers.

It is thought that Canadian soldier, Dr John McCrae, began writing this famous poem on the evening of 2 May, 1915, inspired by the death of his friend, Alexis Helmer.

McCrae's poem led to the poppy becoming one of the world's most recognized symbols for soldiers who have died in conflict.

In Flanders Fields

In Flanders fields the poppies blow
Between the crosses, row on row,
That mark our place; and in the sky
The larks[1], still bravely singing, fly
Scarce heard amid[2] the guns below.

We are the Dead. Short days ago
We lived, felt dawn, saw sunset glow,
Loved and were loved, and now we lie
In Flanders fields.

Take up our quarrel with the foe[3]:
To you from failing[4] hands we throw
The torch; be yours to hold it high.
If ye[5] break faith with us who die
We shall not sleep, though poppies grow
In Flanders fields.

John McCrae

Wordfile

1. A **lark** is a species of songbird.
2. If something happens **amid** noise, shouting, gunfire, etc., it happens while there is a lot of noise, shouting, etc.
3. A **foe** is an enemy.
4. When something is **failing**, it is weak.
5. **Ye** is an old-fashioned form of 'you'.

About the author

John Alexander McCrae (1872–1918) was a Canadian poet, physician, author, artist and soldier during the First World War. He is best remembered for this poem, which is considered the most popular poem written during the war.

Poetry appreciation

1. In the phrase, 'that mark our place', who do you think 'our' refers to?
2. In the first stanza, what can be heard in the sky and on the land?
3. 'Short days ago

   We lived, felt dawn, saw sunset glow,

   Loved and were loved,'

   a. Who is refered to as 'we' here?

   b. What does 'felt dawn' mean?

   c. What happened to the 'we' in these lines?
4. 'To you from failing hands we throw/The torch;'

   a. What do you think the 'torch' symbolizes?

   b. What message is the poet giving to others?
5. 'If ye break faith with us.'

   Here, 'break faith' means:

   a. carry on the legacy of struggle

   b. lie

   c. break religious rules
6. Who or what do you think the 'foe' is in this poem?
7. What do you think 'poppies' stand for in this poem?

   a. the spirit of the dead

   b. flowers for the dead

   c. life after death

   d. the blood that was shed on the fields

   Choose any two options above. Give reasons for your choices..
8. The words 'Flanders fields' are an example of alliteration. Find two more examples of alliteration in the poem.
9. The poet talks about the lives, deaths and duties of soldiers. But victory in war often comes at the cost of precious lives. Do you think it's fair that soldiers are expected to give up their lives for their country? VBQ
10. Do you think war can solve the problems between nations? Give reasons for your answer. VBQ

Activity

In this unit, we have read about how war affects people's lives. Refugees (people who have to live in another country because of war in their own country) are victims of wars. Europe is currently dealing with a refugee crisis, partly as a result of the Syrian war.

A What difficulties might people face as refugees in a new country? In small groups, discuss these points:

- their homes
- their families and friends
- their possessions
- food and drink
- their education and language
- the way others might treat them in their new country

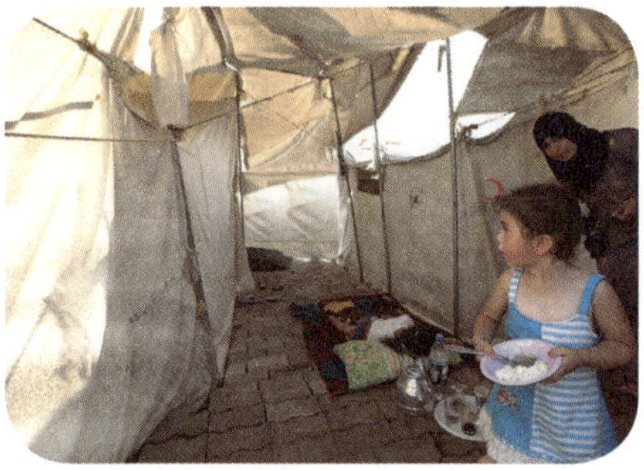

B Imagine that some refugees have moved to your area, and some of the children are about to come to your school. You are part of a committee that has been created to support them.

In groups of four, plan how you can help the children settle into your school and community. Think about the difficulties that you discussed. Once your plans are ready, share them with the rest of the class.

You can make notes here.

Make a wall chart about music

Do you like listening to music? What kind of music do you listen to?

Look at the pictures of musical instruments. Write the name of each instrument under its picture.

1 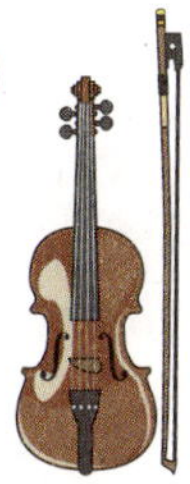 ______________

2 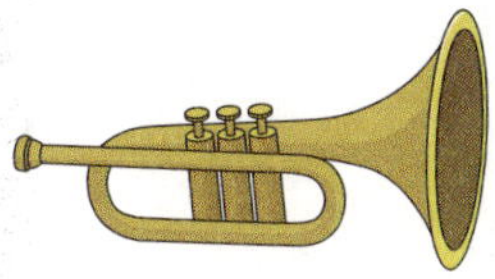 ______________

3  ______________

4  ______________

5  ______________

6  ______________

7  ______________

8 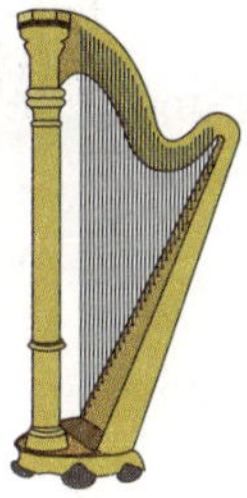 ______________

9  ______________

Look at these styles of music:

jazz hip hop classical rock bhangra rap

Work in groups. Together, select one style of music and make a wall chart for that particular music form. You should include the following information:

- famous musicians who represent that music style
- five of the most popular songs or compositions in that style
- any particular musical instruments that are used in that style
- where the form originated
- any particular countries or regions where it is popular

You could include advertisements, articles, news reports, quotes and pictures to make the wall chart more colourful and informative.

Peer pressure

Roli's birthday is next week.

When her friend Jenny celebrated her birthday a few months ago, she took all her friends to see a film. Everyone came, and they had a great time. Roli wants to take her friends to see a film, too, but she knows her parents will not approve of such an expensive celebration.

Roli is worried that if she doesn't give her friends a special treat too, they may not come to her party at all.

A What should she do? Should she:

1. celebrate her birthday the way she wants to and make it more interesting by adding some other games? ☐
2. make an excuse not to celebrate her birthday at all this year? ☐
3. celebrate her birthday only with her family, and not invite her friends? ☐
4. persuade her parents to give her the money? ☐
5. break up with her friends if they don't come to her party, and then make new friends? ☐

B Have you ever done something just because all your friends were doing it? If yes, what was it?

How did you feel afterwards?

1. happy ☐
2. anxious ☐
3. sad ☐
4. guilty ☐
5. disappointed in yourself ☐

C Which of the following factors make it hard to resist peer pressure?

1. not knowing how the other person will react ☐
2. fear of rejection by the group or the person ☐
3. fear of being made fun of ☐
4. not wanting to upset or hurt another person's feelings ☐
5. not knowing how to get out of a situation ☐
6. ease of doing what others are doing ☐

D Is peer pressure always bad, or can it have a positive effect too? In groups, act out the following situations. Ask your audience to raise their hands if they have faced a similar situation.

1. Annie has been watching television all day. Her friends have come to her house and want her to join them for a game of badminton.
2. Arvind is planning to spend the afternoon playing games on the computer. His friends want to go swimming in the local pool. They refuse to go unless he comes along.
3. Ishani wants to spend her weekly pocket money at the mall. Her friends usually accompany her. But this time, they, as well as Ishani have to prepare a school project about a visit to an old age home. They want to spend their own weekly pocket money on gifts for the residents of the home they will visit. But Ishani is reluctant to join them.

E You might have faced peer pressure in your daily life. You might have also knowingly, or otherwise, exerted peer pressure on others. Tick [✓] the boxes which apply to you and give an example.

Have you ever:

1. used peer pressure to make someone do something? ☐
2. had to do something against your wishes out of peer pressure? ☐
3. used peer pressure to help someone? ☐
4. done something out of peer pressure which had a positive effect on you? ☐

4 Important People

In this unit, I will ...

- practise noun-verb collocations and sentence stress
- learn some synonyms and antonyms related to success
- study present and past perfect tenses
- learn how to express regrets using 'I wish ...' and 'if only ...'
- listen to and act out a historical play, and write a formal letter

Warm-up

Saina Nehwal

J. K. Rowling

Kalpana Chawla

Dhirubhai Ambani

Read this list of famous and important people. What is each one famous for? Put each person in one of the groups below.

C. V. Raman Nelson Mandela J. K. Rowling Rabindranath Tagore Sachin Tendulkar
Ashoka the Great J. R. D. Tata Rani Laxmi Bai Charles Darwin Indira Gandhi
Steve Jobs Dhirubhai Ambani Lata Mangeshkar A. R. Rahman Bachendri Pal

Sport:

Literature:

Music:

Science:

Politics:

Entrepreneurship:

History:

Reading 1

Steve Jobs was an American entrepreneur and inventor. He founded the company Apple, which produce computers and devices such as the iPad and the iPhone. Jobs died in 2011 but his vision and work continue to have great influence in the worlds of music and technology today.

Jobs has also had great influence in the worlds of business and entrepreneurship. You are going to read a report written by one of the students who attended the speech that he gave at the commencement of Stanford University in 2005. In the speech, Jobs tells two stories.

Before you read the report, discuss this question with your classmates:

Jobs' first story is about 'connecting the dots'. Connecting the dots is a children's puzzle. It consists of a series of numbered dots which children connect with a pencil. As the child connects the dots in sequence, a picture is revealed. How do you think this puzzle relates to Jobs' life?

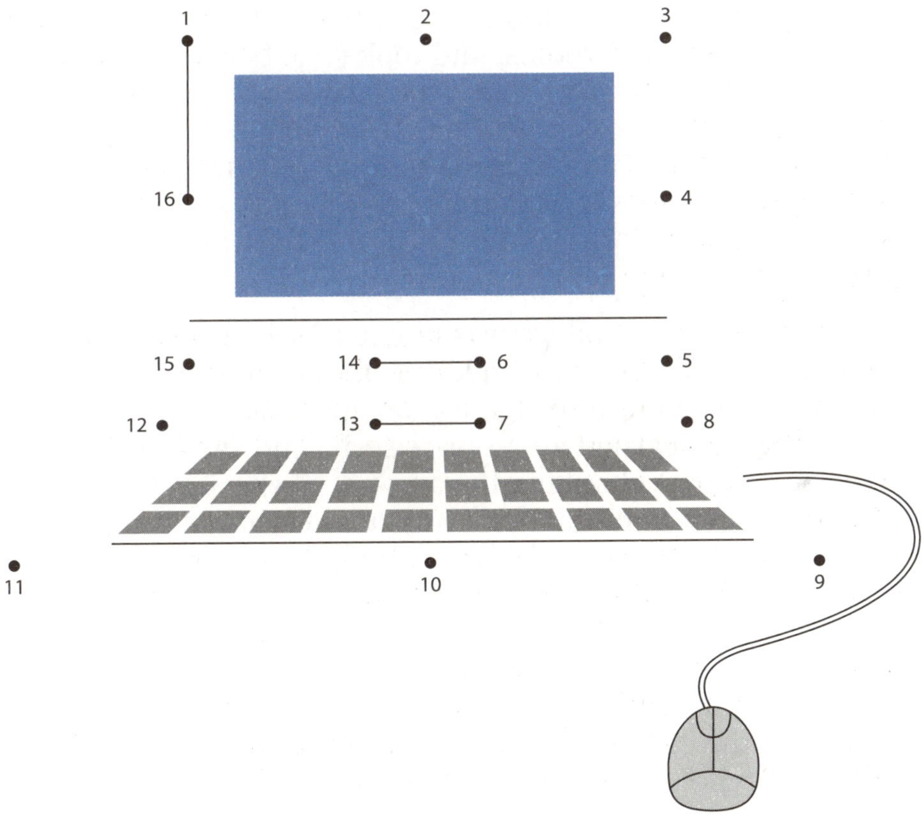

Steve Jobs: Do What You Love

I was honored to be among the audience at Steve Jobs' commencement[1] speech given at Stanford University, one of the finest universities in the world. I was astonished to hear that Jobs had never graduated from college, and that this was the closest he'd ever gotten to a college graduation.

We listened in awe as he told us two stories about his life. The first story was about 'connecting the dots'. I wasn't sure what this meant at first but it became clearer as I listened. Jobs explained that he did go to college but that he naively[2] chose an expensive one, and his working-class parents were spending the money they had saved on his tuition. After six months, he decided to drop out[3] because he didn't know what he wanted to do, nor how college would help him find that out. He admitted that it was scary to do this, but he trusted that everything would be OK, and in the end, he said it was one of the best decisions he ever made.

At first, he didn't have anywhere to live so he slept on the floor in friends' rooms, and took coke bottles back to shops to collect the five-cent deposits in order to buy food. He even walked seven miles across town once a week to get a meal at the Hare Krishna temple. I would find this very hard, but Jobs said that he loved it, and added that following his curiosity and intuition[4] helped him later on. Here's an example that he gave us:

At the time, Reed College was famous for its calligraphy[5] course. Jobs didn't know anything about the subject, but his curiosity led him to sign up for the class. Some of the things he learned about were serif[6] and sans serif[7] typefaces, about changing the amount of space between different letter combinations, and about what makes typography[8] important. When he took the course, it wasn't useful to him, but he was fascinated by the subject, and remembered everything ten years later when he was designing the first Macintosh computer. It became the first computer with beautiful typography, and if Jobs had not done the course, the Mac would never have had all the different typefaces for which it became so famous.

Wordfile

1. **Commencement** is a formal ceremony where students receive their degrees.
2. If you do something **naively**, you do it thinking that it is going to be easy when it is not.
3. If someone **drops out** of university, they leave it without finishing the course.
4. Your **intuition** is a feeling you have that something is true, even when you have no proof.
5. **Calligraphy** is the art of producing beautiful writing.
6. A **serif** is a small line added to the end of a letter for printing. AaBbCc
7. **Sans serif** is a font without the small lines. AaBbCc
8. **Typography** is the design of writing in print or on a computer.

Now I understood what Jobs meant by 'connecting the dots'. When you look back, you can see how things that you did in your past connect, and you have to trust that they will connect in your future. Steve said, 'You have to trust in something – your gut[9], destiny, life, karma[10], whatever.' This made me think about what I'm doing now; will all the seemingly random experiences I'm currently having one day fall into place? Will they, at some point, come together to make a coherent story?

Jobs went on to tell us about his second story, which was about 'love and loss'. He had found that he loved building computers and thinking about how to make them better. He and his friend Woz (Steve Wozniak) started Apple in his parents' garage when he was 20. They worked hard, and within 10 years, Apple had grown into a $2 billion company with over 4,000 employees. When he turned 30, they had just released the Macintosh. And then he got fired. Apple had hired someone to run the company with Jobs, but the two fell out[11] because they had different visions of the future. The Board of Directors agreed with the other person, and Jobs lost his job.

I wasn't surprised to hear that Jobs was devastated to be fired, but I was shocked when he said it was the best thing that could have happened to him. He said, 'The heaviness of being successful was replaced by the lightness of being a beginner again.' Now he was free and could be even more creative.

Over the next five years, he started a company called NeXT, and then another called Pixar. The world's first computer animated film, *Toy Story*, was created by Pixar and the company, according to Jobs, is now the most successful animation studio in the world. Apple bought NeXT, and so Jobs returned to Apple. He would probably never have set up Pixar to make wonderful animated films if he hadn't been fired from Apple.

Jobs finished his speech with some advice: 'Sometimes life hits you in the head with a brick. Don't lose faith.' Jobs believed that it is important to find something that you love. I'll always remember his final, inspiring sentences: 'The only way to be truly satisfied is to do what you believe is great work. And the only way to do great work is to love what you do. If you haven't found it yet, keep looking. Don't settle. Don't give up.'

Did you know?

Jobs visited India in 1974 and stayed for seven months. He developed an interest in Buddhism, and considered becoming a Buddhist monk. He remained a Buddhist for the rest of his life.

According to Steve Jobs, he named his company Apple because he was only eating fruit at the time. He thought the name was fun and spirited.

Wordfile

9. Your **gut** (short for **gut feeling**) is based on instinct or emotion rather than on reason.
10. **Karma** is the belief among Hindus and Buddhists that what you do in this life will influence what happens in the next one.
11. If two people **fall out**, they have an argument that causes them to stop being friendly.

Comprehension 1

A Tick [✓] the correct answer.

1. Steve Jobs did not graduate from college. He left before finishing his course. Why did he drop out?
   a. He wanted to study at the Hare Krishna temple. [ ]
   b. He wanted to make money, so he decided to sell bottles instead. [ ]
   c. His college was expensive, and he did not feel that it was helping him. [ ]

2. Why did he study calligraphy after leaving college?
   a. He was designing his first computer and wanted to learn about typefaces. [ ]
   b. He was just curious about calligraphy and typefaces. [ ]
   c. He wanted to do a course that would be practical in his life. [ ]

3. Why did he leave the Apple company at the age of 30?
   a. He argued with another person who was running the company and was fired. [ ]
   b. He wanted to start other companies. [ ]
   c. He wanted to make an animated movie. [ ]

B Describe what Steve Jobs learnt on the calligraphy course and how it helped him in later life.

C Here are some of the events of Steve Jobs' life. Number them in the order that they happened.

1. He started his companies NeXT and Pixar. ________
2. He was fired from his company. ________
3. Apple bought NeXT and Pixar and he began working at Apple again. ________
4. He started his company Apple. ________
5. He took a course in calligraphy. ________
6. He dropped out of college after six months. ________
7. His company released its first computer, the Macintosh. ________

Comprehension 2

A **Read this line spoken by Steve Jobs and answer the questions.**

'The heaviness of being successful was replaced by the lightness of being a beginner again.'

1. Think of some successful people that you know. How do you think success might be 'heavy'?
2. Why might a person feel 'light' if they have to start all over again?

B **Read these lines spoken by Steve Jobs. Do you agree with them? Discuss with your classmates.**

1. 'You have to trust in something – your gut, destiny, life, karma, whatever.'
2. 'The only way to be truly satisfied is to do what you believe is great work.'
3. 'Keep looking. Don't settle.'

C **Do you think staying optimistic during hard times helps us? Discuss with your classmates.** VBQ

Vocabulary check

Word pairs

A **Circle the stronger word in each pair. Use a dictionary if you need to.**

1. expensive/exorbitant
2. scary/terrifying
3. fascinated/interested
4. useful/indispensable
5. important/essential
6. astonished/shocked
7. attractive/beautiful
8. love/affection
9. good/wonderful
10. devastated/disappointed

Verb + noun collocations

B **Match the verbs with the nouns that they are often used with.**

Verbs	Nouns
1. have	a. (the) fool
2. raise	b. (a) mistake
3. make	c. precaution
4. take	d. (one's) voice
5. play	e. fever

Language skills

Sentence stress

A Listen to these quotes from Steve Jobs. Circle the words which have the most emphasis, and note where there is a pause. Then practise reading them aloud.

1. 'You have to trust in something – your gut, destiny, life, karma.'
2. 'My second story is about love and loss.'
3. 'Sometimes, life hits you in the head with a brick. Don't lose faith.'
4. 'And the only way to do great work is to love what you do. If you haven't found it yet, keep looking.'

B Read these quotes from other famous people. Do you know who they are? Choose three quotes that you like and note the stressed words and pauses. Read them aloud.

1

Clouds come floating into my life, no longer to carry rain or usher storm but to add colour to my sunset sky.

Don't limit a child to your own learning, for he was born in another time.

2

If you want to make peace with your enemy, you have to work with your enemy. Then he becomes your partner.

I learned that courage was not the absence of fear, but the triumph over it. The brave man is not he who does not feel afraid, but he who conquers that fear.

3

There are two kinds of people: those who do the work and those who take the credit. Try to be in the first group; there is less competition there.

You must learn to be still in the midst of activity and to be vibrantly alive in repose.

Reading 2

The Pataliputra Mystery

Pataliputra was a city in ancient India. It was the capital of many dynasties, and during the Mauryan Dynasty it was one of the largest cities in the world. Today, Patna is on the same site.

You are going to read a play that revolves around a mysterious poem. Read on and see if you can interpret the poem.

Read the first part of Scene 1.

Characters

Nakul: Son of Jivaka, a soldier in the army of King Ashoka
Sheila, Laxman: Children of a potter
Aditya: An old Buddhist monk
Bappa: A soldier
Ashoka: The Mauryan King
Bhoja: A nobleman

Scene 1

Noises offstage[1]. Sounds of hooves, dogs barking, horses whinnying[2], children's voices, as the horseman rides away. The children enter. Nakul is carrying a cloth bundle.

Sheila: That rider must have dropped it. And he's gone!

Laxman: Let's open it and see. *(Unties and opens the cloth bundle.)*

What do you think is in the bundle? Discuss your ideas with your classmates, and then read the rest of Scene 1 of the play.

Laxman: Looks like a letter and it's in Brahmi[3]! Wish I could read it. Maybe his name and address are on this.

Nakul: *(taking the scroll[4] from him)* We'll have to find someone who can read Brahmi.

Sheila: Your wish is fulfilled.

(Aditya, a Buddhist monk, enters with his walking stick and his begging bowl.)

Aditya: Laxman! You're just the person I wanted to see. Tell your father to make another begging bowl for me. This one has a crack in it.

Laxman: Already! I gave you one just last month.

Wordfile

1. When something happens **offstage**, it happens behind or at the side of the stage so that the audience cannot see it.
2. When a horse **whinnies**, it makes a soft, high sound.
3. **Brahmi** is the modern name for one of the oldest scripts of ancient India.
4. A **scroll** is a long roll of paper with writing on it.

Aditya: I know, child, I know. But what can I do? The rice and wheat they give me as alms[5] have pebbles in them. People don't seem to have the time these days to clean things up. If your father can't make me another, I'll have to go begging for a begging bowl.

Laxman: Oh stop it, please! *(Bends down to pick up some clay from the ground.)* This lump of clay is for you, all right?

Aditya: Oh, thank you, thank you, my child. May the Buddha enlighten you! What's that in your hand, Nakul?

Sheila: A letter; Laxman thinks it's in Brahmi.

Laxman: Laxman KNOWS it's in Brahmi!

(Nakul gives the scroll to Aditya, who reads it.)

Aditya: This is not a letter, children. It reads like a poem. But I don't know what it means. *(Reads.)*

When the full moon is in Ashara[6]
Follow the river of men to the river bank.
From the city of Ashoka to the vihara[7]
As over the horizon the moon sank.
Bringing the treasures home again.
Fast as a deer, with a leopard's guile[8]
The House of the Lion will then reign
As the twelve pillars of glory smile.

Sheila: I like the poem! It has a nice rhythm to it.

Nakul: *(Laughs and speaks fast in his excitement)* I know! It's about a treasure. We can find the treasure if we solve the puzzle.

Aditya: I don't think so. There are no directions here.

Sheila: How do we find the horseman?

Aditya: Solve the puzzle in the poem. I'm too old to do that.

(Aditya exits, handing over the scroll to Nakul. The children tie up the bundle once again.)

Sheila: Maybe he'll come back looking for this. (*Sound of hooves.*) I was right! That sounds like him.

Wordfile

5. **Alms** are clothing, food or money that are given to poor people.
6. **Ashara** is the month of the monsoon, the rainy season.
7. A **vihara** is a Buddhist temple or monastery.
8. **Guile** is clever but dishonest behaviour.

(Bappa enters searching the ground.)

Nakul: Are you looking for this, sir? (*Extends the bundle. Bappa snatches it from him.*)

Bappa: Did you open it?

Nakul: Yes. But we haven't taken anything.

Bappa (*fiercely*): Are you sure? Because if you have, I'll have you arrested for theft. There is an important letter in here.

Sheila: Yes, we saw it.

Bappa (*angrily*): Did you read it?

Laxman: No, we can't read.

Bappa: (*relieved, smiles*) Oh! (*Gives Laxman a silver coin.*) I'm sorry I yelled at you. This is for returning the bundle. (*Exits.*)

Laxman: What was so important about a poem that made this man so angry?

Sheila: Why did you say you didn't read the letter?

Laxman: (*grins*) I didn't. Aditya did. So there!

Nakul: I still want to solve the puzzle. But I forget the words.

Sheila: (*recites*) *When the full moon is in Ashara*
Follow the river of men to the river bank.

Don't worry. I never forget a poem I like.

Comprehension 1, Part 1

A The poem is important and Nakul thinks it's a puzzle. Read the poem again, and answer questions 1–5. Discuss your answers with your classmates.

1. What do you think a 'river of men' could be?
2. What do you think 'the city of Ashoka' means?
3. What time of day is it when the moon sinks over the horizon?
4. What do you think 'The House of the Lion' means?
5. What do you think 'the twelve pillars' are?

Now read Scene 2.

Scene 2

(Nakul is lying in bed with his head covered in bandages. Aditya is applying medicines to his body while Nakul groans.)

Laxman: How did this happen? You seem lucky to be alive.

Nakul: I am. But I'm more worried about my father in jail.

Aditya: We heard about that too. This was the second time that the emperor's caravan[9] was robbed, wasn't it?

Nakul: Yes, and again under my father's command. You see the caravan was carrying gold, silver and ivory for the new *viharas* that are to be built. There were also sacks of rice and wheat for the workers and silver and copper coins to pay them. My father was especially careful this time. He didn't breathe a word about his plans to anyone. But somehow the robbers caught scent[10] of the whole thing. Our army was no match for them, for they caught us unawares. The robbers lay in wait for us and attacked suddenly.

Aditya: You'll make a great soldier, Nakul. You fought them and didn't run away. *(Pause.)* Did you catch a glimpse[11] of the culprits[12]?

Nakul: No, it was too dark.

Aditya: Think of the night and remember the poem.

Sheila: *When the full moon is in Ashara*

Laxman: Last night was the full moon of Ashara!

Sheila: *Follow the river of men to the river bank*

Nakul: The caravan was like a river of carts and men and we camped on the river bank!

Sheila: *From the city of Ashoka to the vihara*
As over the horizon the moon sank.

Laxman: It matches. Pataliputra is the city of Ashoka and you were going to the *vihara.*

Nakul: And we were attacked at dawn when the moon set.

Wordfile

9. A **caravan** is a group of people and animals that travel together.
10. When you **catch scent of** something, you discover something by intuition rather than evidence.
11. If you **catch a glimpse** of something, you see it very briefly and not very well.
12. The person who committed a crime or did something wrong is called a **culprit**.

Laxman: Aditya, if the first stanza gives us the secret plans of the robbers, maybe the second tells us where they are to hide the loot.

Sheila: *Bringing the treasures home again.*
Fast as a deer, with a leopard's guile
The House of the Lion will then reign
As the twelve pillars of glory smile.

The first two lines don't seem to be a clue. They just describe the treasure being brought home to Pataliputra by clever men – *'Fast as a deer, with a leopard's guile.'* At least we know it's in this city.

Aditya: (*to Nakul*) Maybe your father knows something?

Nakul: I don't think so. All he said was he heard one of the robbers say, 'Bhojavarman should be happy.' He knows an army commander by that name but he is away travelling to Lanka with Prince Mahendra and Princess Sangamitra.

Laxman (*thoughtfully*): There is a nobleman called Bhoja. My father supplies pots to his kitchen. But why would he rob a caravan? He's very rich.

Sheila: What does the House of the Lion mean?

Laxman: A house with a lion gate?

Aditya: It could also be a family.

Sheila: Family of the lion. Of course, *Simhavamsi*! But that's a royal clan. Then he has to be a nobleman.

Laxman: Let's check out Bhoja, the nobleman. And see if his house has twelve pillars.

Comprehension 1, Part 2

B At the beginning of the scene, Nakul is lying in bed and his head is covered in bandages. Describe what happened to Nakul.

C Answer the questions.

1. What is the 'river of men'?
2. What is the city of Ashoka?
3. What time of day is it when the moon sinks over the horizon?
4. What does 'The House of the Lion' mean?
5. What are the twelve pillars?

Now read Scene 3.

Scene 3

The Hall of Justice. King Ashoka is giving alms to a row of bhikshus[13]*. Aditya and the children, all dressed in saffron robes, await their turn. At the other end of the room richly attired*[14] *noblemen sit awaiting the king's audience*[15]*. Bhojavarman is among them. Aditya's turn comes.*

Aditya: Your Majesty, I have a humble request to make.

Ashoka: It's my friend Aditya, isn't it? I can never refuse you anything. Speak.

Aditya: These children have something to say to you. I will be grateful if you listen to them carefully.

(Ashoka nods and sits down on a couch, leaning against a bolster[16]*.)*

Nakul: Your Majesty, what I'm going to say may shock you, but it is the truth. There's a conspiracy against you. One of your trusted men is involved in it.

Ashoka: What! Are you out of your mind? All my men are completely trustworthy.

Laxman: Nakul is right, Your Majesty. We sneaked into this gentleman's house and overheard his conversation with his assistant.

Nakul: Yes, Your Majesty. He is planning to overthrow you and become king. I forget the exact words though.

Sheila: But I remember, Your Majesty. He said, 'We'll use Ashoka's own money to start a rebellion, and in a week I'll be Emperor! We'll finish off this new religion of peace and begin the conquests again.' Your spy at the *vihara* had sent the right information about the caravan.

Laxman: My sister thinks it sounds like a poem. That is why she remembers it so well.

(Sheila recites the poem.)

Ashoka: That's a lot for a little girl to memorise. And who is this audacious[17] 'gentleman'?

Nakul: Bhojavarman. His house has twelve pillars.

Ashoka: Bhoja is one of my most important nobles and these are serious accusations. What proof do you have?

Nakul: Proof? (*They look at each other.)*

Wordfile

13. A **bhikshu** is a Buddhist monk.
14. A person who is **richly attired** is wearing luxurious and expensive clothes.
15. People who are **awaiting the king's audience** are waiting to see and speak to the king.
16. A **bolster** is a long, firm pillow.
17. Someone who is **audacious** is daring and takes a lot of risks.

Ashoka: *(to Nakul)* Wait a minute! You are Jivaka's son, aren't you? *(Nakul nods.)* Jivaka also mentioned Bhoja's name to *senapati*. How do I know it's not a plan to save Jivaka?

Laxman: You could search Bhoja's house, Your Majesty. We heard him order his assistant Bappa to guard the treasure. All the stolen royal treasure is hidden somewhere in his house.

Ashoka: *(to his minister offstage) Mahamantri*, will you call Bhojavarman here?

(Bhoja comes in and bows with folded hands.)

Bhoja: Your Majesty wishes to see me?

Ashoka: Yes, Bhoja. I've heard a lot about your wonderful palace. The twelve pillars are the talk of the town. I wish to visit it tomorrow.

Bhoja: Of course, Your Majesty. It will be a great honour.

Ashoka: But before I visit any place, my guards have to be sure it's safe for me. So I'll have to send them there to search it.

Bhoja: Search my house! You can't do that.

Ashoka: Why not?

Bhoja: Because ... I mean ... Can't they search tomorrow?

Ashoka: Why? (*sternly*) What have you hidden there? We'll search your palace now!

Bhoja: No!

(Bhoja pulls out a dagger and lunges at Ashoka. With lightning speed, Nakul snatches Aditya's begging bowl from his hand and aims it at Bhoja's head as Laxman swings Aditya's walking stick across Bhoja's legs. Bhoja falls to the ground with a moan. The guards surround him, put him in shackles[18] *and take him away.)*

(Jivaka comes limping in through the door. Nakul runs towards him.)

Ashoka: These children saved you, Jivaka, and me too. Your son will make a fine soldier. You'll all be rewarded, of course. Just tell me what you wish to have the most in the world and if I can, I'll get it for you.

Sheila: *(Goes to hug Aditya.)* But we couldn't have done it without Aditya!

Ashoka: I agree. Aditya, my friend, what would you like as a reward?

Aditya: Well, Your Majesty, Laxman just broke my walking stick and Nakul's cracked the handle of my begging bowl. I could do with a new set of those.

Ashoka: *(Laughs.)* Granted!

Wordfile

18. **Shackles** are metal rings that are put around a person's arms or legs to prevent them from escaping.

Comprehension 1, Part 3

D Complete this text about Bhoja. Use suitable words and phrases.

Bhoja was a [1]__________ and one of Ashoka's men. He was very [2]__________ and lived in a house with [3]______________. He wanted to become [4]__________, and so he decided to rob [5]______________ and use it to [6]______________. The money and treasure was taken back to his [7]__________. However, Aditya the monk, with Nakul and his friends, found a poem with clues, and realised what was happening. When they visited Bhoja's house, they heard him [8]______________. When Ashoka suggested that his guards would check Bhoja's house, he [9]______________. Bhoja was [10]__________.

Comprehension 2

Make notes about these questions, and then discuss them with your classmates.

1. The children play a heroic role in solving the mystery and ensuring that the culprit is caught. Who do you think played the most important role? Give reasons with examples from the play.

2. What do you learn about Ashoka the Great from the play?
3. Bhoja says, 'We'll finish off this new religion of peace and begin the conquests again.'

   In the early years of Ashoka's reign, there were many wars, and his empire included India, Pakistan, Afghanistan, Bangladesh, Nepal and parts of Iran. However, he later rejected violence and became a Buddhist. He spent the rest of his reign spreading the Buddhist faith across Asia, and his influence is felt to this day.

   Who are some of the most influential rulers of ancient India? Choose two of them and say why they were famous.

4. VBQ One good turn begets another. Do you agree with this saying? Support your answer with examples from the play.
5. VBQ Do you think it was brave of the children to go to King Ashoka even though the King might not have believed them? Would you take such a risk for a greater good?

Vocabulary

Synonyms and antonyms

Ashoka the Great was a *loyal* and *charitable* man. Steve Jobs was *hard-working* and *creative*. These adjectives describe important and successful people.

A **The table below shows more adjectives that we can use to describe important and successful people.**

Complete the table with synonyms and antonyms.

Remember: synonyms are words which have a similar meaning. Antonyms are words which have the opposite meaning.

You can use a dictionary for this exercise.

Adjectives	Synonyms	Antonyms
talented	smart, brilliant, clever, intelligent, skilled	untalented, dull, unintelligent, unskilled
creative		
hard-working		
trustworthy		
great		
honourable		
charitable		
loyal		
courageous		

B **Look at these famous and influential people. In pairs, use words from Exercise A to describe them.**

Dr Rajendra Prasad

Arundhati Roy

Charles Darwin

Rani Laxmi Bai

Words from the play

C **Complete the crossword with words from the play.**

Across

3. a daring person who takes risks
4. reliable
6. to remove forcibly from power
7. handcuffs, sometimes with a long chain

Down

1. a secret plan to do something harmful
2. a claim that someone has done wrong
5. to hear someone without meaning to
8. to move stealthily

Study tip

When you are reading and you don't know what a word means, try guessing what it means first. You can often guess by looking at the language around the words and thinking about the content of the passage.

Grammar

Present and past perfect tenses

The **present perfect tense** is used to talk about an action which has been recently completed, but whose time is not specified. It shows the effect of a completed action in the present.

*I **have heard** about your wonderful palace.*

*We **have met** before.*

We use the past perfect when we talk about something that happened before another action or event in the past.

*I **had eaten** dinner, when the bell rang.*

Here, the first action (***had eaten** dinner*) was already complete before the second one (*bell **rang***) took place. Hence, the first action is in the past perfect tense, while the second is in the simple past tense.

A Rewrite the sentences using the present or past perfect form of the given verbs.

1. The children ______________ (never see) a tiger before their trip to Tadoba National Park.
2. I ______________ (see) that film already. Let's watch something else.
3. ______________ you ______________ (eat) your breakfast when they arrived?
4. The play ______________ (begin) by the time we got there.
5. ______________ you ______________ (finish) packing? We have to leave for the station immediately.
6. She ______________(read) through the letter and will do what it says.
7. I ______________ (visit) Agra twice by the time I was ten years old.
8. Since she ______________ (prepare) well, she passed the test with flying colours.

Expressing regret: *I wish* ... and *If only* ...

In the play, Laxman looks at the poem written in Brahmi and says: *Wish I could read it!* Discuss these questions in groups.

- Why doesn't Laxman use the word 'I': *I wish I could read it!*
- Can Laxman read the poem? Does he want to be able to read it?
- Laxman is talking about the present. Why does he use the past verb *could*?

Sometimes, when you are talking informally, you can leave out the pronoun 'I', but it is usually better to include it, especially when you are writing in English.

Laxman can't read the poem but he wants to be able to read it. He regrets that he is not able to. When you want to express a regret about the present you can use these structures with a verb in the past tense. They have the same meaning:

***I wish I could** read it!* ***If only I could** read it!*

B **Read these regrets that some people have about the present. Write sentences beginning with *I wish* or *If only*. Remember to use the past tense.**

1. I don't know how to use a computer. I wish I knew how to use a computer.
2. I can't speak Spanish. ____________
3. I don't know how to do my maths homework. ____________
4. My company isn't very successful. ____________
5. I can't swim very well. ____________

Look at this woman's regrets.

When you want to express regrets about the past (*I didn't go to college*), you use **I wish** or **If only** with the past perfect.

If only I had gone to college!

OR

I wish I had gone to college!

C **Read these regrets that some people have about the past. Write sentences beginning with *I wish* or *If only*. Remember to use the past perfect tense.**

1. I didn't study very hard, and now I can't take the exam. What a shame!

   If only I had studied harder for this exam.
2. I didn't trust my friend, but now I know that she was honest.

   ____

3. I dropped out of college and now I don't know what to do.

____

4. I left my job and now I haven't got any money.

____

5. I wasn't very kind to my cousin and now he says I can't come to his party.

____

Listening

Listening to a play

A **Listen to five parts of the play. For each part, write answers to these questions in your notebook. Then discuss your notes with your classmates.**

- Who is talking?
- What has just happened?
- What happens next?

B **Listen to the passage and fill in the blanks.**

1. Ashoka was the third ruler of the ________________
2. He is remembered for ________________ to many parts of the Indian subcontinent and beyond.
3. He conquered many territories in the first ________________ years of his rule.
4. His empire reached to ________________, ________________, ________________ and ________________.
5. Ashoka was transformed after the battle of ________________, in which ________________.
6. After the battle, Ashoka became a ________________ and ________________ king.

Speaking

Acting out a scene from a play

You are going to act out a scene from the play 'The Pataliputra Mystery'.

Work in groups of five, six or seven.

- If you are in a group of five, act out Scene 2. You will act the roles of Laxman, Nakul, Aditya and Sheila. The fifth member of the group will be the director of the scene.
- If you are in a group of six, act out Scene 1. You will act the roles of Laxman, Nakul, Aditya, Sheila and Bappa. The sixth member of the group will be the director of the scene.

- If you are in a group of seven, act out Scene 3. You will act the roles of Laxman, Nakul, Aditya, Sheila, Ashoka and Bhoja. The seventh member of the group will be the director of the scene.

Practise the scene, with advice from your director.

When you are ready, act it out for the rest of the class.

Writing

Imagine that you are Bhoja. You are now in jail, and you regret what happened. Write a letter to King Ashoka in around 150 words, expressing regret, apologizing and asking for forgiveness.

Here are some suggestions:

- Think about how you organize a letter. How do you start and end a letter?
- Divide your letter into paragraphs. In one or two paragraphs, tell King Ashoka about your past and present regrets. Use *I wish ...* and *If only ...*
- In another paragraph, tell King Ashoka how you intend to be have in the future. Apologize and ask for his forgiveness. Use some of the adjectives from vocabulary exercise A.

You can make notes here.

Show your letter to a partner. What does he or she think about it? Does he or she have any advice for how you can improve your letter?

Poem

Invictus is a Latin term meaning 'unconquered'. If a land or a group of people is conquered, they are controlled by force. If a person is 'unconquered', they are *not* controlled by force.

This poem says that no matter who or what tries to control you, you can be the one who is in control.

William Ernest Henley wrote 'Invictus' in 1875. Since then, the poem's message has inspired many people, including Nelson Mandela, who kept a copy of the poem during his 27 years in jail.

Invictus

Out of the night that covers me,
Black as the Pit[1] from pole to pole[2],
I thank whatever gods may be
For my unconquerable soul.

In the fell[3] clutch[4] of circumstance
I have not winced nor cried aloud.
Under the bludgeoning[5] of chance
My head is bloody, but unbowed.

Beyond this place of wrath[6] and tears
Looms but the Horror of the shade,
And yet the menace of the years
Finds, and shall find, me unafraid.

It matters not how strait[7] the gate,
How charged with punishments the scroll.
I am the master of my fate:
I am the captain of my soul.

William Ernest Henley

Wordfile

1. The **pit** in this poem means hell.
2. The earth's **poles** are the two opposite ends of the axis.
3. **Fell** in this poem means cruel. (*literary*)
4. If you are in the **clutch** of something, it has control over you.
5. If you **bludgeon** someone, you hit them repeatedly with a weapon.
6. **Wrath** means anger.
7. **Strait** means narrow. (*archaic*)

Poetry appreciation

A **The poem begins with the lines, 'Out of the night that covers me/Black as the Pit from pole to pole'. What is the 'night' that he refers to here?**

B **The poet describes many difficulties that we may face in life. Describe them.**

1. the fell clutch of circumstance	
2. the bludgeonings of chance	
3. wrath and tears	
4. the menace of the years	
5. a strait gate	
6. a scroll charged with punishments	

C **The poet believes that we can face and overcome the various difficulties that we come across in life. Find words and phrases which show how the poet feels or behaves.** I have not winced nor cried aloud.

D **The poem ends with these inspirational lines:**

VBQ

'I am the master of my fate:

I am the captain of my soul.'

Do you agree that it is possible to be master of your own fate? Discuss with a partner.

Activity

Think of a person who has inspired or influenced you. This person may be a famous personality from the world of sport, literature, music, art or film; or perhaps a hero from history. The person may not be famous at all. They might be a person in your family, school or neighbourhood.

Make a poster about this person. You can include:

- a photo, picture or drawing of the person
- some quotes by the person that inspired you
- reasons why they have inspired or influenced you

5 Wildlife

In this unit, I will ...

- practise word stress in three-syllable words
- learn about the form and use of the active and the passive voice
- learn about *-ed* and *-ing* adjectives
- listen to a girl talking about pet care and conduct a survey about owning a pet

Warm-up

A **Certain animals are found only in particular regions in the world. Look at the pictures and write the names of the regions where these species are found. Can you say what is common to all of them?**

black spider monkey ________

Narcondam hornbill ________

Asiatic cheetah ________

giant panda ________

Sumatran orangutan ________

African penguin ________

B **Humans often use animals to test products. Can you name four products where animals are used in testing?**

C **Think of some other ways that humans affect animal populations.**

Reading 1

You are going to read an article about Kaziranga National Park in Assam, India. The park is a World Heritage Site and is home to the largest population of tigers in the world.

About the author

Born in New Delhi in 1952, Valmik Thapar is a conservationist who has spent nearly 40 years studying and serving the tigers of India. Over that time, he has written more than 20 books and presented and produced wildlife documentaries for the BBC, Animal Planet, Discovery and National Geographic.

Wordfile

1. The **proportions** of something describe its size.
2. A **dynamic** person is full of energy and has a positive attitude.
3. When you are **enveloped** by something, you are surrounded and covered by it completely.
4. When you are **oblivious** of something, you are not aware of it at all.

Kaziranga, Grassland of the Giants

1 Kaziranga is the land of the megafauna – the rhino, tiger, elephant and the wild buffalo – and the greatest story of India's wildlife conservation.

2 Nothing can prepare you for the experience of Kaziranga National Park. You have to visit it to believe it. When I went there for the first time, I was very lucky – old friend and colleague S. Deb Roy, an amazing man who had put his life into saving Assam's incredible wildlife, was with me. This was the early 1990s, when the severe crisis that now threatens wildlife in general hadn't set in. Kaziranga was stunning. It is a grassland of immense proportions[1] and dotted around are patches of superb forests with the mighty Brahmaputra river flowing on one side.

3 My first day was a journey from the western range, then administered by a remarkable ranger called Pankaj Sarma, to the eastern range under another dynamic[2] character called Bodo. Deb Roy and I spent 10 hours from dawn to dusk enveloped[3] in the beauty of this unique wilderness system. I will never forget that day. Nature wove its spell around me like never before. In that one day, we saw 108 rhinos. At a watchtower called Bahubil in the western range, we sipped some hot tea and suddenly a burst of alarm calls on the far side of the tall grass revealed a tiger striding along the edge of a water body. Kaziranga has the highest density of tigers in India and they are enormous in size. We peered out, as the tiger padded across, oblivious[4] of our presence. Later, when we stopped for lunch at an old forest rest house, a herd of elephants was bathing in another water body.

4 Kaziranga is the only place in India that reminds me of Africa – wildlife comes out of everywhere. It is the great land of the giants, the megafauna, be it rhinos, elephants, wild buffaloes, and even a few gaur with lots of smaller ungulates[5] and a host of tigers that

are huge and generally look well-fed. And it is these large animals that guard the grassland. Unlike many other forests of India, you rarely find locals wandering around Kaziranga since the big animals will charge to kill. Even while driving around in a jeep, at least six rhinos tried to charge us. And it is even more frightening when a tiger charges. As we drove around, I noticed that all the forest staff were well armed, unlike in any other national park. They live on forest posts on stilts and eat a jungle menu of cane and bamboo shoots that are deliciously spiced. The human intruders[6] are poachers armed with automatic rifles who come mainly to kill rhinos for their horn. Big gun battles rage between the forest staff and poachers and every year there are injuries and fatalities. This is a rare example of how wildlife can be saved; protection at its very best and a lesson for the rest of India.

5 For me, Kaziranga is a veritable[7] Noah's Ark and has been India's greatest story in wildlife conservation. Let us never forget that in the early 20th century the population of rhinos was down to 12 and today it is between 1,600 and 1,800, if not more. And it is not just rhinos or other megafauna. The birdlife is among the finest to be found anywhere in India, as lesser and greater pied hornbills screech through the air and an endless array[8] of fishing eagles swoops into fish-laden water bodies and red jungle fowl dart in and out of lush green foliage[9]. Thousands of pelicans fish the water in abandon and near the swamps the swamp partridge waddles in its exquisite finery.

6 If you are lucky, you can watch otters scamper across the land into water, with heads bobbing up and down as they start to fish. A grey-headed eagle swoops into the water and comes out with a fish caught firmly in its talons[10]. Pockets of forest within the grasslands are a frenzy[11] of green and so much of what grows is coiled, looped and encircled in an endless embrace.

7 In the hilly forests nearby are troops of hoolock gibbons and capped langurs and there could even be the elusive[12] clouded leopard. Emerald doves and imperial pigeons dive in and out of the forest canopy[13]. The smaller grasslands are dotted with hog deer and swamp deer. Hundreds of thousands of hog deer once roamed the flood plains of India. Now they are only found in places where their habitat has survived the

Wordfile

5. **Ungulates** are any animals that have hooves, such as deer, pigs, sheep, goats, etc.
6. An **intruder** is a person who enters a place without permission.
7. **Veritable** means true or real.
8. An **array** is a large number of things.
9. **Foliage** is the leaves of a plant or tree.
10. **Talons** are the claws of a bird of prey.
11. A **frenzy** of colour is an exciting show of colour.

Did you know?

Although India has only 2.4% of the world's surface, it holds about 8.1% of the world's animal and plant life, ranking sixth among the 12 mega biodiversity centres of the world. India has more than 40,000 plant species, or about 12% of the plants on the earth. About 1.7 million animal species have been identified on the planet, and about 127,570 have been reported in India.

exploitation by man. Small herbivores in these grasslands follow in the steps of the giants. It is interdependency at its best. The elephants and rhinos make inroads into the high grass and create areas for smaller animals to graze. The sambar hide in the evergreen forest glades[14]. What a magical assortment of life it is.

The peace is suddenly shattered by the sharp calls of the hog deer. And, lo and behold[15], from the grass emerges that mesmeric[16] image of a tiger, catching the rays of the setting sun. 8

Will Kaziranga survive the pressures of today? Will there be enough political will to keep this unique paradise alive? I'm not sure, but this is more than a World Heritage Site – it is a true wonder of the world and needs all the support we can give it. Future generations must be able to witness its magic, for it is the true jewel in India's wildlife crown. 9

Valmik Thapar

Wordfile

12. When something is **elusive**, it is difficult to find, catch or achieve.
13. The **canopy** is the top layer of a forest that is formed by the trees.
14. A **glade** is an open space in a forest.
15. We use the phrase **lo and behold** to express a sudden change in the situation.
16. Something that is **mesmeric** fascinates us and holds our attention.

Comprehension 1

A Answer the questions.

1. In paragraph 1, which word does the writer use to refer to the large animals in the park?
2. In paragraph 2, which two phrases does the writer use to show that Kaziranga National Park is a wonderful place to visit?
3. When did the writer first visit Kaziranga National Park?
4. How are these people described in the article?
   a. S. Deb Roy ____________________
   b. Pankaj Sarma ____________________
   c. Bodo ____________________
5. According to paragraph 4, why is this forest different from other forests in India?
6. Name any five animals and five birds that the writer sees at Kaziranga.
7. In paragraph 5, the writer describes the park as a 'veritable Noah's Ark'. Why does he say this?

B Correct the statements that are incorrect.

1. Valmik Thapar visited Kaziranga in 1909.
2. Kaziranga has the highest density of elephants in India.

3. You will find many locals wandering about the Kaziranga National Park.
4. The population of rhinos was 1,600–1,900.
5. Like at all other national parks, the forest guard at Kaziranga was not well armed.
6. The protection of Kaziranga is a task for everyone.

Comprehension 2

A **The resources of this planet belong to animals and birds as much as they belong to human beings. Do you agree with the statement? Give reasons for your answer.** VBQ

B **Imagine you are a ranger at Kaziranga National Park and you have been asked to speak to a group of secondary school students about the park. What would you say to the students? Think about the difficulties in managing the park and the support that is needed.**

C **Imagine that you recently visited Kaziranga National Park. Make a presentation on your visit to the sanctuary.**

You can include these points in your presentation:

- the various animals you saw in the national park
- factors threatening the biodiversity of the park
- conservation efforts made by the government for the park
- how students can raise awareness about the problems facing national parks in the country

Vocabulary check

Find these words in the article. Match them with their meanings (a–f). Use your dictionary to help you.

Words	Meanings
1. superb	a. awesome in size or power
2. mighty	b. without end or limit
3. remarkable	c. worthy of attention
4. great	d. attitude of wild or complete freedom
5. endless	e. impressive, splendid
6. abandon	f. large in size

Language skills

Word stress: three-syllable words

Some words in English are broken into smaller chunks of sound called syllables. When you pronounce words that have two or more syllables, you stress only one of the syllables.

For the word *completely*, we stress the second syllable (com-**PLETE**-ly).
For words with three syllables, the stress most often falls on the first or second syllable.

A **Which syllables are stressed? Practise saying the words and then put them in the correct column. Check your answers in a dictionary.**

abandon	canopy	exquisite	enormous	enveloped	guarantee
habitat	paradise	proportion	refugee	volunteer	wilderness

O o o	o O o	o o O
______	______	______
______	______	______
______	______	______
______	______	
	______	

B **Practise saying these words and underline the stressed syllables. Then listen and check your answers.**

1. ev·er·green
2. a·maz·ing
3. un·der·stand
4. her·bi·vores
5. dy·nam·ic
6. ma·gic·al
7. rec·om·mend
8. pro·tec·tion

Spelling

C **Unscramble these words. and write their correct spelling**

1. egrevener
2. desutandr
3. nicdamy
4. moncremed
5. gazmian
6. vohierbser
7. cimagal
8. tenoprioct

Reading 2

Have you ever seen a hornbill? Do you know what a hornbill looks like? Describe it to your friends.

You are going to read about a hornbill named Harold and how he finds a new home when he falls out of his nest.

Harold: Our Hornbill

Harold's mother, like all good hornbills, was the most careful of wives; his father, the most easy-going of husbands. In January, long before the flame tree flowered, Harold's father took his wife into a great hole high in the tree trunk. In this weather-beaten hollow, generation upon generation of hornbills had been raised, and Harold's mother, like those before her, was enclosed within the hole by a sturdy wall of earth, sticks and dung. Walled up in her uncomfortable room, Harold's mother was a prisoner for over two months. During this period an egg was laid, and Harold was born.

In his naked boyhood, Harold was no beauty. His most promising[1] feature was his flaming red bill, matching the blossoms of the flame tree. He had a stomach that could never be filled, despite the best efforts of his parents, who brought him pieces of jackfruit and berries from the banyan tree.

As he grew bigger, the room became more cramped, and one day his mother burst through the wall, spread out her wings, and sailed over the treetops. Her husband pretended he was glad to see her about, and played with her, expressing his delight with deep gurgles[2] and throaty[3] chuckles. Then they repaired the wall of the nursery so that Harold would not fall out.

Harold was quite happy in his cell, and felt no urge for freedom. He was putting on weight and feathers, and acquiring a philosophy of his own. Then something happened to change the course[4] of his life.

Wordfile

1. Something that is **promising** is likely to develop favourably or turn out well.
2. A **gurgle** is a sound that is similar to water moving over rocks or through a pipe.
3. A **throaty** sound is a deep or rough sound made at the back of the throat.
4. A **course** is the path or direction that someone or something moves along.

One afternoon, he was awakened from his siesta by a loud thumping, a sound quite different from that made by his parents. Soon the wall gave way, and there was something large and yellow and furry staring at him – not his parents' bills, but the hungry eyes of a civet cat.

Before Harold could be seized, his parents flew at the cat, both roaring lustily and striking out with their great bills. In the ensuing melee[5], Harold tumbled out of his nest and landed on our garden path. Before the cat or any predator could get to him, Grandfather had picked him up and taken him to the sanctuary[6] of the veranda. Harold had lost some wing feathers and did not look as though he would be able to survive on his own, so we made an enclosure for him on the front veranda of our north Indian home, and Grandfather and I took over the duties of his parents.

Harold had a simple outlook[7], and once he had got over some early attacks of nerves, he began to welcome the approach of people. Grandfather and I meant the arrival of food, and he greeted us with craning neck, quivering open bill, and a loud, croaking, 'Ka-ka-kaee!' Fruit, insect, or animal food, and green leaves, were all welcome. We soon dispensed with[8] the enclosure, but Harold made no effort to go away; he had difficulty flying. In fact, he asserted his tenancy rights, at least as far as the veranda was concerned. One afternoon, a veranda tea party was suddenly and alarmingly convulsed[9] by a flash of black and white, and noisy flapping; and behold, the last and only loaf of bread had been seized and carried off to his perch[10] near the ceiling.

Harold's best friends were those who fed him, and he was willing even to share his food with us, sometimes trying to feed me with his great beak. While I turned down his offers of beetles and similar delicacies[11], I did occasionally share a banana with him. Harold loved bananas and dates and balls of boiled rice. I would throw him the rice balls, and he would catch them in his beak, toss them in the air, and let them drop into his open mouth. He perfected this trick of catching things, and in time I taught him to catch a tennis ball thrown with some force from a distance of 15 yards. He would have made a great baseball catcher.

Wordfile

5. A **melee** is a confused struggle or fight that usually involves many people.
6. A **sanctuary** is a place where someone or something is protected and given shelter.
7. A person's **outlook** is their attitude towards life.
8. When you **dispense with** something, you get rid of it.
9. If someone or something is **convulsed**, they are violently affected by something.
10. A **perch** is a place where a bird lands or rests.
11. A **delicacy** is something that is pleasing to eat.

Harold would toy with anything bright or glittering, often swallowing it afterwards. On one occasion, he seized a rupee coin from me (a week's pocket money in those days) and swallowed it neatly. I never saw the coin again. Only once did he really misbehave. That was when he removed a lighted cigar from the hand of an American cousin who was visiting us. Harold swallowed the cigar. It was a moving experience for Harold, and an unnerving[12] one for our guest.

Although Harold never seemed to drink any water, he loved the rain. We always knew when it was going to rain, because Harold would start chuckling to himself about an hour before the first raindrops fell. This used to irritate my Aunt Ruby. She was always being caught in the rain. Harold would be chuckling when she left the house. And when she returned, drenched to the skin, he would be in fits of laughter.

As the storm clouds gathered, and gusts of wind shook the banana trees, Harold would get very excited, and his chuckle would change to an eerie whistle. 'Wheee ... wheee,' he would scream. And then as the first drops of rain hit the veranda steps, he would start roaring with pleasure. The wind swept the rain into the veranda, and Harold would spread out his wings and dance, tumbling about like a circus clown. Many years later, I still miss Harold's raucous[13] bark and the banging of his great bill. If there is a heaven for good hornbills, I hope he is getting all the summer showers he could wish for, and plenty of tennis balls to catch.

Ruskin Bond

Wordfile

12. When a situation is **unnerving**, it upsets you and you are unable to think clearly.
13. A **raucous** noise is one that is loud and unpleasant to listen to.

About the author

Ruskin Bond was born in Kasauli, India in 1934. He is one the most loved English writers in India, and one of the most prolific. When he was only 17, Bond wrote his first novel, *The Room on the Roof*, which received the John Llewellyn Rhys Memorial Prize in 1957. Since that time, Bond has written more than five hundred short stories, essays and novellas, and more than forty books for children. He has received several awards in his lifetime, including the Padma Shri in 1999 for his contribution to children's literature, and the Delhi government's Lifetime Achievement Award in 2012. He now lives in Landour, Mussoorie, with his extended family.

Comprehension 1

A List six items that Harold ate in the story.

1. ____________ 3. ____________ 5. ____________

2. ____________ 4. ____________ 6. ____________

B Complete the statements.

1. Harold's mother was enclosed in a tree because ____________
2. Harold's mother left the hole in the tree trunk as ____________
3. When Harold fell out of the tree, Grandfather ____________
4. Harold's mother was in the tree trunk for two months because ____________

   ____________.
5. Harold's distinguishing feature as a chick was ____________
6. Harold's parents saved him by ____________
7. Harold asserted his tenancy rights by ____________.

C Answer the questions.

1. Why does the writer say Harold 'would have made a great baseball catcher' ?
2. What did Harold do that surprised the visitor?
3. What would Harold do when it started to rain?
4. Did Harold enjoy living with Grandfather and the boy? Explain your answer.
5. How is Harold's family similar to human families?
6. Did the author miss Harold after he went away? Support your answer with examples.

Comprehension 2

A Imagine that one day an injured bird lands in your garden. What would you do? How would you take care of it?

B Imagine that you are Harold. Write a summary of the story from the bird's point of view.

VBQ **C Our pets can often become like family members. Is it good to become attached to them? How do you think we would cope with the pain of separation when they leave us?**

Vocabulary

Forming adjectives from verbs and nouns

We can form **-ed** and **-ing** adjectives from verbs. We use **-ed** adjectives to talk about how we feel. We use **-ing** adjectives to talk about the person, thing or situation that caused the feeling.

*Leela is **interested** in biology.* *Leela thinks biology is **interesting**.*

We can form adjectives from nouns using suffixes like **-ful**, **-ish**, **-less**, **-ly**.

*It is a **colourful** painting.* *The **foolish** man wasted all his money.*

A Complete the table with related -*ed* and -*ing* adjectives.

Verb	-*ed* adjective	-*ing* adjective
1. annoy		
2. bore		
3. confuse		
4. interest		
5. worry		

B Choose the correct adjectives.

1. This book about dinosaurs is really (fascinated/fascinating).
2. We felt much more (relaxed/relaxing) after our holiday in the hills.
3. The long journey was very (tired/tiring) but it was worth it.
4. Just look how (excited/exciting) Maria is about her new bicycle.
5. I'm always (surprised/surprising) to meet people who don't like travelling.

C Complete the sentences by forming adjectives from the given nouns using suffixes.

1. The ______________ man did not think of anyone else except himself. (self)
2. The ______________ man was begging for food. (home)
3. The traveller threw a ______________ of sand into the fire and put it out. (hand)
4. The neighbours in our new colony are very ______________. (friend)
5. In the potter's ______________ hands, a lump of clay was transformed into a beautiful vase. (skill)

Grammar

Active and passive voice

Remember that when we want to talk about someone or something that is the performer of an action, we make them the subject of the verb, and we use the **active** form of the verb. The receiver of the action is the object of the verb.

The dog	*ate*	*our dinner.*
↓	↓	↓
performer of action	action	receiver of action

However, we sometimes want to focus on the receiver of the action (here, 'our dinner'). In this case, we make that person or thing the subject, and use a **passive** form of the verb.

Our dinner	*was eaten*	*by the dog.*
↓	↓	↓
receiver of action	action	performer of action

Passive structures consist of a form of **be + the past participle of the verb**.

Active		**Passive**
*The teacher **marks** our tests.*	→	*Our tests **are marked** by the teacher.* (present)
*Ruskin Bond **wrote** the story.*	→	*The story **was written** by Ruskin Bond.* (past)
*The students **will perform** a play.*	→	*A play **will be performed** by the students.* (future)
*Raj **has repaired** our car.*	→	*Our car **has been repaired** by Raj.* (present perfect)
*Sheila **was writing** a letter.*	→	*A letter **was being written** by Sheila.* (past continuous)

Sometimes, we use the passive voice to avoid mentioning the performer of the action, perhaps because we do not know who the performer is, because the performer is not important, or because we do not want to say who the performer is. In this case, we do *not* use **by +** performer.

*My car **was stolen**.* (I don't know who stole it.)

*The vase **was broken**.* (I know who did it, but I don't want to say the person's name.)

A **Complete the sentences with the verbs in bold. Use the tenses given.**

1. The park rangers ______________________________ with automatic rifles. (**arm**, present simple)
2. The package ______________________________ by my mother earlier today. (**post**, past simple)
3. A new sales manager ______________________________ by our company. (**hire**, present perfect)
4. Last week, two rhinos ______________________________ by poachers. (**kill**, past simple)
5. The garden wall ______________________________ soon. (**repair**, future)
6. He ______________________________ by a snake. (**bite**, present perfect)

B **Rewrite the sentences using the passive voice. Decide whether you need to add 'by' + performer.**

1. The burglar stole all of my jewellery.
2. The noise woke the baby up.
3. Someone took the tourists on a jungle walk.
4. They have cancelled the game because of rain.
5. Earlier today, I sent a letter to my grandfather.
6. They will demolish the old warehouse next month.

Listening

VBQ

Pet care

A **Listen to a girl talking about her pet. Are the sentences true (T) or false (F)?**

1. Mina's feathers are yellow and green. ________
2. The girl and her father bought the bird at the pet shop. ________
3. The girl's father said the bird would be scared at first. ________
4. Singing can help to calm birds. ________
5. The girl's cousin suggested stroking the bird. ________
6. Chewing on things is good for a bird's beak. ________

B **Listen again. Complete the notes about taking care of a pet with words from the recording.**

Taking care of a pet

- You should remember a bird might be [1]____________ at first and may even [2]____________ when you get near her cage.
- You can [3]____________ or [4]____________ to your bird to help it relax.
- You can also build your relationship by [5]____________ food with your bird.
- Birds like it when you gently [6]____________ the back of their head.
- Birds need to develop their [7]____________, so it's good to buy them some chewy [8]____________.
- Birds enjoy playing [9]____________ and can easily be taught to play [10]____________ and hide-and-seek.

Speaking

A survey

Conduct a survey among your classmates about pets. Then work in groups and discuss the results.

1. Do you like animals?
   a. Yes, I do. ☐ b. They're OK. ☐ c. No, I don't. ☐
2. Would like you to have a pet if you could?
   a. Yes. ☐ b. No. ☐ c. Not sure. ☐

3. Do you have a pet?
   a. Yes. ☐ b. No. ☐
4. What kind of pet would you like to have?
   a. dog ☐ b. cat ☐ c. bird ☐
   d. fish ☐ e. turtle ☐ f. none ☐
   g. any other ____________

5. Which animals do you think make the best pets?
   a. dog ☐ b. cat ☐ c. bird ☐
   d. fish ☐ e. turtle ☐ f. lizard ☐
   g. any other ____________

6. Do you think it's a good idea to have a pet?

   a. Yes. ☐ b. No. ☐

   Reason: ____________________

7. At what age would you like to have a pet?

   a. 1–3 years ☐ c. 8–11 years ☐

   b. 4–7 years ☐ d. 12–15 years ☐

8. What are the benefits of owning a pet?
9. What are the drawbacks of owning a pet?

Writing

Harold fell out of tree and got hurt.

Write about a time that you got hurt, or make up a story about a time you got hurt.

Were you taken to a hospital? Did you break a bone? Who looked after you? How were you treated? How were you taken care of? Who took care of you?

Use the passive form where appropriate.

Useful phrases

I was taken to the hospital right away.
An X-ray of my leg was taken.
The cut was washed and then bandaged.
My ankle was wrapped in a cold towel.
My arm was put in a sling.
My leg was set in a cast.
I was given medication three times a day.
I was driven to school every day.

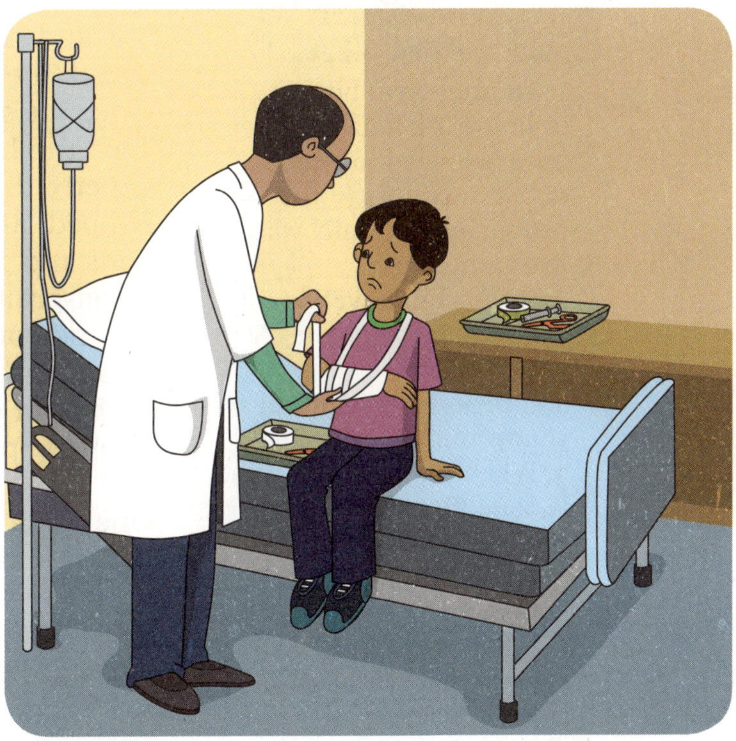

Plan

1. Describe how you got hurt. What were you doing? What happened?
2. Describe what happened after you got hurt. Who helped you? What did they do?
3. Describe how you were taken care of until you recovered.

Poem

You are going to read a poem about a louse and a mosquito.

While reading the poem, think about the louse and the mosquito. How would you describe their personalities?
You may read *The frog and the nightingale* by Vikram Seth, that deals with a similar theme.

About the poet

Vikram Seth was born in 1952 in Kolkata, India. After his public schooling, Seth earned degrees in philosophy, politics and economics at Oxford University in the UK. Later, he pursued a PhD in economics at Stanford University in the US, but did not complete it. Seth published his book of poetry, *Mappings*, in 1980, and his first novel, *The Golden Gate*, in 1986.

The Louse and the Mosquito

In the King's bed, Creep the louse
Lived in her ancestral[1] house.
They had dwelt[2] here as of right
For three decades, and each night
She and her enormous brood[3]
Drank the King's blood for their food.
Once the signal came from Creep
That the King was fast asleep,
Quietly, discreetly[4], they
Nipped[5] and sipped and drank away.
Sons and grandsons, sisters, brothers,
Great-granddaughters, great-grandmothers,
Second cousins and their wives
Thus pursued their gentle lives.
—Lives of undisturbed delight—
Growing plump and smooth and white.

One day a mosquito flew
Through the window. As he drew
Closer to the velvet bed
Canopied with gold, he said:
'Lovely! Just the place for me.
Ah, what perfume—let me see—
Rose—no, jasmine. And the quilt—
Smooth as banks of Ganges silt!

Wordfile

1. An **ancestral** house or home is a house that once belonged to one of our ancestors (= the people in our family who lived before us).
2. If someone **dwells** somewhere, he or she lives there.
3. A **brood** is a family of young animals.
4. When something is done **discreetly**, it is done so that others will not notice what is happening.
5. When you **nip** something, you take a small bite out of it.

Let me test the bedsprings now.'
So he jumped up—and somehow,
In a parabolic[6] leap,
Landed not too far from Creep.

'Sir Mosquito, flap your wings.
Leave at once. This bed's the King's.'
'Who may you be, Lady Louse?'
'I'm the guardian of the house.'
'House?' 'This quilt. It's mine,' said Creep.
'There's no place for you, Sir Leap.'
'Let me sleep here for one night
And I'll catch the morning flight.'
Thus the sad mosquito pleaded,
And at last his prayers were heeded[7]
For the tender-hearted Creep
Could not bear[8] to watch him weep.

'Well, come in,' she said at last,
'But tonight you'll have to fast[9],
For on no account[10] may you
Bite him, as we're trained to do.
We can drink and cause no pain,
Loss of royal sleep, or stain.
You, I fear, would cause all three.
I can't risk my family.'

But the glib[11] mosquito cried:
'Now you've let me come inside,
Lady Louse, how can you be
Cold in hospitality?
Just one bite—I ask no more—
For I've learned from learned lore[12]
That the royal blood contains
Remedies for aches and pains—
Ginger, honey, sugar, spice,
Cardamom, and all things nice.
Save me. I'm in broken health.
Let me bite him—once—by stealth[13].
He won't even shift or sigh.
Cross my heart and hope to die.'

Wordfile

6. **Parabolic** means curved.
7. To **heed** something means to take notice of it.
8. When you **bear** something, you manage to tolerate it.
9. If you **fast**, you do not eat for a period of time.
10. The idiom **on no account** means 'under no circumstances'.
11. When someone is **glib**, they speak in a smooth and easy manner but they are not sincere.
12. **Lore** is knowledge that is passed down through generations.
13. When something is done **by stealth**, it is done secretly.

Finally the louse agreed.
'Right!' she said, 'but pay close heed.
Wait till wine, fatigue, or deep
Dream-enriched, unbroken sleep
Has enveloped him. Then go:
Lightly nip his little toe.'
'Yes, yes, yes. That's all old hat,'
Said Sir Leap, 'I know all that.
Keep your stale advice.' He smiled:
'Seriously—I'm not a child.'

It was only afternoon
—Fairly early, fairly soon—
When the King came for a snooze,
Doffed[14] his crown and shirt and shoes,
Lay down on the bed, and sighed.
The mosquito almost died
From excitement, shock, and sweat.
'No!' the louse cried: 'No! Not yet!'
But too late! The self-willed bumbler[15]
—Oh, if only he'd been humbler—
Rushing to the rash[16] attack,
Leapt upon the royal back,
And with fierce and fiery sting
Deeply dirked[17] the dozing king.

'Help! a scorpion! a snake!'
Screamed the King, at once awake.
'I've been bitten! Search the bed!
Find and strike the creature dead!'
When they made a close inspection
The mosquito foiled[18] detection,
Hidden in the canopy;
But the louse clan could not flee,
All were killed with ado[19].
    Meanwhile, the mosquito flew,
Looking out for further prey,
Humming mildly on his way.

Vikram Seth

Wordfile

14. If you **doff** an item of clothing such as a hat, you take it off.
15. A **bumbler** is someone who makes a lot of mistakes.
16. **Rash** behaviour is done quickly without much thought.
17. When someone is **dirked**, they are attacked with a knife.
18. When you **foil** something, you prevent it from happening.
19. When something is done with **ado**, it is done with great fuss and attention to detail.

Poetry appreciation

A Match the sentence halves.

1. Creep and her family have lived
2. Every night, Creep and her family
3. The mosquito likes the bed because
4. Creep asks the mosquito
5. Creep says the mosquito can stay
6. The mosquito attacks the King
7. The mosquito escapes by hiding
8. Creep and her family

a. the quilt is soft and smooth.
b. to leave the bed.
c. and stings him on the back.
d. in the King's bed for three decades.
e. are all killed by the King's men.
f. drink the King's blood.
g. if he does not bite the King.
h. in the canopy of the King's bed.

B Answer the questions.

1. What does the mosquito mean when he says the following to Creep?
   a. 'Cross my heart and hope to die.' (line 62)
   b. 'That's all old hat.' (line 69)
2. 'The self-willed bumbler
   —Oh, if only he'd been humbler—
   Rushing to the rash attack,'
   a. Who is the 'self-willed bumbler' here?
   b. Why is he called this?
   c. Whom does he rashly attack and why?
   d. What happens after this?
3. Why do you think Creep insists that the mosquito should fast or just take one small bite after the King is fast asleep?
4. Find a simile used in the poem.
5. Write the rhyme scheme of any one stanza of the poem.
6. Pick out lines from the poem to show that it is a narrative.
7. What do you think the moral of this poem is?

C Imagine you are Creep or the mosquito. Write your thoughts and feelings during the conversation.

Activity

Writing a narrative poem

The poem 'The Mosquito and the Louse' is a **narrative poem**. A narrative poem is a poem that tells a story. Read another narrative poem, 'The Frog and the Nightingale' by Vikram Seth.

Now, write your own narrative poem where the characters are animals. Read the guidelines and make notes below.

1. Think of a conflict or event that you would like to write about. Write a short paragraph about why the conflict or event is interesting or important to you.
2. Think of a character or characters that would fit well with the conflict or event. Write a short paragraph about the character or characters and why they are appropriate for the conflict or event.
3. Think of a setting (place and time) for your poem. Write a short paragraph about why that setting is appropriate.
4. Write an outline for your poem so that you have an idea of the sequence of events.
5. Start writing. Don't force the poem to rhyme as it is not necessary for narrative poems to rhyme.

Conflict or event:

Character(s):

Setting:

6 Think Differently

In this unit, I will ...

- learn about idiomatic expressions and expand my knowledge of words with the prefix *bio-*
- learn about simple, compound and complex sentences and talk about my hopes for the future
- learn about oxymorons
- discuss alternative forms of education and make a presentation about it
- write a blogpost about experiences at school

Warm-up

A Look at these pictures of some new inventions. Match each invention with its name.

1.

a. pencil printer ________
b. rocking lamp ________
c. eco cab ________
d. water clock ________
e. Corky, the little brown mouse ________

2.

3.

4.
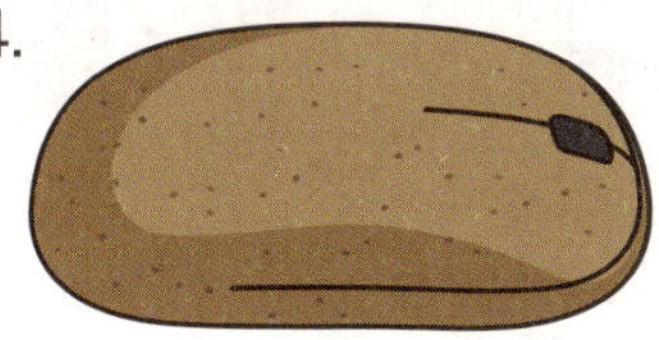

5.

B These inventions are all 'green'. This means they are less harmful to the environment than traditional devices that perform the same functions. Can you guess how each one is green?

Reading 1

You are going to read about three 'innovations' in the field of education. These ideas have helped underprivileged children learn better.

Wordfile

1. The basic systems of an organization, such as buildings, power supply and communication form its **infrastructure**.
2. **Accessibility** is how easy a place is to reach or enter.
3. The position of the body while sitting or standing is called **posture**.
4. Something that is not convenient or comfortable is **awkward**.
5. A **portable** object can be easily moved or transferred.
6. **Recycling** is converting waste into reusable material.
7. A **retail outlet** is a store where goods are sold to individual customers.

A Helping Hand for Children in Need

Cardboard book bags unfold into desks

Many schools in rural areas lack basic necessities like infrastructure[1], good teachers and accessibility[2].

They also lack school bags, chairs and desks. This kind of situation in the classroom also affects children's posture[3] and their concentration levels. They also end up with bad eyesight and bad handwriting because of their awkward[4] position.

To help solve this problem, a Mumbai-based non-profit organization called Aarambh came up a few years ago with the Help Desk, a portable[5] desk made out of recycled[6] cardboard boxes. The desk can also be turned into a school bag in which children can keep their books and notebooks instead of the plastic bags that many of them carry.

The organization collects used cardboard cartons from retail outlets[7], corporate offices, and recycling centres. They have created a stencil design for the desk and cut out the design from the used cardboard boxes. The cut pattern can be folded into a small desk for students. At the end of the school day, students can re-fold the portable desk into a brief case like book bag. The Help Desk does not cost an arm and a leg. Help Desks can be an eco-friendly, economical, and portable solution to one of the most common problems in rural areas - and it costs less than Rs 20.

Floating school in Bangladesh

Mosammat Reba Khatun teaches Bengali, Maths and English on Shidhulai Swanirvar Sangstha's floating school on the Gumani river in the Pabna district in northwest Bangladesh. Hers is one of 70 such moving schools run for free by the NGO. In total, the school teaches 90 students between six and nine years of age. Almost two-thirds of the pupils are girls. Started in 2002 by Mohammed Rezwan, the NGO's founder, the boat schools have helped thousands of children in the country.

The floating schools work in the remote[8] river basin where access to education is hard, particularly during the monsoon season. From late June to October, one third of the country goes underwater, making access to basic services very difficult. 'It is the main reason for school drop outs in rural[9] Bangladesh,' Mosammat says. Were it not for innovative inventions such as this floating school, many of these children would find accessing education impossible.

The school collects children from their homes, teaches them on board and returns them at the end of the session. Mosammat describes the boat's architect's philosophy as 'if the children couldn't come to school, then the school should come to them.' As a further innovative step, the boat is solar-powered, allowing the school to have Internet-linked computers, making learning more interactive. 'I think technology makes learning easier for children from disadvantaged backgrounds,' Mosammat says. Being solar-powered also enables the boat to have solar lanterns, allowing children to have light by which they can do their homework in the evening.

E-learning in Sudan

In Sudan, Africa, millions of children cannot go to school because they live in remote areas, in nomadic[10] tribes, on the streets or in prison. In order to reach these children, War Child, an NGO, makes education available through digital learning materials. Together with local partners and the Ministry of Education, it started an e-learning pilot project[11] in 2012, focusing on the maths curriculum.

Wordfile

8. A **remote** place is located far away from the main city or town.
9. **Rural** relates to villages.
10. A **nomad** is a person who wanders from place to place and has no fixed address or place of living.
11. A **pilot project** is a study done as a test before the launch of the project on a bigger and full scale.

Wordfile

12. **Facilitation** is the process of making an action easier or more accessible.
13. To do something strictly is to do it **rigorously**.

Through this project, children are able to access education from a distance via laptops and new media. The children learn to read and write, which allows them to join regular schools as soon as they have the chance.

The programme provides a creative and fun applied-gaming instruction method combined with in-community facilitation[12]. It is based on part of an out-of-school mathematics curriculum and is aimed to test rigorously[13] whether children can learn using this methodology. The participating children have never been to school. Informal teaching rather than traditional teaching is used in the village. Today, the programme has been extended to many more states in Sudan.

Comprehension 1

A What are the biggest problems faced by the schools for underprivileged children? Tick the correct options.

1. lack of infrastructure ☐
2. high school fees ☐
3. too much food ☐
4. accessiblity ☐
5. poorly trained teachers ☐
6. broken, damaged or no furniture ☐
7. lack of transport ☐

B **Read the statements and mark them as true (T) or false (F).**

1. The Help Desk school bags are made of recycled plastic. ________
2. Children can use the Help Desk as both desks and bags. ________
3. The Help Desk bags are very expensive. ________
4. The process of making the school bags is very complicated. ________
5. The main reason for school drop outs in Bangladesh is war. ________
6. The e-learning programme launched in Sudan focuses on maths. ________
7. The e-learning program in Sudan started in 2015. ________
8. Under the e-learning program, students are given tablets to access the Internet. ________

C **Answer the questions.**

1. What problems do students face when schools lack basic infrastructure?
2. How has Aarambh helped students in rural areas?
3. Who are Mosammat Reba Khatun and Mohammed Rezwan? What does Shidhulai Swanirvar Sangstha do to further the cause of education in Bangladesh?
4. How has solar power helped the organization's work?
5. How has War Child helped to overcome the problem faced by Sudan's students?

Comprehension 2

1. What do the three organisations have in common?
2. What advantage does a floating school have over a traditional school?
3. NGOs work to help the underprivileged. Do you think charity is important in daily life? Should we spend our own money to help those less fortunate than us? Give reasons for your answer. VBQ

Vocabulary check

Idiomatic expressions

A **In the passage, you came across the idiom, 'cost an arm and a leg'. Something which costs an arm and a leg is very expensive. Look at these idiomatic expressions and match them with their meanings.**

Idioms	Meanings
1. to be as sick as a dog	a. to joke with someone
2. raining cats and dogs	b. to reveal a secret
3. to drive someone up the wall	c. someone who is unpredictable
4. to pull someone's leg	d. to be very ill
5. to hold one's horses	e. to be terribly annoying
6. a loose cannon	f. raining heavily
7. let the cat out of the bag	g. to be patient

B **Fill in the blanks with the correct idiomatic expressions.**

have an axe to grind
bag of tricks
dog's life
come hell or high water
a new lease of life
beyond one's wildest dreams
clean as whistle
pressed for time

1. Use your ______________ to get us out of this problem.
2. She couldn't stay longer because she was ______________
3. After a week of staying home because of the rains, Haroun was determined to go out, ______________
4. No matter what the topic of discussion is, he always ______________
5. They could not find anything bad about him. He was ______________
6. The injured dog got ______________ when the doctors saved him.
7. They became rich ______________
8. Thomas works 12 hours a day, and then does all the chores at home. His is a ______________

Language skills

Prefix *bio-*

Bioplastic is a kind of plastic made with a biological substance such as banana peels.

Bio- is a prefix that you see at the beginning of many words. It is used to show that the word relates to life and living things.

A Can you think of any words that begin with *bio-*? Discuss with your classmates and write them down.

B Look at these words that have the prefix *bio-*. What do they mean? Discuss with your classmates.

biochemistry	biography	biology
biometric	biotechnology	bioweapon

Check the meanings of the words in this extract from a dictionary.

biochemical /ˌbaɪəʊ'kemɪkəl/ ADJ BEFORE N **Biochemical** processes are the chemical processes that happen in living things.

biochemistry /ˌbaɪəʊ'kemɪstri/ N-UNCOUNT **Biochemistry** is the study of the chemical processes that happen in living things. • **biochemist** (**biochemists**) N-COUNT ❑ *Other enzymes were identified by biochemists.*

biographer /baɪ'ɒgrəfə/ (**biographers**) N-COUNT Someone's **biographer** is a person who writes an account of their life.

Word Link	*bio ≈ life : antibiotic, biography, biology*

Word Link	*graph ≈ writing : autograph, biography, graph*

biography /baɪ'ɒgrəfi/ (**biographies**) N-COUNT A **biography** of a person is an account of their life, written by someone else. • **biographical** /ˌbaɪə'græfɪkəl/ ADJ ❑ *...a biographical film.*
→ see **library**

biological /ˌbaɪə'lɒdʒɪkəl/ 1 ADJ **Biological** is used to describe processes and states that occur in the bodies and cells of living things. ❑ *...a natural biological response.* • **biologically** ADV ❑ *Humans are biologically programmed to eat.* 2 ADJ BEFORE N **Biological** studies are connected with research in biology. ❑ *...biological sciences.* 3 ADJ **Biological** weapons and **biological** warfare involve the use of organisms which damage living things. ❑ *...biological weed control.*
→ see **war, zoo**

Word Link	*logy, ology ≈ study of : anthropology, biology, geology*

Word Link	*ist ≈ one who practices : biologist, journalist, pharmacist*

biology /baɪ'ɒlədʒi/ N-UNCOUNT **Biology** is the science concerned with the study of living things. • **biologist** (**biologists**) N-COUNT ❑ *Biologists are studying the fruit fly.*

biometric /ˌbaɪə'metrɪk/ ADJ **Biometric** tests and devices use biological information about a person to create a detailed record of their personal characteristics. ❑ *...the use of biometric information such as fingerprints.*

biotechnology /ˌbaɪəʊtek'nɒlədʒi/ N-UNCOUNT **Biotechnology** is the use of living parts such as cells or bacteria in industry and medicine. [TECHNICAL]
→ see **technology**

bioweapon or **bio-weapon** /'baɪəʊˌwepən/ (**bioweapons**) N-COUNT **Bioweapons** are biological weapons.

C Read the dictionary extract again and answer the questions.

1. Where is the main stress on these words? Circle the syllable with the main stress. Practise saying the words.

biochemistry   biography   biology   biometric   biotechnology   bioweapon

2. Complete the table.

Noun	Noun (person)	Adjective
biochemistry		
	biographer	
		biological
biotechnology		

Study tip

Knowing the meanings of common prefixes and suffixes can help you to understand and make new words. Find out the meanings of common prefixes and suffixes, and keep lists of words that contain them.

Prefix/suffix	Meaning	Examples
bio-	relating to life and living things	biology, biotechnology, biographer, biochemistry

Reading 2

1 Rearrange the spellings of the words below to form words found commonly in ghost stories. Then, write a brief description of each.

1. shbanee ____________
2. hguol ____________
3. dinjn ____________
4. gerpoltiest ____________
5. phsacgusroa ____________

Satyajit Ray's *Professor Shonku* stories, written as diary entries, explore the realm of science fiction and adventure. The stories are originally in Bengali.

This story delves into Professor Shonku's curiosity about ghosts and life after death.

How would you feel if you could talk to ghosts? Read the story to find out what Professor Shonku does when he sees a particular ghost.

Professor Shonku and the Spook

10 April

I have believed, for a long time, that one day things such as ghosts and spectres[1], telepathy[2] and clairvoyance[3] will become subjects for scientific study. I have heard first-hand accounts of encounters with ghosts, from people who are sensible and trustworthy, and not given to irrational flights of fancy. So I have not been able to dismiss the concept of ghosts, or life after death, as complete nonsense.

Mind you, I have never had such an experience myself. A Chinese magician was once successful in hypnotising me; I have, on one occasion, had to struggle with an invisible adversary[4], and seen a sadhu turn a heap of bones into a living, breathing creature. But I have never come face to face with the ghost of a dead man.

It was possibly for this reason that, of late, the desire to see a ghost was growing stronger in my mind. I kept wondering if there might be a scientific way to make an apparition[5] present itself.

Wordfile

1. A **spectre** (here) is a ghost.
2. **Telepathy** is the direct communication of thoughts and feelings between people's minds without the need to use speech, writing, or any other normal signals.
3. **Clairvoyance** is the ability to know about future events or to be able to communicate with dead people.
4. Your **adversary** is someone you are competing with, or arguing or fighting against.
5. An **apparition** is the ghost or image of a dead person

Naturally, in this case, chemicals and scientific instruments alone could not achieve anything. What was required was concentration. I had to have that—as much as I could muster—for there would be no point in being able to see any ordinary ghost. I wanted to call the departed souls of specific people to my room, talk to them, and then send them back to the other world. If I could bring them as real people who could be felt and touched, if I could shake hands with them, that would be my biggest achievement. An achievement for science!

As a result of my hard work over the last three months, all my careful research and craftsmanship, my new machine called Neo-spectroscope is now ready. The term 'spectro' is related to 'spectre' here, not 'spectrum'. And it is 'neo', for no one has ever built such a machine before.

A detailed description of this machine is already given in my main notebook.

There is no need to repeat that here in my diary. Briefly, what I did is this: I built a metal helmet to fit my head. Two electric wires come out of the helmet, which go into a glass bowl filled with a solution that I have made. Soaking in that solution are two flat pieces of copper. The two wires are connected to the copper.

A variety of ingredients have gone into making the solution. The most important of these is the juice from the roots of some trees in our cremation ground, which have been nourished by the smoke from several funeral pyres, over many years.

When this solution is heated over a gas burner, thick coils of green smoke rise from it forming a column that shoots up to a height of five and a half feet. Rather extraordinarily, it does not spread anywhere, but remains hovering over the glass bowl. It is through this column of smoke that a ghost is supposed to appear.

This morning, I tested my machine for the first time. I cannot say I was entirely successful, chiefly because I failed to concentrate fully. Just as I was going into my laboratory, I saw Newton pounce upon a cockroach in one corner of the veranda and kill it with his paw. As a result, when I put the helmet on and began to think of a suitable ghost, all I could think of was the lifeless form of the cockroach.

Probably for this reason, five minutes later, I could clearly see a huge cockroach taking shape in the column of smoke, waving its antennae at me. This spectre of the cockroach remained visible for nearly a minute. Then it disappeared.

Obviously, it was pointless to try for a proper ghost after that.

I shall try again tomorrow morning. Today, I must spend as much time as I can in practising mental exercises. I must not lose my concentration tomorrow.

11 April

Unbelievable.

This morning, I had a conversation for almost three and a half minutes with my dear, departed friend, Archibald Ackroyd, the British scientist. He died in Norway under suspicious circumstances.

Today, incredibly, the same Ackroyd appeared amidst the coils of green smoke in my lab. [...]

12 April

Today, I had meant to get Siraj-ud -daula in my laboratory to find out the truth behind the episode of the black hole in Calcutta. But my neighbour, Avinash Chatterjee, arrived and ruined all my plans.

I had just finished my coffee in the living room, when he turned up. I doubt if there is another person in the entire world with an attitude that is as completely unscientific as that of Avinash Babu's. All I have ever seen him do is express complete indifference to my successes as a scientist, and mock me for my failures.

He entered the room and promptly sat down on a sofa. 'Why were you loitering[6] near the Usri?' he asked.

Usri is the name of the river that flows through Giridih. It is true that I go there sometimes on my morning walks, but over the last twenty days or so, I haven't been there. As a matter of fact, I haven't set foot outside my house at all.

So I said, 'When did you see me loitering?'

'Today. Only about an hour ago. I called out to you, but you didn't reply.'

'What! How is that possible? I did not leave the house this morning, not even once.'

Avinash Babu burst out laughing. 'What's the matter with you? Why are you denying your movements? The man I saw was about five feet two inches tall like you, had a beard exactly like yours, and was bald, just like you. How many men in Giridih fit that description?'

Wordfile

6. If you **loiter** in a place, you remain there or walk up and down without any real purpose.

A combination of wonder and annoyance rendered me speechless. What did Avinash Babu take me for? A liar? I, Trilokeshwar Shonku?

'And it wasn't just I who saw you,' Avinash Babu went on, 'Ramlochan Banerjee saw you, too. But it was not by the river. He found you in the mango grove behind our judge's house. That was after I saw you. He just told me, on my way here. You can ask him, if you like.'

I remained silent.

Prahlad appeared with a cup of coffee. Avinash Babu suddenly asked him a question, 'Prahlad,' he said, 'was your babu at home all morning, or did he go out?'

'Last night he was pottering in the lab until quite late,' Prahlad replied, 'so how could he go out early this morning? No, he was at home.'

I must mention something here. I did not go to my laboratory after yesterday morning. I never go there without a reason. All I did yesterday, after my encounter with Ackroyd, was practise concentrating. But I did that in my bedroom. At nine last night, I went to bed and rose this morning, as always, at five. How could Prahlad say that I was pottering in the lab late last night?

'When I was working in the lab,' I asked Prahlad, 'did you bring me coffee?'

'Of course. You were fiddling with your things in the dark, so I ...'

'In the dark?' I interrupted him, 'If it was dark, how can you be so sure that it was me, and not someone else?'

Prahlad grinned. 'How could I not recognise you, babu? There was so much moonlight. It fell on your bald head, and it was shining like ...'

'All right, all right.'

'Once I saw a film,' Avinash Babu told me, 'it had a funny story. There was this man, who got split in two. So, at any given time, you could see one half in one place, and the other somewhere else. Do you think a similar thing has happened to you? I shouldn't be surprised. How many times have I told you not to do these weird experiments? One's brain gets affected by such things. But would you listen? Oh no!'

I smiled a little foolishly, and offered an imaginary explanation for my supposed preoccupation[7] this morning. Then I said goodbye and made my way to the river.

Wordfile

7. If you have a **preoccupation** with something or someone, you keep thinking about them continuously or frequently.

After dinner, I couldn't help going into the laboratory once more. The Neo-spectroscope was lying exactly where I'd left it. My notebooks, papers and all the apparatus were in their places.

Did I come here last night? If I did, how could I have forgotten all about it? It was impossible.

I switched the light off. Moonlight came streaming through the southern window and fell on the table. I walked towards the window, my mind full of anxious thoughts.

I could see my garden from here. I sat in that garden every evening, on my favourite deck chair, under a colourful umbrella. That umbrella was still there, as was the chair. It should have been empty. But I could see someone sitting in it.

There was no one in my house except Prahlad and Newton, my cat. Prahlad would never sit in my chair, unless he was out of his mind.

The man sitting there was old. He was bald, except for a little hair around his ears. He had an unkempt[8] beard and moustache. Although I could only see his profile[9], and he did not turn his face towards me even once, it was clear that there were startling resemblances between his appearance and my own.

Suddenly I had an idea. Could it be that some youngster had put on a disguise to look like me and was simply playing a practical joke? That must be it. I decided to catch him red-handed. So I stole out silently, crossed the passage outside and reached the garden.

But it was in vain. When I got to the chair, it was empty. I touched the canvas and found it warm. It could only mean that someone was sitting there just a few moments ago. I looked around quickly. There was no one. In that bright moonlight, everything was clearly visible. There was nowhere that a man could hide!

Had my own eyes played tricks? I returned to my bedroom feeling more agitated than ever. If I don't take a pill, I will not be able to sleep tonight.

14 April

The manner in which the mystery of the double Shonku was solved is something that no other experience in my entire life can match.

Over the last two days, I did not step out of my bedroom for fear of running into the second 'me'. I told Prahlad to lock the door of my bedroom from outside and place a

Wordfile

8. If you describe something or someone as **unkempt**, you mean that they are untidy and not looked after well.
9. A **profile** is the outline of a person's face seen from the side.

large, heavy table against it, to stop myself from leaving the room by mistake. Prahlad did as he was told, and brought my meals, as well as cups of coffee, directly to my bedroom. Each time, he had to remove the table and unlock the door. He waited in the room until I finished eating, then took the used plates and cups away, locking the door behind him and replacing the table.

In spite of these measures, each day Prahlad received news of people having seen 'me' in various places in Giridih, but chiefly by the river. Everyone who had seen me, was convinced that I had gone completely crazy, which was the reason why I was not responding to their greetings. Last evening, Prahlad said, the doctor had come to my house out of his own desire to examine me. But Prahlad told him I was asleep.

This morning, I could not bear it any more. So I called Prahlad and had him unlock the door. Then I went straight to my laboratory.

My chair, my table, the new machine, the electric wires, the container for the solution—everything was where it should be. The empty chair seemed inviting.

I went and sat in it. Then I poured some of the solution into a beaker and lit a burner. When I placed the beaker over the burner, green smoke began to rise from it almost at once.

Then I wore the helmet, and made sure that the wires remained in contact with the copper plates placed in the beaker.

My eyes remained fixed on the spiralling smoke. In my mind was a picture of the unfortunate Nawab of Bengal in the eighteenth century, Siraj-ud-daula.

All other thoughts were banished.

Slowly, a skeleton appeared in the column of smoke. As soon as its hazy outlines became clear, it was obvious that only the top half had appeared. There was the skull, the neck and the ribcage, but nothing else.

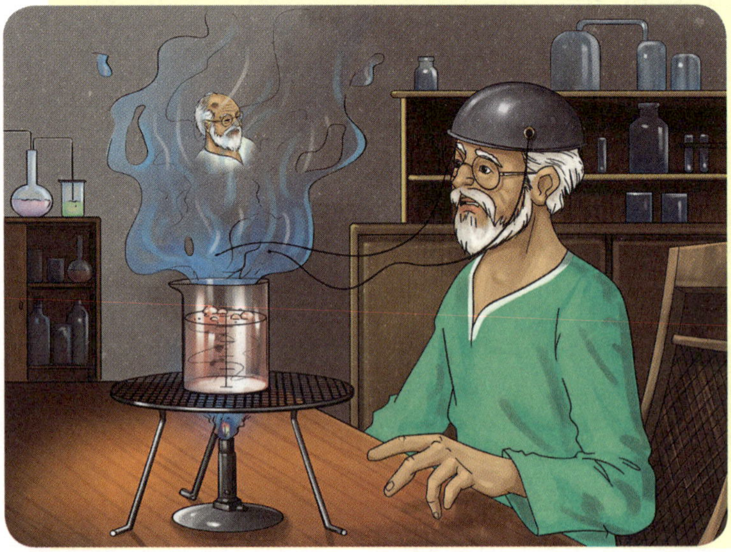

How very strange! How did this happen?

A few moments later a turban, embroidered with gold thread, appeared on the skull. This was followed by two glittering diamond studs on its earlobes.

It came to me in a flash. All the pictures of Siraj-ud -daula that I have seen in history books show only his face and torso. That was the picture I had in mind and so only those portions of his body, as seen in the picture, had now appeared before my eyes.

I was still staring at the skeleton and had just noticed the pupil in one of the eyes being formed, when a sudden guffaw[10] broke my concentration. In the next instant, the upper half of Siraj-ud-daula's body vanished. Then quite unexpectedly, a figure emerged from the green smoke, stepped out of it and walked towards my table. Who was this? Was it my own reflection in a mirror? Or was it someone else? I had no idea that two different men could look so much like carbon copies of each other.

The stranger spoke. The sound of his voice told me at once that it was no reflection. He cast an unnaturally sharp glance in my direction and said, 'Trilokeshwar, I am grateful to you. You have helped me fulfil a long-cherished dream.'

I swallowed and somehow managed to find my voice. 'Who are you?' I asked.

'I will tell you, be patient. Once upon a time, I used to sit by the Usri for my meditation. One day, a vicious hailstorm started while I was sitting there, lost in my meditation. A hailstone fell on my head with such force that it killed me.'

'Killed ...?'

'Yes. Ever since that day, I have often wanted to return here. But it wasn't possible for me to assume a bodily form again. Your scientific skills have now made that possible. I was here on the very first day when you were sitting in that chair although I did not let you see me.'

'But ... but ... please tell me who you are!'

'I am your great-great-great-grandfather, the late Botukeshwar Shonku. Born in 1730, died in 1807. Come, let us shake hands.'

My ancestor, whose appearance was totally identical to mine, offered me his hand. As soon as I touched it, I felt a tremor run through my body. Botukeshwar's hand was freezing cold. He laughed. 'Does that feel cold? All right, I'd better go.'

He dropped my hand and sprang back into the smoky column. In a few seconds, his body was reduced to a skeleton. Before that skeleton disappeared from view, it bent its head and showed me a little hole in its crown.

Having met a ghost in the flesh, I lost my interest in meeting an intangible[11] form. So I locked up my Neo-spectroscope in the almirah. To tell the truth, the mental strain that was being caused by this entire business was beginning to affect me too much.

I was playing with Newton in the living room a little later, when Avinash Babu turned up. He looked both worried and agitated. After sitting down, he remained silent for one entire minute. All he did was stare at the floor and frown. Then he spoke, 'You know my nephew, Shibu, don't you?'

'Yes.'

Wordfile

10. A **guffaw** is a crude and boisterous laugh.
11. If something is **intangible,** it cannot be perceived by touch.

'He ... well, he likes taking photos. So, when he heard that you had denied being outdoors even though various people had seen you here and there, Shibu decided to ... to play a prank. He took his camera to the riverside and hid behind a tree, until he saw you arrive. Then he quickly took your picture'.

'Good. Have you brought it with you?'

'No. There was no point in bringing it. All the picture shows is the river, the sandy bank and rocks. Shibu saw you standing quite close to those rocks. You should have been in the picture, but you're not. You've vanished!'

I smiled. 'Shall I tell you who it was?' I remarked, 'It wasn't me, but the ghost of one of my ancestors. Come on now, have a cup of coffee. Prahlad!'

Satyajit Ray

About the author

Satyajit Ray (1921–1992) was a renowned filmmaker who directed several films that were acclaimed internationally. The author of several short stories and novels, primarily aimed at children and young adults, Ray was also a publisher, calligrapher, illustrator, music composer and film critic. Felu*da* and Professor Shonku are two of his most popular fictional characters.

Comprehension 1

A Read the questions and tick the correct answers.

1. What was the reason behind the narrator's wish to see a ghost?
   a. He was bored and looking for a distraction. ☐
   b. He wanted to scientifically prove the existence of ghosts and life after death. ☐
   c. He wanted to come face to face with the ghost of a dead man. ☐
2. What was the most noticeable ingredient in the solution prepared by the narrator?
   a. Chemicals prepared by the narrator in his laboratory. ☐
   b. A mixture of rare herbs. ☐
   c. Juice from the roots of the trees in the cremation ground. ☐
3. Why was the first experiment by the narrator unsuccessful?
   a. He was interrupted by his neighbour, Avinash Babu. ☐
   b. He could not concentrate as he had seen Newton kill a cockroach. ☐
   c. The machine designed by the narrator failed to function. ☐

4. How was Avinash Babu's attitude towards the narrator and his scientific experiments?
   a. He was friendly and appreciative. ☐
   b. He was indifferent and unappreciative. ☐
   c. He played a key role in the experiments. ☐
5. Why did the narrator lock himself in the bedroom?
   a. He was afraid of running into his second self. ☐
   b. He wanted to concentrate on his work. ☐
   c. He was feeling distressed. ☐
6. What was the narrator's great-great-great grandfather's wish?
   a. To meet the narrator. ☐
   b. To be able to walk on the banks of the Usri. ☐
   c. To become immortal. ☐

Comprehension 2

Answer the questions.

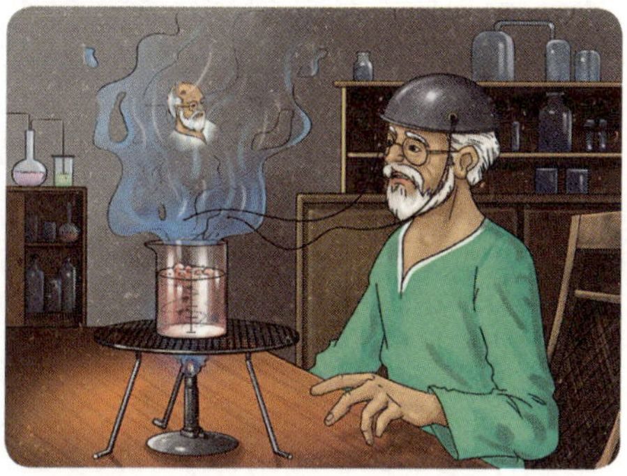

1. The narrator believed in the concept of ghosts and life after death. What were the reasons behind his belief?
2. Who was the narrator's double? How did the narrator help him through his invention?
3. How was the narrator's experience of meeting a ghost in flesh? What made him lock up the Neo-spectroscope?
4. What is your impression of Professor Shonku? What kind of person do you think he is?
5. The narrator believed that his experiment would be an achievement for science. Are new scientific discoveries always good for humanity? Give reasons for your answer. VBQ

Vocabulary

Oxymorons

Oxymorons are phrases that place together two words that are opposite to each other in meaning. They are used for draw attention to an idea or to provoke thought.
same difference

A Identify the oxymoron in each sentence.

1. My brother always thinks that I have the larger half of every share.
2. It is an open secret that Sara dislikes cream buns.
3. The deafening silence that greeted me when I entered the room was scary.
4. Please act naturally when you meet him.
5. Climbing the mountain was his only choice.
6. Please bring original copies of the sale deed.
7. The students were clearly confused by the professor's explanation.
8. Virtual reality is the future.

B Replace the words in italics with a single word from the story with the same meaning.

1. Stefan and *the person he was fighting with* were exhausted at the end of the duel.
2. The child *walked up and down with no purpose* on the beach.
3. The old man was *untidy and not looked after carefully.*
4. Her *ability to know about the future and communicate with dead people* is well known.
5. The scientist was *occupying himself with his inventions* in his laboratory.
6. Avinash always *laughs at people in a scornful way.*
7. The police found him under *questionable, probably dishonest* circumstances.

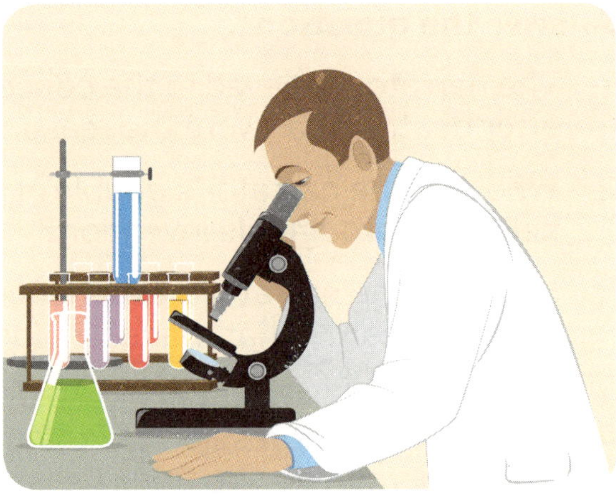

Grammar

Simple, compound and complex sentences

Sentences are of three kinds, depending on their structure.

A **simple** sentence has a subject and a finite verb. It has one main clause.

The sun shines brightly.
Jack went up the hill with Jill to fetch a pail of water.

A **compound** sentence contains two or more main clauses joined by a coordinating conjunction like *and, but, so, for, nor, or* and *yet*.

The sun shines brightly ***and*** *it gives us warmth and light.*
Jack and Jill went up the hill ***yet*** *they did not fetch a pail of water*

A **complex** sentence contains one main clause and one or more subordinate clauses. A subordinate clause begins with a subordinating conjunction such as *because, until, unless, although, since* or *after*. Subordinate clauses do not make complete sense on their own, unlike main clauses.

Although *she was hungry, she waited until her brother joined her.*
Though *Jack and Jill went up the hill, they did not fetch a pail of water.*

A Identify whether the sentences are simple (S), compound (Cd) or complex (C).

1. I washed my hands before I ate breakfast.
2. She ran fast yet she came second.
3. After the party, he went to his friend's house.
4. The apparition became clearer and clearer.
5. The professor was puzzled because he had not gone to the laboratory.
6. As it was late, I decided to stay back with my friend.
7. I called Prahlad and I asked him to lock the door.
8. I went and sat on the chair.

B Join the following simple sentences to form compound or complex sentences.

1. The boy saw a lizard. The boy yelled in fright.
2. The moon shone brightly on Professor Shonku's head. It made his head shine.
3. The man went for a walk. He saw the professor then.
4. You must sleep early. You have to wake up early.
5. Many people witnessed the crime. In spite of that, he denied it.
6. The roads are blocked. We have to find an alternate route.
7. Sana knew she was in trouble. She ran as fast as she could.

Expressing future time

Arvind is asking some questions about the future. He uses the verb **will** (or the short form **'ll,** like *you'll*) to ask about what might happen in the future. What form of the verb follows **will**?

Now read Gopa's answers to Arvind's questions. Note the different phrases that she uses to talk about her hopes for the future.

What will you do when you finish school?

Do you think you will go to college? What will you study?

I hope I'll continue to study. **I'd like to** get a good job!

I think I'll go to college but **I'm not sure** what I'll study. **Maybe I'll** study medicine but **I'll need to** get good marks in school!

C **Work with a partner. Ask and answer Arvind's questions. Use these expressions to talk about your hopes for the future, and make notes about your classmates' hopes in your notebook.**

I think I'll ...
I hope I'll ...
I'd like to ...
I'm not sure. Perhaps I'll ...
Maybe I'll ...

D **Write seven sentences about your partner's hopes for the future. You can follow these structures while writing your sentences.**

Pooja expects that she will work in a bank when she leaves school.

Salman hopes he will go into the army.

Vincent thinks he will have his own business.

Shania will maybe go to college, but she will need to pass her exams.

The future perfect tense

Read what Sushil says about his future. Note the tense he uses.

We use the future perfect tense when we talk about something that will already have happened by a specific time in the future. For example, Sushil is in school now, but he is predicting that when he is 19 years old, he will no longer be in school.

The future perfect tense has this structure:

person		past participle
I You He/She/It We They	will have	**left** school. **graduated** from college. **trained** to be a doctor. **got** married. **finished** their course.

C **In your notebook, write some sentences about your own future using this table. You can use different past participles if you like.**

By the time I'm 18, By the time I'm 24, By the time I'm 30, By the time I'm 40, By the time I'm 60,	I will have	left school. graduated from college. studied ... learned ... trained to be a ... discovered ... won ... got married. travelled to ...

Listening

Interview

A You are going to listen to an interview with a student who goes to an alternative school. As you listen, answer the questions. Write Y (yes) or N (no).

1. Do the students have to wear a uniform? __________
2. Do all students get up early for exercise? __________
3. Do students have to go to classes? __________
4. Which classes does this student enjoy? __________
5. Do students follow a compulsory schedule? __________
6. Do students have any help? __________
7. Do students have exams? __________
8. What will this student do when he finishes school? __________

B Listen to the interview again, and complete the table with notes. (These are your opinions, so there are no right or wrong answers!)

Things that are good about the school	Things that can be problematic

Speaking

Making a presentation

Form groups of equal number and discuss the advantages or disadvantages of alternative methods of schooling. Prepare a presentation that you will share with your classmates.

Some of the groups will be in favour of NGOs and alternative methods of schooling, while others will be against this.

Think about:

- school grounds and environment
- class size
- enjoyment of school
- pressure to study and pass exams

- equal opportunities for all students
- opportunity to study non-traditional subjects such as arts and crafts, dance, singing, exercise and sport
- development of skills such as taking and passing exams
- development of values such as independent thought and responsibility
- preparation to function in traditional life outside school

You can use these phrases while presenting your views.

We believe that ...
Firstly, we feel that ...
In our opinion, alternative schools ...
Secondly, we would argue that ...
Next, we do not believe that ...
Finally, some people would argue that ...

As you listen to your classmates' presentations, note down any points that your group has not considered.

After listening to all of the presentations, discuss this question with a classmate:

Would you like to go to an alternative school? Why/Why not?

Writing

Writing a blogpost

A Imagine that you are a student in your final year at an alternative school. Write a post for your school blog about your experience at the school. Write around 200–300 words.

Write about:

- the things that you have enjoyed about the school
- the things that you or your friends have found difficult at the school
- your plans for the future

Useful phrases

Well, it's been [...] years, but it's gone by so quickly!
Looking back ...
When I arrived at Suru Valley School ...
At first ...
Since then, I have ...
Now, I am ...
I am looking forward to ...
I will always ...

B Imagine that you are Professor Shonku's ancestor. Write a diary entry about returning to Giridih and meeting your descendant. Mention your experience about walking on the banks of the Usri, and being seen by various townspeople.

Poem

You are going to read a poem about following your dreams without giving up.

You Can be Whatever You Want to be!

There is inside you
All of the potential[1]
To be whatever you want to be;
All of the energy
To do whatever you want to do.

Imagine yourself as you would like to be,
Doing what you want to do,
And each day, take one step
Towards your dream.

And though at times it may seem too
difficult to continue,
Hold on to your dream.

One morning you will wake up to find
That you are the person you dreamed of,
Doing what you wanted to do,
Simply because you had the courage
To believe in your potential[1]
And to hold on to your dream.

Donna Levine

Wordfile

1. If someone or something has **potential**, they are capable of being successful or useful in the future.

Poetry appreciation

Answer the questions.

1. According to the first stanza of the poem, what are the things that can help us in becoming whatever we want to be?
2. What does the poet advise us to do while trying to achieve our dreams?
3. 'One morning you will wake up to find
   That you are the person you dreamed of
   Doing what you wanted to do'
   Explain the given lines. What kind of person do you dream of becoming?
4. In the last stanza, what kind of 'courage' is the poet referring to?

VBQ

5. What does the poet mean by the words 'each day, take one step towards your dream'? Why do you think persistent hard work is important for achieving our dreams?

Activity

Some people are happy to see where life will take them and others have a dream that they are determined to achieve. Which type of person are you?

If you have a special dream, write about it and explain how you plan to achieve it.

If you do not have a special dream, find someone who has one. Ask that person about his/her dream and how they plan to achieve it.

Ask your parents, grandparents, aunts and uncles if they had a dream when they were young. Ask these questions:

- What were their dreams?
- Did they achieve their dreams?
- Are they still trying to achieve their dreams or did they abandon it?

Making a scrapbook on birds

In Unit 5, we read about a bird called the hornbill. A hornbill has a long, downward-pointing, curved beak.

Create a descriptive photo scrapbook about birds based on questions A, B and C.

A Find out about five other birds which have distinct beaks.

In your scrapbook, paste their pictures and add a few lines to describe each bird. Name the section 'Birds and their beaks'. You could mention these points:

- where they are found
- the style of their beak
- what they eat
- predators that they must escape from

Hornbill

____
____
____
____
____
____
____

B Visit a zoo. Observe the birds there and gather information about the following questions. Compile the information and/or your photos in your scrapbook under the section 'Birds in the zoo'.

1. How many different kinds of birds can you see? Identify the birds using the information written outside their enclosures. Note down their description and try to find out more about them.
2. Are there any birds that you have seen before?
3. Which are the birds found in and around water and which are the ones found in enclosures or on trees?
4. Which species are the most numerous and which are the rarest?
5. Which are the migratory birds and which are the residents?
6. If you have a camera, take photos of the birds you observe.

C Gather the following information about birds that are extinct and those that are on the verge of extinction. Compile the information under the section 'Endangered birds'.

1. What measures have been taken by the government or other organizations to save such birds?
2. How can people in general help in maintaining bird populations?

Honesty and trust

One afternoon, Deepak goes out to buy groceries for his mother.

He is in a hurry because his friends are waiting for him in the park. He brings home the groceries and runs off to play cricket.

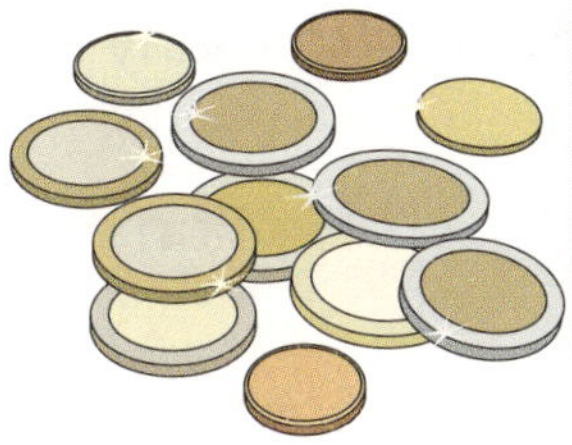

When he comes home in the evening, he realizes that the shopkeeper has mistakenly given him too much change.

A What should he do? Should he:

1. keep the money because it's just a small amount? ☐
2. go back to the shop immediately and return the money? ☐
3. keep the money and add it to his savings to buy a new game? ☐
4. keep the money because it is the shopkeeper's fault that he didn't count carefully? ☐
5. donate the money to charity because it is not his money? ☐

B Have you ever found yourself in a similar situation? What happened? What did you do?

C Imagine you are Deepak. You have decided to keep the extra money, convincing yourself that it's the shopkeeper's fault.

Which of these thoughts might cross your mind later?

Corruption is defined as 'dishonest or illegal behaviour, especially by people in a position of power'. We take various kinds of corruption, both small and major, for granted in daily life, such as paying extra money for processing an application or to get a job done faster.

D Conduct a survey among your peer group in class and in your neighbourhood, asking them the following questions:

1. Is corruption a necessary part of functioning in today's society, whether we like it or not?
2. Do you know anyone who has engaged in corruption or bribery to get something done?
3. Do young people have a duty to speak up against corruption?
4. Would you pay someone extra money to get an important task done quickly, or would you get it done in the honest way, even though it might take longer?

Note the total number of people who participate in your survey. Then, count the number of people who say 'yes' to each question and the number who say 'no'. Find out the percentage of each and display your information in the form of a pie chart for each question.

Display the results of your survey in class.

Total number of participants:

Corruption is a necessary part of society

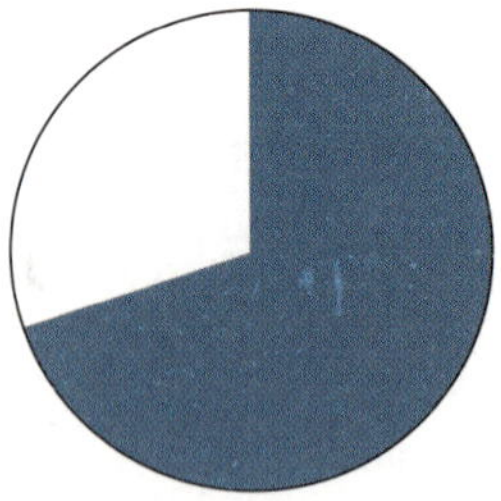

_____% say YES
_____% say NO

Do you know anyone who has engaged in corruption?

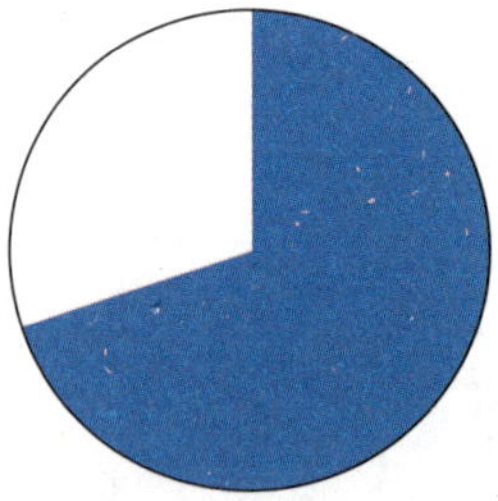

_____% say YES
_____% say NO

Would you pay someone to get something done?

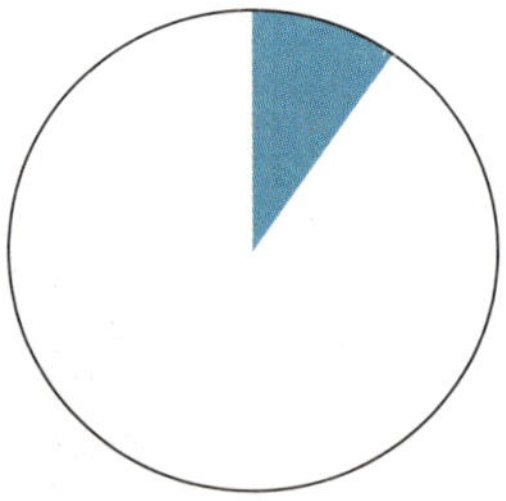

_____% say YES
_____% say NO

Should young people speak up against corruption?

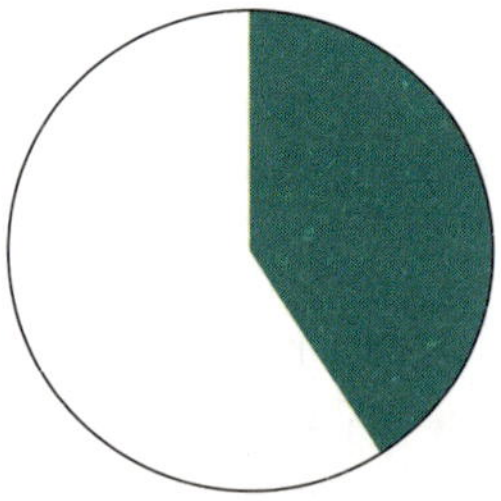

(these are representative pie charts)

_____% say YES
_____% say NO

Way with Words

- Includes exercises on contextual application of language encountered in the reading text
- Fosters appreciation of literary devices and figures of speech (simile, metaphor, personification, etc)

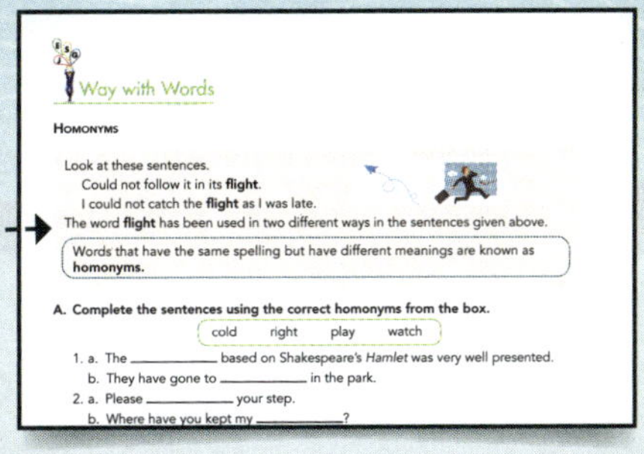

Grammar in Use

- Imparts formal understanding of language structures and syntax
- Includes easy-to-understand explanations of grammar concepts, graphic organisers and plenty of practice exercises

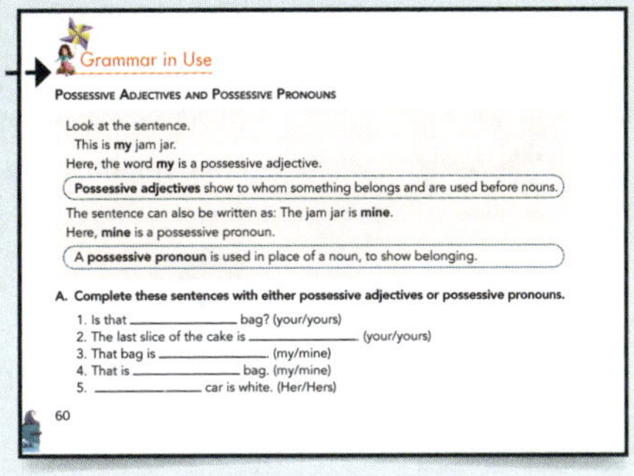

Study Skills

- Develops the sub-skills of language study
- **Spell Check** and **Pronounce Well** include phonics drills and exercises on spelling
- **Use Your Dictionary** develops dictionary referencing skills

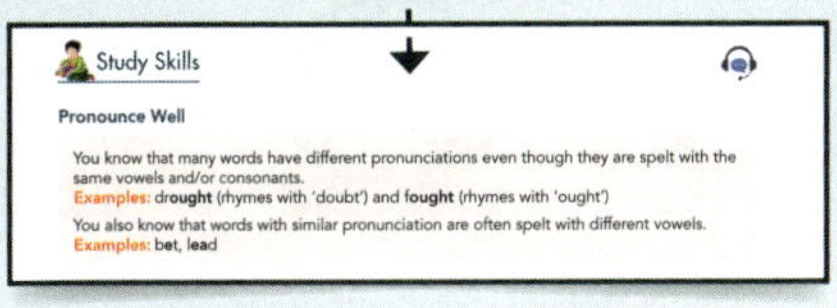

Listening and Speaking

- Facilitates fluency in oral and aural communication
- Includes conversation practice, role plays, debates and listening comprehension
- Exercises on rhyme and meter in poetry chapters

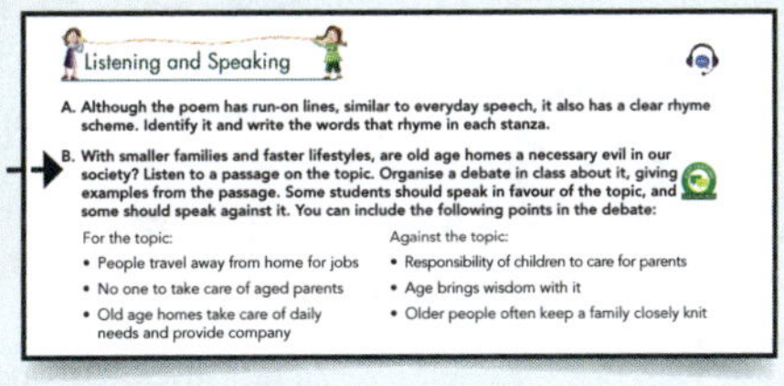

Literary Genres and Terms

- Includes a glossary to introduce literary genres and explain literary devices and narrative tools

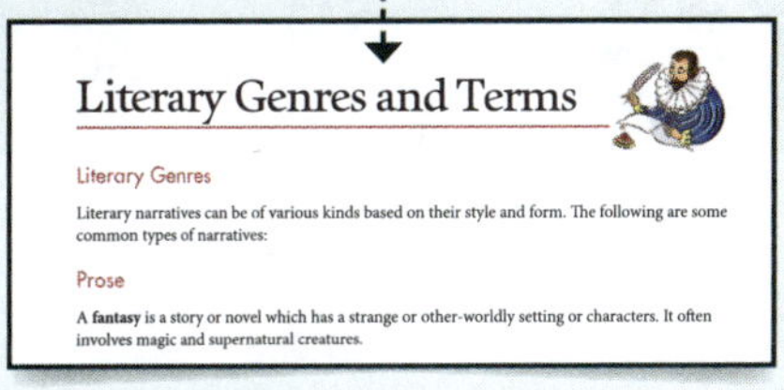

Pen it Down

- Includes guided and free writing tasks, to enable learners to express themselves creatively, logically and coherently

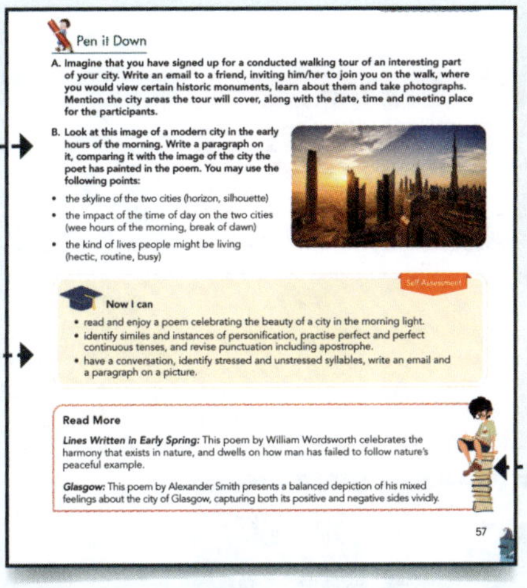

Read More

- Contains extra suggested reading for the avid learner to foster love for literature

Now I can

- Self-assessment of learning objectives for the chapter

Assessments

- Includes a Test Paper in Workbooks 3-8 based on the principle of SAFAL that encourages competency-based learning

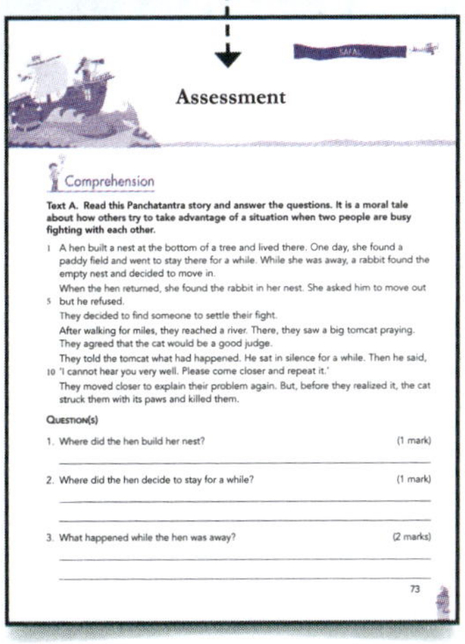

Poster

- Literature and vocabulary games, and activities based on distinct themes

Icons

Revised Engaging English aims to equip students with various skills outlined in the National Education Policy, 2020, that target the holistic education of the learner. Take a look at the various icons used to showcase these skills.

Twenty-first Century Skills

Mastering these skills will equip learners to face the challenges of a rapidly changing, digital society.

Happiness Content

The idea underlying 'Happiness Content', a part of the 'Happiness Curriculum', is that learning should be an enjoyable process. For knowledge to bring joy, learning must focus on concept-based rather than rote learning.

1 HC **Learning and Awareness**

Exploring happiness through Learning and Awareness

2 HC **Feelings**

Experiencing happiness in relationships through Feelings

3 HC **Active Participation**

Happiness through Active Participation

The Sustainable Development Goals (SDGs) were adopted by the United Nations in 2015 as a universal call to action to end poverty, protect the planet, and ensure that by 2030, all people enjoy peace and prosperity. The 17 SDGs recognize that development must balance social, economic and environmental sustainability.

Art Integration

The arts, or the fine arts, are painting, sculpture, architecture, poetry, music, literature and dance. Art-integrated experiential learning uses concepts from the arts to provide learners a multi-disciplinary experience.

Cross-curricular Content

The cross-curricular approach to teaching recognises that subjects are inter-linked, and for effective concept-acquisition, they must be taught in synergy with each other.

Acknowledgements

The publishers wish to thank and acknowledge the following for granting us permission to use copyright material:

Bittu Sahgal, Editor, Sanctuary Asia & Founder, Sanctuary Nature Foundation, for *Where Tigers Swim*, from the book, *The Sundarbans Inheritance*. First published by Sanctuary Asia. Reprinted with the permission of Sanctuary Asia. Roald Dahl for *Dar es Salaam to Nairobi by Ford Prefect*, taken from *Going Solo*, published by Jonathan Cape Ltd and Penguin Books Ltd. Copyright © The Roald Dahl Story Company Limited, 1986; Gareth Owen for *Uncle Alfred's Long Jump* Copyright © Gareth Owen. Reproduced by permission of the author c/o Rogers, Coleridge & White Ltd., 20 Powis Mews, London W 11 1JN; Maureen Lee for *Miss Smith and the Black Pearl* © 1982 Maureen Lee; Mary Kom for *Unbreakable*. Reproduced in arrangement with HarperCollins *Publishers* India, from the book *Unbreakable* © Mary Kom.

The publishers have applied for permission for the following:
Looking for Vultures' Eggs by Bibhutibhushan Bandopadhyay, *Grannie* by Vernon Scannell, *Grandpa Learns to Read and Write* by Michael Morpurgo, *At the Theatre: To the Lady Behind Me* by A. P. Herbert. Acknowledgements for these texts will be made in the future editions of the book.

Every effort has been made to trace copyright holders and to obtain their permission for the use of copyright material. However, in some instances, we have been unable to trace the owners of the copyright pieces published here. The authors and publishers will gladly receive any information enabling them to rectify any error or omission in subsequent editions.

Illustrations

Inside: Page 6: SDG logo and icons: https://www.un.org/sustainabledevelopment/
The content of this publication has not been approved by the United Nations and does not reflect the views of the United Nations or its officials or Member States. Page **11:** Natalie_; **12:** johnwoodcock; **14:** beastfromeast, dedMazay; **16:** artbesouro; **17:** naphoart naphoart, mi_007, rustemgurler; **18:** sabelskaya; **20:** tachyglossus; **22:** Benjavisa, Karma15381; **24:** Gleb Kosarenko; **25:** vectornation; **26:** LMPC / Contributor; **31:** hisa nishiya; **34:** 1970s; **40:** Yutthana Gaetgeaw; **41:** JohnPitcher; **50:** kbeis, mammoth, evenfh, David Chang, AROYBARMAN, owngarden; **53:** rhoon; **55:** Alfadanz; **56:** duncan1890; **57:** duncan1890; **58:** Big_Ryan; **67:** lemono; **70:** suriya9 **71:** suriya9; **74:** PCH-Vector; **76:** Mervana; **95:** PoulCarlsen; **102:** klyaksun; **108:** Irina Cheremisinova; **109:** bobbyperu; **112:** Historical Picture Archive / Contributor, The India Today Group / Collaboratore, Getty Images News, Colorfuel Studio; pijama61; **125:** Vik_Y, Nayanba Jadeja; **127:** Claudiad; **133:** Dana Kulbayeva; **135:** prawny, Samarskaya; **135:** yelet; **141:** The India Today Group; **144:** chekat; **145:** Olga Naumova; **146:** Christian Petersen / Staff; **147:** MANAN VATSYAYANA / Stringer, Jack Vartoogian/ Getty Images / Contributor, fotomedia, ozgurdonmaz; **151:** Smashing Stocks; **154:** akuzone; **164:** JakeOlimb; **166:** Getty Images.

Detailed Contents

Unit	Theme	Comprehension	Way with Words	Grammar in Use	Study Skills	Listening and Speaking	Pen it Down
1. Three Questions	Neighbourhood and Community	• Completing sentences • Questions	• Forming abstract nouns using suffixes • Synonyms	• Transitive and intransitive verbs • Using *few/a few, little/a little, little/less*	• Pronounce Well: syllables	• Conversation using close-ended and open-ended questions	• Email writing
2. Hope is the Thing with Feathers	Selfhood	• Reference to context • Explaining literary terms	• Imagery	• Determiners • Phrases and clauses	• Use Your Dictionary: colloquial expressions	• Listening comprehension: answering questions • Debate on a given topic	• Message writing • Paragraph writing
3. Looking for Vultures' Eggs	Adventure and Imagination	• Reference to context • Character sketch • Questions	• Collocations • Word association	• Converting adjectives to nouns • Transformation of sentences: interrogative and assertive	• Use Your Dictionary: alphabetical order	• Listening to a description and guessing • Describing a scene • Conversation: speaking on a given topic	• Describing an incident • Writing an alternate ending to a story
4. Coromandel Fishers	Professions	• Questions • Reference to context	• Idioms with *call* • Phrasal verbs with *call*	• Transformation of sentences: exclamatory and assertive	• Use Your Dictionary: words of Indian origin	• Listening comprehension: answering questions • Recitation	• Writing a factual essay
5. Where Tigers Swim	Endangered Animals	• Matching points • Questions	• Compound adjectives • Commonly confused words	• Types of adjectives • Tenses	• Pronounce Well: stressed syllables	• Listening comprehension: true/false • Research and presentation on a given topic	• Writing an essay on a given topic
6. Composed upon Westminster Bridge, September 3, 1802	Tales of the City	• Questions • Reference to context	• Simile • Personification	• Perfect and perfect continuous tense • Punctuation • Apostrophe	• Spell Check: long *a*	• Conversation: expressing admiration • Stressed and unstressed syllables	• Email writing • Picture composition
7. Mary Shelley	Creatures of the Dark	• Questions • Reference to context	• Word meanings • Forming antonyms with prefixes	• Adjective phrases • Transformation of sentences with adjective phrases • Noun phrases	• Spell Check: commonly confused spellings	• Speaking on a given topic	• Writing a notice
Research and Write							
8. Grannie	Family	• Questions • Reference to context	• Emotive language	• Question tags • Comparison of adjectives	• Pronounce Well: /v/ and /w/ sounds	• Rhyme scheme • Debate on a given topic	• Making a poster
9. Grandpa Learns to Read and Write	Books and Reading	• Questions • Reference to context	• Crossword • Expressions related to studying	• Prepositions • Prepositional phrases	• Spell Check: plurals of foreign words	• Listening comprehension: fill in the blanks	• Informal letter
10. Dar es Salaam to Nairobi by Ford Prefect	Travel	• Reference to context • Questions	• Onomatopoeia • Crossword	• Infinitives • Transformation of sentences using infinitives • Gerunds	• Use Your Dictionary: animal expressions and their meanings	• Listening comprehension: answering questions	• Letter to the editor

Unit	Theme	Comprehension	Way with Words	Grammar in Use	Study Skills	Listening and Speaking	Pen it Down
11. Uncle Alfred's Long Jump	Humour	• Questions • Reference to context	• Irony • Proverbs	• Coordinating and subordinating conjunctions • Indefinite pronouns	• Pronounce Well: words with silent letters	• Listening comprehension: answering questions • Class discussion on a given topic	• Writing a report
12. The Invisible Man	Scientific Pursuits	• Questions • Reference to context	• Figurative language • Nominalisation	• Present and past participles • Active and passive voice	• Use Your Dictionary: looking up word entries	• Conversation: asking for help	• Essay writing
Research and Write							
13. The Model Millionaire	Art and Culture	• Reference to context • Questions	• Contextual usage: fill in the blanks • Antonyms • Multiple meanings of *perfect*	• Modals • Transformation of sentences using *if* and *unless*	• Pronounce Well: the letter *g*	• Conversation: expressing surprise	• Diary entry
14. The Human Seasons	Cycle of Life	• Questions • Reference to context	• Idioms related to nature • Word meanings	• Main and subordinate clauses	• Pronounce Well: *th* sound • Different pronunciations of words starting with *c-*	• Rising and falling intonation in *yes/no* and *wh-* questions	• Writing a poem
15. Miss Smith and the Black Pearl	Race and the Arts	• Questions • Reference to context	• Multiple meanings of *good* • Homographs • Making sentences	• Simple, compound and complex sentences and their transformation • Adjective clause	• Use Your Dictionary: abbreviations, acronyms	• Conversation: speaking on a given topic	• Writing a letter
16. Unbreakable	Women in Sports	• Questions • Reference to context	• Contextual usage: fill in the blanks • Expressions related to sports	• Noun clause • Adverb clause	• Use Your Dictionary: words of Greek origin	• Listening to and enacting an interview	• Picture composition
17. At the Theatre: To the Lady Behind Me	On the Stage	• Questions • Reference to context	• Idioms with *play* • Collective nouns	• Adverb phrases • Transformation of sentences with adverb phrases • Transformation of sentences: simple, complex and compound	• Pronounce Well: homophones, homographs	• Listening comprehension: fill in the blanks • Enacting a poem	• Descriptive account
18. Twelfth Night	New Beginnings	• Questions • Reference to context	• Archaic words	• Direct and indirect speech		• Conversation: thanking for help • Intonation: stressing on different words in a sentence	• Writing a report • Making a poster
Research and Write							
Literary Genres and Terms							

Contents

1

Three Questions

Leo Tolstoy

Let's Get Started

A. The United Nations Sustainable Development Goal 16 highlights the importance of safe and sustainable communities, where people live in harmony. Think about ways how we can help our neighbours, as this leads to building of communal bonds. Write two lines each in the given space, and also mention what your idea of a 'good neighbour' is.

What we can do to build stronger bonds	Good Neighbour	Situations where we might need help from others

B. One of the most important inventions of man is the concept of time. What is your definition of time? Draw a symbol or choose an image which shows the impact that the passing of time has. Share and explain your symbol to the class. Avoid commonly used objects like clocks and watches.

HC **Learning and Awareness:** Understanding our desire for clarity and prosperity

Reading

Do you ever wonder about the future or think what might have been the best way to have done something? Read this story about a king who wants to know who the most important people for him are and the right time for doing the most important thing.

It once occurred to a king that if he always knew the right time for every action, the right people to listen to and who to avoid, and above all, what the most important thing to do was, he would never fail in anything.

proclaimed: announced

councillors: advisors

hermit: a person who lives alone, away from people and society

frail: weak and thin

recommenced: started again

What did the king announce throughout his kingdom?

He had it **proclaimed** throughout his kingdom that he would give a reward to anyone who would teach him these truths. Many learned men came to the king. In reply to the first question, some said that one must draw up a table of days, months and years, and live strictly according to it. Others declared that it was impossible to decide beforehand the right time for every action; one should be attentive to all that was going on and do what was the most needed. Some said that the king should have a council of wise men to help him decide the proper time for everything. Yet others said there were things one had to decide at once, for which one must know beforehand what was going to happen. Since only magicians knew that, one must consult magicians.

Equally varied were the answers to the second question. Some said that the people the king most needed were his **councillors**; others said it was the priests; yet others, the doctors; while some said the warriors were the most necessary.

To the third question, some replied that the most important occupation was science. Others said it was skill in warfare; and others, again, said that it was worship.

The king was dissatisfied with all the answers. He decided to consult a **hermit** renowned for his wisdom. The hermit lived in a wood and he received none but common folk. So the king put on simple clothes, and leaving his horse and bodyguards behind, went alone.

When the king arrived, the **frail** hermit was digging the ground in front of his hut. He greeted the king and went on digging, breathing heavily.

The king went up to him and said, 'I have come to you, wise hermit, to seek answers to three questions: How can I learn to do the right thing at the right time? Who are the people I most need? And what affairs are the most important?'

The hermit listened to the king, but did not answer. He just **recommenced** digging.

'You are tired,' said the king, 'let me take the spade and work awhile for you.'

'Thank you,' said the hermit and giving the spade to the king, sat down on the ground.

A little later, when he had dug two beds, the king stopped and repeated his questions. The hermit again gave no answer, but rose and said, 'Now rest awhile and let me work a bit.'

But the king did not give him the spade and continued to dig. One hour passed and then another. The sun began to sink behind the trees. The king at last stuck the spade into the ground and said, 'I came to you, wise man, for an answer to my questions. If you can give me none, tell me so and I will return home.'

'Here comes someone running,' said the hermit, 'let us see who it is.'

Who did the king and the hermit see?

The king turned round and saw a bearded man come running out of the woods. When he reached the king, he fell to the ground, moaning feebly. The king and the hermit **unfastened** the man's clothing. There was a large wound in his stomach. The king washed and bandaged it several times till the blood ceased flowing. Meanwhile, the sun had set and it had become cool. The king, with the hermit's help, carried the wounded man inside the hut and laid him on the bed. The king also fell asleep, tired as he was. When he awoke in the morning, he saw the bearded man gazing **intently** at him.

unfastened: opened

intently: carefully

executed: (here) killed

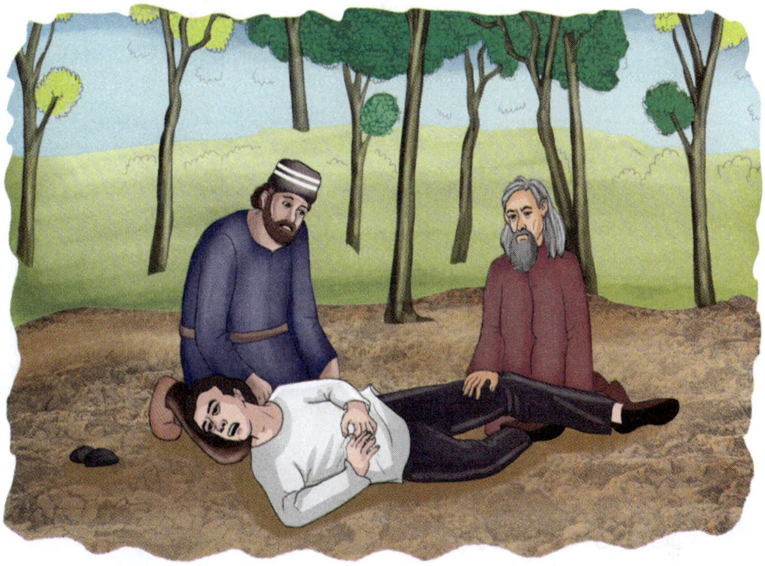

'Forgive me!' said the man in a weak voice.

'I do not know you and have nothing to forgive you for,' said the king.

'But I know you. I am that enemy of yours who swore to revenge himself on you, because you **executed** my brother and seized his property. I knew you had gone alone to see the hermit and I resolved to kill you on your way back. But the day passed and you did not return. So I came out from my hideaway to find you. I came upon your bodyguards. They recognised me and wounded me. I escaped from them and would have bled to death had you not dressed my wound. I wished to kill you, but you have saved my life. If I live, I will serve you as your most faithful servant and will bid my sons to do the same. Forgive me!'

The king was very glad to have made peace with his enemy and to have gained him for a friend. Having taken leave of the wounded man, the king went out and looked around for the hermit. He was outside, on his knees, sowing seeds in the beds that had been dug the day before.

The king approached him and said: 'For the last time, I pray you, answer my questions, wise man.'

'You have already been answered!' said the hermit, looking up at the king, who stood before him.

'What do you mean?' asked the king.

Wordwise

The meaning of the word 'question' has changed with time. In the 13th century, it meant a philosophical or a divine problem. A century later, it also came to refer to a difficulty or a doubt.

According to the hermit, for what purpose was man sent into this life?

'Do you not see?' replied the hermit. 'If you had not pitied my weakness yesterday and dug those beds, but had gone your way, that man would have attacked you. So the most important time was when you were digging the beds. I was the most important man. To do me good was your most important business. Afterwards when that man ran to us, the most important time was when you were attending to him, for if you had not bound up his wounds, he would have died without having made peace with you. So, he was the most important man. What you did for him was your most important business. Remember: there is only one time that is important—now! It is the only time when we have any power. The most necessary man is he with whom you are, for no man knows whether he will ever have dealings with anyone else and the most important affair is to do him good because for that purpose alone was man sent into this life!'

About the author

Leo Tolstoy (1828–1910) was a Russian author best known for his novels, *War and Peace* and *Anna Karenina*. He also authored short stories, essays and plays. A man with great sympathy for the downtrodden and the poor, Tolstoy was a social reformer too. His ideas about non-violent resistance influenced social leaders like Mahatma Gandhi.

Comprehension

Quick Recap

A. Complete the sentences with suitable words and phrases.

1. The king wanted to know the right ________________, ________________ and the ________________ to do.
2. Some people advised the king to consult magicians because ________________.
3. The king did not give any reward to the learned men because ________________.
4. The king offered to help the hermit because ________________.
5. The man who fell in front of the king was ________________.
6. The hermit taught the king that the most important work ________________.

B. Answer the questions in a few lines.

1. Why did the king want the answers to his three questions?
2. What were some of the answers offered for the first question?

3. According to the various learned men, who were the most important people?
4. What arrangements did the king make to meet the hermit?
5. What was the condition of the stranger who came running suddenly?
6. How did the king help the stranger? What surprising confession did the stranger make?
7. How did the hermit answer the three questions?
8. Explain these lines with reference to context.
   a. *'Now rest awhile and let me work a bit.'*
   b. *'I do not know you and have nothing to forgive you for.'*
   c. *'If you had not pitied my weakness yesterday and had not dug those beds for me, but had gone your way, that man would have attacked you.'*

Life Skills and Values importance of time, forgiveness

Think and answer.

1. The change of heart in the bearded stranger illustrates a simple truth. What is it?

HC **Feelings:** gratitude

2. Do you think the three questions of the king were important? Why?
3. According to the story, which way of answering questions is more effective: telling someone the right answer or guiding people to arrive at the answer themselves?

Way with Words

Forming Abstract Nouns Using Suffixes

We often form abstract nouns from adjectives and verbs by adding suffixes.

Suffixes like **-tion**, **-ment** and **-ion** can be added to verbs to form abstract nouns.
Examples: action, arrangement, discussion

Suffixes like **-ness** and **-ity** can be added to adjectives to form abstract nouns.
Examples: faithfulness, reality

A. Form abstract nouns from these words, using suffixes.

exhaust reconcile forgive proclaim complex hostile

B. Complete the sentences with the abstract nouns you have formed.

1. The two friends had a teary ____________ after their bitter fight.
2. ____________ within team members lessens productivity.

3. By the new king's ________________, everyone who had worked for more than ten years in the kingdom was given a house of his own.
4. The ________________ of the question paper made it difficult for the students to finish it within the allotted time.
5. The convict begged the judge for ________________, but to no avail.
6. After working continuously through the day, the man fainted from ________________.

Synonyms

C. Choose the most appropriate synonyms for these words, as used in the story.

1. **proclaimed:** declared, indicated, protested, advertised
2. **frail:** withered, weak, sick, irritable
3. **tired:** weary, irritated, worn, distressed
4. **ceased:** ended, stopped, closed, shut down
5. **faithful:** religious, reliable, loyal, steady

Grammar in Use

Transitive and Intransitive Verbs

You know that certain verbs need an object to complete their meaning, while there are others that do not. An **object** of a verb is a noun or pronoun that receives the action of the verb.

Transitive verbs are those that need one or more objects to make complete sense. When a verb has two objects, one is a direct object, while the other is an indirect object.

A direct object can be identified by asking the question **who** or **what** receives the action of the verb. To identify the indirect object, we have to ask the question **to/for whom**.

Examples: The hermit **greeted** the *king*. (direct object: **king**)
Ram **bought** a *racquet* for Shyam. (direct object: **racquet**; indirect object: **Shyam**)

Intransitive verbs are those which do not need an object to make complete sense.

Intransitive verbs can stand alone or may be followed by a phrase that gives information about the action. Some common intransitive verbs are *appear*, *arrive*, *belong*, *disappear*, *exist*, *remain*, *respond*, *rise*, *sleep*, *fall*, *go*, and *happen*.

Examples: The hermit **lived** in a wood.
The man **fell** to the ground, moaning feebly.

A. Underline the verbs in these sentences and state whether they are transitive or intransitive.

1. My aunt bought me a bag.
2. The girl danced beautifully.
3. We went to the circus.
4. I can play tennis well.
5. She sings in the choir.
6. We found a briefcase under the stairs.
7. These cupcakes are tasty.

Using few/a few, little/a little, little/less

The words **few**, **a few**, **little**, **a little**, **less** and **more** all indicate quantity. However, their usage is quite different.

Examples: **Few** men in the kingdom could match the hermit's wisdom.
She had only **a few** pennies left after buying groceries.
Little is known about the origin of the Loch Ness monster.
Can I have **a little** sugar?
The **less** people know about the incident, the better.
The **more** you practise the piano, the better you will be.

B. Complete the following sentences with these often confused words. Some of the words may be used more than once.

a little	a few	few	less	more	little

1. We had ________________ participants than we expected.
2. I have ________________ suggestions to make.
3. ________________ people know of Kolkata's origins.
4. The ________________ I see him, the ________________ I like him.
5. There was ________________ doubt about his role in the crime.
6. ________________ good men is all it takes to change the world.
7. We could do ________________ to convince him.
8. Why don't you taste ________________ bit of the cake?

Study Skills

Pronounce Well

You know that a **syllable** is a word, or part of a word, that contains a single vowel sound. It is a single unit of speech. A word can contain one or more syllables.

Look at the way these words have been divided into syllables. Say them aloud, noting the syllables.

king: one vowel sound, hence one syllable
be-gin: two vowel sounds, hence two syllables
imp-or-tant: three vowel sounds, hence three syllables

Say these words aloud and divide them into syllables.

1. photograph
2. reference
3. inhabit
4. bravado
5. patron
6. permitted

Listening and Speaking

We ask questions to get information. Questions can be close-ended or open-ended. Close-ended questions that end with a 'yes' or a 'no' do not give much information. Open-ended questions encourage people to talk in detail and share their opinion.

Listen to a conversation between two friends who ask each other questions. Note the use of close and open-ended questions.

Then, work in pairs to enact a conversation between two people who ask questions to find out more about each other's past. Use as many open-ended questions as you can.

21ST CENTURY Communication

Pen it Down

Imagine that you have recently received help from someone you least expected to come to your aid. Write an email to your friend telling him about the experience and the impact it has left on you.

Remember to use these components of an email:

- sender's and recipient's email addresses
- subject of the email
- salutation
- introduction
- body of the email
- closing phrase

HC **Feelings:** gratitude

Self Assessment

Now I can

- read and understand a story about the importance of making the best of every moment.
- observe that an example can teach more effectively than discussion.
- form abstract nouns using suffixes, identify transitive and intransitive verbs and use words such as *few, a few, little* and *a little* correctly.
- converse using close and open-ended questions, and write an email.

Read More

The Greatest Short Stories of Leo Tolstoy: This book includes stories with a moral lesson, such as 'How Much Land Does a Man Need?' which is about a greedy man who makes a deal with the Devil.

The Dalai Lama's Cat: This book by David Michie shows that wisdom can come from unexpected sources, including a cat. Narrated by a pet cat in the Dalai Lama's household, it offers an often-humorous glimpse into the spiritual leader's life.

2

Selfhood

Hope is the Thing with Feathers

Emily Dickinson

Let's Get Started

How well do you know yourself? Look at this 'me-tree' which consists of roots, a trunk and branches with leaves. The roots stand for the qualities that nurture your growth. The trunk stands for qualities that make you strong and sensible. Finally, the leaves stand for the qualities you should cultivate in order to develop as a person.

Complete the 'me-tree' as a way to understand yourself better. Share your 'me-tree' with the class.

List the qualities that you want to see in yourself.

List the values you believe in.

List your main personality traits.

Did you refer to yourself as 'optimistic' or 'hopeful'? Give two reasons for your choice.

HC **Learning and Awareness:** Exploring the relation between self-reflection and knowledge

Reading

Life has its ups and downs, however hope is what keeps us going. Read this poem which celebrates hope and its selflessness.

'Hope' is the thing with feathers[1] –
That **perches** in the soul –
And sings the tune without the words –
And never stops – at all –

And sweetest – in the Gale – is heard –
And **sore** must be the storm –
That could **abash** the little Bird
That kept so many warm –

I've heard it in the chillest land –
And on the strangest Sea[2] –
Yet – never – in **Extremity**,
It asked a crumb – of me.

What is being referred to as 'the little Bird'?

perches: rests

sore: painful

abash: make someone feel ill at ease or confused

extremity: an extreme condition or state

Literary terms

1. This is a **metaphor**. The quality of hope is being imagined as a bird that sings words of courage to lift one's spirit.

2. This is an example of **alliteration**, where the 's' sound is repeated at the beginning of consecutive words.

About the poet

Emily Dickinson (1830–1886) is one of the greatest American poets. Only ten of her 1800 poems were published in her lifetime. Her poems talk about life, love, nature and death. Dickinson's poetry is characterised by its frequent use of pun, irony, humour and satire. Some of her famous poems are 'She Went as Quiet as the Dew', 'Of all the Souls that Stand Create' and 'To Hear an Oriole Sing'.

Comprehension

Quick Recap

A. Answer the questions with reference to context.

1. *'Hope' is the thing with feathers –*
   That perches in the soul –
   a. Why has 'Hope' been described as 'the thing with feathers'?
   b. What are the similarities one may see in 'Hope' and a bird?
   c. How, according to the poet, does 'Hope' behave in the 'soul'?
2. *That could abash the little Bird*
   That kept so many warm –
   a. What does the poet refer to by the word 'abash'?
   b. What could 'abash' the 'Bird'?
   c. How do you think the 'Bird' kept 'so many warm'?
3. *Yet – never – in Extremity,*
   It asked a crumb – of me.
   a. Where has the poet heard the 'Bird'?
   b. What compliment does the poet pay to the 'Bird'? What do these lines convey about 'Hope'?
   c. What does 'Extremity' mean? What figure of speech has been used here?

B. Read the poem carefully. Find instances of these literary terms in the poem and explain them in your own words.

Term	
metaphor	**Line:** **Explanation:**
symbol	**Line:** **Explanation:**
personification	**Line:** **Explanation:**

Life Skills and Values being hopeful, positivity

Think and answer.

1. Why is hope important to us? Explain with reasons.
2. What are the traits of hope that the poet has highlighted in the poem? Can you add two more to the list?
3. Suggest an alternative title for the poem. Give reasons for your answer.

Critical Thinking

Way with Words

Imagery

Imagery is the use of descriptive language to help the reader visualise what has been described in a story or poem.

Example: 'Hope' is the thing with feathers.

In this line, the phrase 'thing with feathers' creates a visual image of hope being as free and light as a bird.

Imagery may pertain to different senses—visual, sound, smell, taste or touch.

Example: My heart pounded like a drum before the battle started.
The word 'pounded' creates a sound imagery of the heart thumping rapidly from a state of anxiety, similar to drum beats during a battle.

Identify the types of imagery in these lines and explain them in your own words.

Imagery	Type and Explanation
1. Like a painted ship on a painted ocean	
2. Her dreams crashed like a thousand mirrors cracking.	
3. It was her first book – soft and velveteen to the touch.	
4. The sun had become a light yellow yolk.	
5. After the blizzard, the blanket of snow covered everything in sight.	

Grammar in Use

Determiners

Determiners are words placed before a noun or a noun phrase. They tell us whether the noun or noun phrase is general or specific.

The following are the most commonly used determiners:

Articles: a, an, the

Example: It asked for **a** crumb.

Demonstratives: this, that, these, those

Example: **That** little bird kept so many warm.

Possessives: my, your, his, her, its, our, their

Example: Hope is **our** biggest ally.

Quantifiers: some, many, few, most, more

Example: Hope keeps us going through **many** situations.

Distributives: each, every, either, neither

Example: Hope perches in **every** soul.

Interrogatives: which, what, whose

Example: **Which** events in life make one sad?

A. Complete the sentences with suitable determiners.

1. ____________ red dress are you talking about? Is it the one that belongs to Katie?
2. I haven't bought ____________ new books ____________ year because I have no money.
3. Of ____________ the trees in grandma's garden, I love ____________ gulmohar the best.
4. The Kenilworth or The Grand, ____________ venue is suitable for the party?
5. Although there are ____________ guests, we must be careful about ____________ person's needs.
6. On ____________ of the more hectic days, I dream of travelling across the world.
7. ____________ hopes of winning the race soared when I saw the rival jockey falling behind.
8. ____________ students thanked ____________ beloved class teacher, Mrs Sen, for ____________ kindness and support.

Phrases and Clauses

A **phrase** is a group of words that conveys some meaning, but does not make complete sense by itself as it does not have a subject or a verb.

Examples: without the words, in the gale, the chillest land

A **clause** is a group of words that contains a subject and a finite verb. It can be a sentence by itself, or a part of a sentence and stand on its own, or be dependent on the rest of the sentence for its meaning.

Examples: **'Hope' is the thing with feathers.** (a clause which is a sentence by itself)
One should never lose hope and **they should always be positive.** (a clause which is a part of the sentence)
It sings the tune **which has no words.** (a clause which is dependent on the rest of the sentence for its meaning)

B. Identify whether the underlined words are phrases or clauses.

1. She rushed outside when she heard the noise.
2. The player who scores the winning run will be declared the Man of the Match.
3. She is my best friend.
4. I will agree to whatever they decide.
5. The boy whose arm was in a sling ran faster than everyone else.
6. I want to visit the city where the Taj Mahal is situated.
7. I will read the article on new scientific discoveries that appeared in the newspaper today.

Study Skills

Use Your Dictionary

Writers often use colloquial words to make their writing sound true to real life.

Example: I've heard it in the **chillest** land (Here, the word 'chillest' is used in the sense of 'coldest'. However, it also creates an image of a land that is bitterly cold.)

Underline the colloquial expressions in these sentences. Using your dictionary, write what they mean.

1. I would like to have a chat with you about your plans for the summer camp.
2. Radha is out for the day with her friends.
3. Ironing my uniform every day is such a drag.
4. It's a long way to Japan from where we stand.
5. This rattrap is a far cry from the elegant hotel it used to be.
6. Be a good chap and bring back my car from the mechanic's.

Listening and Speaking

A. Listen to a passage and answer these questions.

1. Whose story did the narrator's grandfather like to recount?
2. What was the profession of the poor boy's father?
3. Why was the father referred to as 'Kala Babu'?
4. How did the mother help out?
5. Where did the narrator's grandfather stay and with whom?
6. What exam had he passed?
7. Where did he study medicine and whom did he meet there?

B. **Do you think that the ability to look at a situation in a practical manner helps us to deal with it better, rather than hoping that the situation would get better?**

Work in two groups and have a debate in class on the topic. You can use the following expressions:

- the reality is...
- to my knowledge...
- looking at it this way...
- I believe that...
- I have to disagree...
- We may conclude...

21ST CENTURY Communication

Pen it Down

Messages are short letters sent to communicate with people.

Read this message from Ishita to Ashna.

Dear Ashna,

Please meet me at the library at 4 p.m. today for the study session.

Ishita

A. **Imagine that you and your friend regularly volunteer to care for animals in your locality. Write a message to your friend informing him/her of an injured bird in your area and requesting their help to get it treated.**

HC Participating in Neighbourhood/Society

B. **When we face difficult situations in life, it is important to not let go of hope. Write a paragraph on the importance of being hopeful in life. You can talk about the following points:**

- how a change in mindset helps to deal with the situation
- how hope begets hope
- how one should not feel lonely and seek help when needed

Self Assessment

Now I can

- read and understand a poem on the significance of hope.
- understand types of imagery, use determiners and revise phrases and clauses.
- participate in a debate, write a message and a paragraph.

Read More

Work Without Hope: This poem by Samuel Taylor Coleridge is about how one should strive to find something to aim for in life, and then hope would follow naturally.

I Dwell in Possibility: This poem by Emily Dickinson is about the positive qualities of creativity and illustrates how hope gives us numerous chances to express ourselves.

novel

3

Looking for Vultures' Eggs

Bibhutibhushan Bandopadhyay

Let's Get Started

ART INTEGRATION

***Pather Panchali*, Satyajit Ray's first film as a director, is based on Bibhutibhushan Bandyopadhyay's novel of the same name. Read this fact file about the film and the books they are based on. Work in pairs and fill in the blanks with the correct information.**

Ray cast Chunibala Devi, an 84-year-old former actress in the role of Indir Thakrun, the children's much-loved ____________. She became the first ____________ to win the best actress award in an international film festival, for this role.

The books are set in ____________, and the incidents have certain similarities with the ____________ own life.

Satyajit Ray turned the first book into a film, which went to ____________ Film Festival, in Paris. This gained him worldwide ____________.

Pather Panchali first appeared as a ____________ in a Bengali periodical in 1928. In the ____________ *Aparajito*, the family shifts to Varanasi, where Apu grows up. The story then shifts to ____________ in the 1940s, where he aspires to be a writer.

Ray went on to make ____________ more films covering the later parts of the ____________.

HC **Learning and Awareness:** Evaluating our assumptions and preconditioning about life and situations around us

Reading

This story is taken from a translation of the Bengali novel, Pather Panchali (The Song of the Road), *by Bibhutibhushan Bandhopadhyay. The novel traces the journey of a poor young boy, Opu, who lives in a village with his mother, Shorbojoya and sister, Durga. But his poverty does not*

limit his imagination. In this excerpt, Opu finds a book that mentions a formula to make people fly. Opu is fascinated and sets about collecting the necessary items. He is sure that he will be able to fly.

There was one piece of information which Opu had not passed on to anybody, not even to his sister.

One day, at about noon, he had opened a wooden chest, which belonged to their father. The chest was **crammed** with books. He opened the books one by one and turned over the pages to see whether there were any pictures to look at or perhaps a good story. It was in one of them that he had come across this amazing piece of information. The book had a title on the cover, *An Anthology of Ancient Philosophical Works*. He had not the slightest **notion** of what the title meant, but the cover was faded and **mottled** like marble; and as he turned it back, a **swarm** of **silverfish darted out** and disappeared as fast as they could.

Opu raised the book to his nose. It had a peculiar old smell. The pages were thick and dust-coloured, and he loved their smell. There was something about it which made him think of his father. It was the book in the damaged board cover which attracted him the most, so he hid it under his pillow. He read it when he was alone and one day he came across an amazing statement. If somebody had told him about it, he would have been astonished, but this was not **hearsay**, it was in cold print. The writer was describing the properties of mercury. If you put some mercury in a vulture's egg, leave it out in the sun for a few days, and then hold it in your mouth, you can fly high up in the sky.

Opu could not believe his eyes. He read the passage again and again. He hid the book in his own broken box and went outside to think.

He asked his sister, '*Didi*, do you know where vultures build their nests?' She did not know. One of boys in the village said, 'They build nests at the top of big trees in the open country.'

His mother was cross with him. 'Where have you been wandering in this heat?' He moved into his room and pretended to lie down. He opened the book. There it was! Astonishing! It was so easy to fly and yet nobody knew about it. Perhaps nobody had a copy of this book except his father. Or it might be that

crammed: stuffed

notion: idea

mottled: spotted

swarm: a large group of insects

silverfish: a small, silvery, wingless insect that feeds on food scraps and bookbindings

darted out: ran away suddenly and rapidly

hearsay: rumour

Why did Opu love the smell of the old book?

Did You Know? **Science**

Mercury is a fast-moving, poisonous, liquid metal. In ancient times, people believed that it could be turned into gold when combined with other metals.

all this time nobody's eye had fallen on this particular place in the book. He thrust his nose into the book again and smelt it. That same old smell! It never occurred to him to question the truth of what was written in such a book.

There was no problem about mercury. He knew that mercury was used on the back of mirrors. There was a broken mirror in the house and he would be able to get some from there. The problem was where to get vultures' eggs from.

The cowherd boys used to tie their cattle to Hiru the barber's jackfruit tree, and go into the village to get oil and tobacco. Opu knew one of them. 'You go all over the countryside. Have you ever seen a vulture's nest? If you can get me some vultures' eggs, I'll give you two pice,' he told him.

A few days later, the cowherd boy turned up at the house. He produced two small black eggs from a bag in his waistband. 'Look at what I've brought for you, Sir,' he said.

Opu stretched out an eager hand to take them. He turned them this way and that, and murmured, 'Vultures.' Then he said to the boy, 'They are real, aren't they?'

'I got them from the top branch of a very high tree and a very risky job it was. But I can't let you have them for less than two annas.'

darkened: (here) reduced

Where would Opu get the mercury from?

Opu's face fell when he heard the cost. 'I'll give you two pice,' he said, 'and you can have my cowries. I'Il let you have all of them and the tin box I keep them in.'

The cowherd boy was more experienced in worldly matters than Opu. He was not prepared to sell the eggs except for cash. Eventually, the price was fixed at four pice. Opu managed to get two pice from his sister and completed the deal. The cowherd took some of Opu's cowries as well. These cowries were Opu's life. At any other time, he would not have parted with them for half a kingdom. But playing with cowries seemed poor sport in comparison with flying in the sky.

He had the eggs in his hand and his mind felt as light as a balloon. Then, slowly, a little shadow of doubt **darkened** his joy. That evening, before dark, he was in Nera's orchard, sitting on a branch that had been cut off a rose apple tree. His mind was busy with questions. 'Shall I really be able to fly now? Where shall I fly to? To my uncle's house? Or to where Baba has gone? Or shall I fly across the river? Or shall I fly to where the stars rise in the sky, as the sparrows or the mynas do? Shall I do it today or tomorrow?'

Later that same evening, Durga was looking for an old piece of cloth to use as a **wick**. While she was rummaging among some torn rags, something rolled from the back of the shelf and fell on to the floor. 'Goodness, Ma,' she exclaimed, 'there are two big eggs here. They fell and broke. I wonder what bird came into the house and laid its eggs here.'

It is best to pass over what happened later. Opu cried and refused to touch his food for a whole day. Shorbojoya talked about it when she went down to the pond for her bath. 'Opu's making an enormous fuss. I've never heard the like of it. He says that if you have a vulture's egg, you can fly. That cowherd boy's a proper **scoundrel**. He collected a couple of eggs from a crow's nest or somewhere and said they were vultures' eggs. And he made Opu pay four pice for them. I can't tell you what a **simpleton** the lad is, *Shejbou*. I don't know what I'm going to do with him.'

How could poor Shorbojoya know? Everybody had not read the *Anthology of Ancient Philosophical Works* and not everybody knew the properties of mercury. It is as well they did not because in that case everybody would be able to fly[1].

Did You Know? History

Cowries, or polished, brightly coloured shells, were once used in India and other countries as currency. The word 'cowrie' is derived from the Hindi word, *kauri*.

wick: a strip of cloth used in a candle or lamp

scoundrel: a dishonest person

simpleton: a person who is not very intelligent and can be tricked easily

Why did Shorbojoya call her son a simpleton?

Literary term

1. This is an example of **irony**. Everyone wouldn't be able to fly even if they read the *Anthology of Ancient Philosophical Works*. It gently pokes fun at books that made such false claims and at Opu's willingness to believe them.

About the author

Bibhutibhushan Bandopadhyay (1894–1950) was a writer of novels, short stories and travelogues. His first novel, *Pather Panchali*, is a landmark in Bengali fiction and was adapted into an award-winning film by Satyajit Ray. *Chander Pahar* and *Aranyak* are among his other famous novels.

Comprehension

Quick Recap

A. Answer the questions with reference to context.

1. *It was in one of them that he had come across this amazing piece of information. The book had a title on the cover,* An Anthology of Ancient Philosophical Works.
   a. Where was this book found? Who found it?
   b. What 'information' is being spoken about here?
   c. Why was it amazing?

2. *He asked his sister, 'Didi, do you know where vultures build their nests?'*
   a. Who was the speaker?
   b. Why was he asking about vultures?
   c. What reply did his sister give?

B. Read the story carefully and complete this character sketch of Opu.

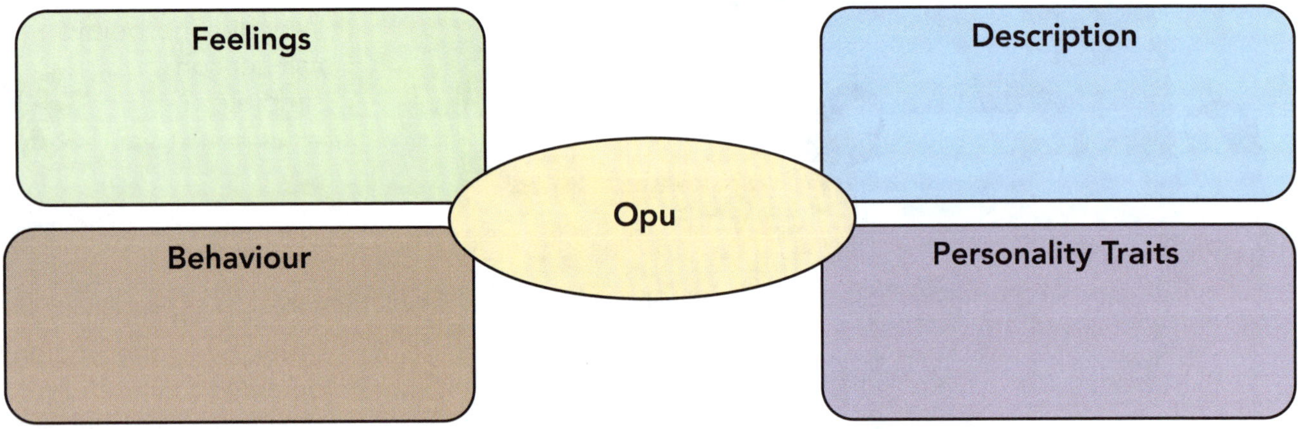

C. Answer the questions.

1. Describe the condition of the book that Opu found in the wooden chest.
2. What did the boy in the village tell Opu about the vultures?
3. How much did the cowherd want for the eggs? With what did Opu pay him?
4. What were the thoughts that ran through Opu's mind after he got the eggs?
5. What happened to the eggs? What was Opu's reaction?

Life Skills and Values imagination, innocence

Think and answer.

1. Why do you think Opu did not tell anyone what he had found in the book?
2. Why didn't Opu question the truth of what was written in the book?
3. Explain in your own words why the author is being ironic when he says that everyone would be able to fly if they had read the *Anthology of Ancient Philosophical Works.*

21st Century Critical Thinking

21st Century Information Literacy

Way with Words

Collocations

A **collocation** is a combination of words that are commonly used together.

Example: We say 'heavy rain' and not 'big rain' or 'strong rain'.

A. In the story, you have come across the collocation, 'slightest notion'. Identify five other collocations from the story.

B. Match the words in the two columns to form collocations.

A	B
1. useful	a. progress
2. remember	b. shame
3. make	c. remarks
4. spiteful	d. advice
5. hopeless	e. vaguely
6. crying	f. situation

Word Association

C. Circle the odd word in these word sets. Give reasons for your choice.

1. worship	kinship	friendship	partnership
2. sisterhood	neighbourhood	parenthood	motherhood
3. autobiography	travelogue	anthology	newspaper
4. continuous	courageous	rebellious	purposeless
5. adjective	adverb	paragraph	verb

Grammar in Use

Converting Adjectives to Nouns

You know that we can convert adjectives to nouns by adding suffixes like *-ity*, *-ment*, *-tion*, or dropping suffixes like *-y*, *-ic*.

Examples: real → reality   lengthy → length

A. Convert these adjectives into their noun forms. Then, make sentences with the nouns.

1. astonishing 2. tolerable 3. imaginative 4. artistic 5. cosmic 6. active

Transformation of Sentences

You have learnt that there are four types of sentences: assertive, interrogative, imperative and exclamatory.

An **assertive sentence** simply makes a statement.

Example: A few days later, the cowherd boy turned up at the house.

An **imperative sentence** issues an order, command, or request.

Example: Don't stay out in the heat, Opu.

An **interrogative sentence** asks a question.

Example: Shall I really be able to fly now?

An **exclamatory sentence** conveys a strong or sudden emotion.

Example: It was that same old smell!

We can interchange assertive and interrogative sentences, without changing their meanings.

Examples:
1. Do you know which bird came into the house and laid its eggs? (**interrogative**)
   I don't know which bird came into the house and laid its eggs. (**assertive**)
2. These cowries were Opu's life. (**assertive**)
   Weren't these cowries Opu's life? (**interrogative**)

B. Change these sentences according to the instructions.

1. Rita was sure she would win. (Begin: Wasn't Rita…)
2. Is this the way a person should behave? (Begin: This is…)
3. Isn't it terrible that the garbage has not been removed? (Begin: It is…)
4. Can our freedom fighters ever be forgotten? (Begin: Our…)
5. We should always fight for justice. (Begin: Shouldn't…)
6. I can't believe that Srilatha didn't win the singing contest. (Begin: Can…)
7. Watching whales in their natural habitat was the best part of our holiday. (Begin: Wasn't…)
8. Is there anyone who hasn't heard of Darwin? (Begin: There is…)

Study Skills

Use Your Dictionary

Words are always arranged alphabetically in the dictionary. When the first letter in a set of words begin with the same letter, we ignore the first letter and then, arrange the words alphabetically by starting with the letters which are different from each other.

Example: bath bend board build

Arrange the words in each set alphabetically.

1. assume amuse assist assess
2. require register rapid robot

3. convert combine compass collapse
4. darkness demand delete destination

Listening and Speaking

A. Listen to the description of a city seen from the sky. Can you guess which city it is?

Now, imagine that you have been given the power to fly. You are soaring over a city. Describe what you see. After listening to your description, your classmates will identify the city.

B. Imagine you are Opu. You come home to find that your sister has dropped and broken the eggs. In pairs, write and enact a conversation between Opu and his sister.

Pen it Down

A. Like Opu in the story, people often associate a smell with a memory. A smell might remind us of a person or an incident, or recall a feeling of sadness or happiness.

Describe an incident when you associated a smell with a memory. Explain why it was memorable for you.

B. What if the eggs that Opu bought had remained intact? In about 200 words, write an alternate ending to the story. You should include the following points:

- Opu's difficulties in preparing the formula for flying
- his attempt to fly and its outcome

Self Assessment

Now I can

- read about the innocence of a village boy and the power of imagination.
- understand collocations, create nouns from adjectives, and practise transformation of interrogative and assertive sentences.
- describe a scene, speak and write on a given topic and frame an alternate ending to a story.

Read More

David Copperfield: This novel by Charles Dickens is about a boy making his way in the world in 19th-century Britain. The story follows young David, as he struggles to cope with boarding school and his stepfather's cruel treatment, until he finds a stable home with his aunt.

Swami and Friends: This novel by R. K. Narayan is about ten-year-old Swami's adventures with his friends in the fictional town of Malgudi. The stories, set in British India, describe Swami's love for cricket and his dislike for the routine of school.

lyric poem

Professions

4

Coromandel Fishers

Sarojini Naidu

SUSTAINABLE DEVELOPMENT GOALS

10 REDUCED INEQUALITIES

Let's Get Started

The United Nations Sustainable Development Goal number 10 aims to ensure that all professions provide a steady and sufficient income for those who practise it. However, there are many occupations like handicraft or fishing, which do not yield much income. The Indian coastline particularly abounds with fishermen, who practise various unique ways of fishing and are known for their local produce.

Read this passage on the unique Chinese fishing nets that can be found at the harbour's mouth at Fort Kochi, Kerala. Fill in the blanks with the given words.

bamboo	spellbinding	delicately	emperor	operated
balancing	popular	evening	explorer	huge

The Kochi coast is known for ________ cantilevered Chinese fishing nets that droop down over the water. They have become a ________ tourist attraction. It is believed that they were first introduced around 1350-1450 AD by a Chinese ________. He was a member of the court of Kublai Khan, the great Mongol ________. These nets are carefully attached to teak wood and ________ poles and are spread over 20 meters. Lights are attached to the poles to attract the fish. Each fishing net is ________ by more than four fishermen. Fishing is usually done in the morning and early ________. The net is lowered into the water for a short time and then raised ________ by pulling on the ropes. The slow rhythm and ________ of the net appears ________ to a first-time viewer.

HC **Learning and Awareness:** Evaluating our assumptions about happiness

Reading

Sarojini Naidu wrote about people who lead difficult lives, but who teach us important human values in the way they overcome their hostile environment. In this poem, the speaker inspires

his fellow fishermen to take their boats out to sea, leaving behind the comfort of land.

Rise, brothers, rise; the wakening skies pray to the morning light,
The wind lies asleep in the arms of the dawn like a child that has cried all night.[1]
Come, let us gather our nets from the shore and set our **catamarans** free,
To capture the leaping wealth of the tide, for we are the kings of the sea!

No longer delay, let us hasten away in the track of the seagull's call,
The sea is our mother, the cloud is our brother, the waves are our **comrades** all.
What though we **toss** at the fall of the sun where the hand of the sea-god drives?
He who holds the storm by the hair, will hide in his breast our lives.

Sweet is the shade of the cocoanut **glade**, and the scent of the mango grove,
And sweet are the sands at the full o' the moon with the sound of the voices we love;
But sweeter, O brothers, the kiss of the **spray** and the dance of the wild foam's glee;[2]
Row, brothers, row to the edge of the **verge**, where the low sky mates with the sea.

Coromandel: a broad coastal plain in Tamil Nadu

catamaran: a type of fishing boat

comrades: friends who one works with

toss: move from side to side or back and forth

glade: an open space in a forest

spray: jet of water

verge: a limit beyond which something occurs

Whose call do the fishermen hear?

Literary terms

1. This is a **simile**. Here, the wind is being compared to a child asleep in the arms of its mother (the dawn) after crying all night.

2. This is an example of **personification**. Here, the waves are being imagined as dancers dancing with unrestrained joy.

About the poet

Sarojini Naidu (1879–1949) was a poet, orator and a freedom fighter. Also known as the 'Nightingale of India', she wrote about humble folk living ordinary but vivid lives. Her famous poems include 'Indian Weavers' and 'In the Bazaars of Hyderabad'.

Comprehension

Quick Recap

A. Answer the questions in a few lines.

1. Explain the line, 'the wakening skies pray to the morning light'.
2. What will the fishermen do when they hear the seagull's call?
3. Which lines in the poem highlight the courage of the fishermen?
4. Write down one example of visual imagery and another that appeals to the sense of smell, and explain them.

B. Answer the questions with reference to context.

1. *Come, let us gather our nets from the shore and set our catamarans free,*
   To capture the leaping wealth of the tide, for we are the kings of the sea!

   a. Who is the speaker in these lines?

   b. What is described as the 'leaping wealth of the tide'? What is the figure of speech used in this phrase?

   c. What kind of weather had the people in the catamarans recently experienced?

   d. Why does the speaker call himself and the others the 'kings of the sea'?

2. *The sea is our mother, the cloud is our brother, the waves are our comrades all.*

   a. Why does the speaker call the sea their mother, the cloud their brother and the waves their comrades?

   b. What is being referred to as the 'fall of the sun' later in this stanza?

   c. Who is being referred to as 'he' in this stanza? What will 'he' do?

3. *Sweet is the shade of the cocoanut glade, and the scent of the mango grove …*

   a. What are the different meanings of the word 'sweet' as used in this stanza?

   b. What, according to the speaker, is 'sweeter' than sitting in the shade of coconut and mango trees? Why?

   c. Where does the speaker ask his brothers to row towards in this stanza? Find a single word for this place.

Life Skills and Values facing challenges at work, appreciating nature

Think and answer.

1. What hardships do fishermen often face at sea?
2. How is the fishermen's love for their work indicated in the poem?
3. What kind of relationship do fishermen have with nature? Is it a friendly or a hostile one?

21ST CENTURY Productivity

HC complementarity among entities in nature

Way with Words

Idioms

Expressions where verbs and prepositions carry a specific meaning when used together are known as **idioms**.

In the poem, the speaker asks the fishermen to row in the direction of the seagull's call. The verb **call** has different meanings depending on the preposition with which it is used.

A. Match these idioms using call with their meanings.

Idioms	Meanings
1. call a spade a spade	a. be the person who controls a situation
2. call someone names	b. doubt something or make others doubt it
3. call into question	c. say exactly what one thinks without hiding one's opinion
4. call the shots	d. challenge someone to give proof of his or her claims
5. call someone's bluff	e. use insulting words about somebody

Phrasal Verbs

B. Complete the sentences using these phrasal verbs with call. Change the tense where necessary.

call in   call up   call for   call away   call off

1. The police have ________________ an investigation into the robbery.
2. I had not spoken to my friend for a while. So, I decided to ________________ her ________________.

3. The party had to be ________________ at the last minute.
4. They decided to ________________ a specialist when the general physician was unable to diagnose Beatrice's illness.
5. Raghu had to miss lunch because he was ________________ for a meeting.

Grammar in Use

Transformation of Sentences

You have learned what exclamatory and assertive sentences are. Each of these types of sentences can be changed into the other.

Examples: 1. How sweet is the scent of the mango grove! (**exclamatory**)
The scent of the mango grove is sweet. (**assertive**)
2. The morning light is beautiful. (**assertive**)
How beautiful is the morning light! (**exclamatory**)

Rewrite these sentences according to the instructions given.

1. What a pretty dress! (Begin: It...)
2. It is very sad that we lost the match. (Begin: How...)
3. The sky looks beautiful today. (Change into an exclamatory sentence.)
4. What a disaster! (Change into an assertive sentence.)
5. Alas! She is no more. (Begin: It is...)
6. It is a touching moment. (Change into an exclamatory sentence.)
7. How odd that actor looks in his purple jacket and white shoes! (Begin: That...)
8. It is a lovely night. (Change into an exclamatory sentence.)

Study Skills

Use Your Dictionary

You know that 'catamarans' are fishing boats. The name came into use in the early 17th century, from the Tamil word, *kattumaram*.

The following words are of Indian origin. Using your dictionary, find out what they mean and which Indian language they come from. Remember to use an advanced English dictionary.

juggernaut	bandicoot	pariah	patchouli
dinghy	lacquer	bungalow	jaggery
doolally	sorbet	mandarin	cheetah

Listening and Speaking

A. Listen to a passage about imaginary sea monsters and answer these questions.

1. How were the stories of terrifying sea monsters created?
2. Name any two monsters mentioned in the passage.
3. Which famous book is mentioned in the passage? Name its author.
4. Name one striking feature of the giant squid.
5. Which feature of the squid was a 'whim of nature'? Why?
6. How did the squid's colour change?

B. Recite the poem with the correct intonation. Try to recognise the jaunty rhythm of the poem, which resembles the movement of a boat.

Pen it Down

Today, most professions are dependent on technology, but there are some occupations that still rely heavily on nature, such as fishing and agriculture.

Write a factual essay about one such occupation, highlighting the hardships faced by those who practise it. You may use the following points:

- non-seasonal rains
- sudden storms
- large sea animals
- drowning

21ST CENTURY Information Literacy

Self Assessment

Now I can

- understand the hardship faced by fishermen at sea and recognise their unbreakable spirit.
- enjoy the imagery and rhythm of the poem.
- identify idioms and phrases having the verb *call* and practise transformation of sentences.
- recite a poem with correct intonation and write a factual essay.

Read More

The Chimney Sweeper: This poem by William Blake is about a little boy who cleans the chimneys in houses. The dreams of a happy future help the boy bear the difficulties in his life.

Wandering Singers: This poem by Sarojini Naidu portrays the life of a band of folk singers who travel from one village to another, singing about the deeds of men and the laughter of women long dead. They have no interest in the material world, yet are content.

5

Where Tigers Swim

Bittu Sahgal

Let's Get Started

SUSTAINABLE DEVELOPMENT GOALS 15 LIFE ON LAND

Throughout history, cyclones and severe storms have wreaked havoc on India, particularly battering the Odisha and Bengal coastlines and the Sundarbans mangrove forest. In recent years, we faced Cyclones Fani (2019), Amphan (2020) and Yaas (2021), to name a few. Once a cyclone has hit, the rescue and rehabilitation efforts should start immediately, to help the affected people get back on their feet.

Look at the different measures that are taken in cyclone-affected areas and sort them under the correct categories. Then, add one measure of your own for each category.

Rehabilitation

people and animals	transport and communication	relief and aid

- rescue people from collapsed buildings and flood water
- remove uprooted trees to clear roadblocks
- treat injuries at hospitals
- collect fund for repair work
- air-drop relief materials at unreachable areas
- shift people to higher ground
- repair phone lines
- distribute food, water, clothes, medicines and dry ration
- restore electricity
- rescue animals from drowning
- remove live wires from water to prevent electrocution

HC **Active Participation:** Exploring uniqueness of animal order

Reading

Have you ever seen a tiger in the wild? The Royal Bengal tiger is our national animal. But due to human neglect and cruelty, they are an endangered species today. This account is taken from the book, The Sundarbans Inheritance. *It narrates the author's experience of encountering this*

magnificent beast and explains how the tiger's habitat is shrinking due to human intrusion.

January 2001: It is three in the afternoon and a **brisk** breeze whips my hair as I stand behind the **prow** of the Project Tiger patrol boat. I am making my way along the blue-green waters of the Netidhopani river in the Sundarbans Tiger Reserve, having charted the day's course on a large map a few minutes earlier. Happy to be alive, I see a dragonfly and a common wanderer butterfly navigate the strong wind to cross our boat's path, 100 metres from the shore. Pulling on a windcheater against the cold, I marvel at the magic of nature that gifts such fragile creatures with their amazing flying capabilities.

About 250 metres ahead of our vessel, I spot a floating log. We are moving against the current about 30 metres from shore. I watch the log in a disinterested way, waiting for it to drift closer to our boat. That never happens. Instead, I begin to notice that it is moving at a 90 degree angle to us and to the powerful current. Strange! At a distance of 150 metres, I peer through my binoculars and see a small round shape—certainly not a log. It takes me a full 10 seconds to realise that a childhood dream has come true. I am in the Sundarbans and there before me, in flesh and blood, is a wild tiger.

brisk: (here) cold but refreshing

prow: the pointed front part of a ship

silhouetted: outlined as a dark shape against a brighter background

remorse: a feeling of deep regret or guilt

Name the river the narrator was travelling on.

No one sees tigers in the Sundarbans. Everyone knows you come here for the experience, or to birdwatch, or just to escape urban life. Yet, against all probability, there she is. The cat's head, **silhouetted** and dark like some ancient god, is perhaps 500 metres to our left from the far shore. As we draw nearer, I can see her ears twitching. When she turns her head to stare at our boat, I am struck by the yellow of her beautiful eyes. She is headed straight for the far bank but then, to my utter surprise, she turns and begins to swim back in the direction whence she came.

Remorse now takes the place of the pure joy I had just experienced on seeing the cat. How much energy has that cat already spent swimming against the powerful current? And I have disturbed and forced her to do just the opposite of what she had wanted.

Did You Know? G.K.

Project Tiger is a conservation programme for tigers, started by the Indian government in 1973. The project aims to maintain the population of tigers in their natural habitat and protect them from extinction.

What instructions does the narrator give to the boatman?

propelling: pushing something forward

momentarily: for a very short time

predators: animals that prey on others

crustaceans: a class of animals that have hard, crust-like shells, such as lobsters, crabs

slick: glossy and slippery

mudskipper: a fish that can survive both in water and on land

benthic: relating to creatures living in the bottom of a body of water

Everyone is now on deck. I shout harsh instructions to the boatman to maintain a distance of at least 30 metres from the cat and yell at him *not* to cut off her path to 'get a better look'. But the cat has other ideas. As our boat comes to a near halt, she actually begins to swim back towards us with the current! She approaches as close as ten metres to our left, glancing up at us just once before heading for the shore from *behind* our vessel.

Tigers are very powerful swimmers. I can imagine her huge, paddle-like paws **propelling** her forward underwater. Her heart must be fit to burst from the effort and anxiety. Avoiding a second Project Tiger vessel positioned between our boat and the shore, she heads for the mud bank. Great paws touching the earth, the tigress struggles **momentarily** in the slippery mud and then bounds, tail up, into the mangroves and is swallowed by her emerald forest.

The whole episode takes no more than three or four minutes, during which I am granted momentary access into the life of one of the world's most secretive, most threatened **predators**. I have seen tigers in the wild scores of times across India, but for some reason that I cannot quite explain, this experience leaves me marked for life.

The Sundarbans is a birder's paradise and before daylight faded, I found myself identifying birds, comparing their beaks with the foods they sought. Curlews and whimbrels dug deep into the mud for **crustaceans**, sandpipers picked off smaller creatures closer to the surface, brown-winged kingfishers waited patiently for a fish or crab to come within striking distance before swooping down on them like multicoloured stealth bombers.

On **slick** mud banks that melt like chocolate into the water, crocodiles, monitor lizards, **mudskippers** and fiddler crabs revealed themselves from time to time, like so many 'earth jewels'. A snake painstakingly made its way towards a gathering of mudskippers, but lost its chance at the very last moment when the fish, specially adapted for movement on land, darted away.

This utterly fragile, strange and magical ecosystem is geologically new and still evolving. Rivers and tides circulate nutrients like a chef might stir a great soup, with nothing wasted, as living creatures join the **benthic** flora in metabolising everything organic.

Even the air is thick with drama as the sun begins to set. Above me, competing with swifts for the bounty of an insect-stocked sky, pigmy **pipistrelles** scan the horizon. Clearly, all is well with the world as darkness descends on Ghazikhali where we drop anchor for the night.

A conflict of interest?

(*Here, the author narrates an incident from an earlier visit to the Sundarbans.*)

By the time we reached the Matla Four Forest Compartment, all thoughts of heaven had been forgotten. Here, scores of labourers were busy hacking a huge, sweet water pond out of the mangrove swamp. I wondered why, since every Sundarbans creature had learned to survive very well in the **brackish** water environment, without well-intentioned but ecologically risky 'handouts' from humans.

Half an hour later, we docked at the Haldibari Camp **jetty** and walked through a net-protected walkway to inspect a fleet of fishing boats. Laden with logs, the boats had been **confiscated** from wood **poachers** by the Forest Department. There are almost 300,000 people who **scour** the Sundarbans swamps to **eke out** a living each day and some clearly are no longer satisfied with farming or fish. At this rate, the forest will soon vanish, I thought darkly, sold to the highest bidder.

A deltaic patch of low-lying mud and silt, the Sundarbans is a tropical **estuarine** swamp forest where as many as 65 mangrove plant species grow, making it the most **biodiverse** mangrove forest in the world. It is also a world heritage site as declared by UNESCO. It is situated on the **confluence** of three rivers – the Ganga, Brahmaputra and the Meghna. Not only is it significant as a wildlife habitat but it also protects the region against the direct onslaught of cyclones.

When Cyclone Amphan made **landfall** in the Ganges delta in 2020, it caused massive devastation by pushing water levels up to

pipistrelle: a type of small brown bat

brackish: salty

jetty: landing platform to which boats can be fastened

confiscated: (here) captured something as punishment

poachers: illegal hunters

scour: search thoroughly

eke out: (here) manage to make (a living) with difficulty

estuarine: relating to the mouth of a large river where it meets the sea

biodiverse: having a wide range of plant and animal life

confluence: (here) the place where the rivers join and become one larger river

landfall: the act of arrival or nearing land, especially from the sea

Did You Know? Geography

The Matla, Ghazikhali and Netidhopani are rivers in the Sundarbans, while Haldibari is an area known for tiger sightings.

Who had confiscated the boats of the poachers?

salinity: amount of salt dissolved in a body of water

buffer: something that lessens shock or protects from damages

What prevented excessive damage due to Cyclone Amphan?

15 kilometers inland in parts of this delta. Wind blowing at over 150 kmph wreaked havoc on the Sunderbans, claiming countless lives, houses and livestock. The ferocity of the storm brought the sea water onto the lands increasing their **salinity** and rendering them useless for agriculture for the next few years.

However, more extensive damage was prevented by the presence of the mangroves. The ecosystem nurtured and sustained by the mangroves not only adds to the wealth of flora and fauna in this area but the swamps themselves act as a **buffer** zone to cyclones as well.

About the author

Bittu Sahgal (1947–) is an environmental activist and writer. In 1981, he started *Sanctuary Asia*, India's first wildlife and environment-conservation magazine. He has co-authored books such as *India Naturally* and *The Bharatpur Inheritance*. He founded 'Kids for Tiger', a project that tries to involve school children in environmental issues.

Comprehension

Quick Recap

A. Match the following.

A	B
1. fiddler crabs	a. pushed water levels up to 15 kilometers inland
2. adapted for movement on land	b. place to drop anchor
3. Haldibari Camp	c. a floating log
4. water of the Sundarbans	d. digging a sweet water pond
5. a Royal Bengal tiger	e. confiscated boats of logs
6. Ghazikhali	f. mudskippers
7. Matla Four Forest Compartment	g. as many as 65 different species
8. mangroves	h. earth jewels
9. Cyclone Amphan	i. brackish

B. Answer the questions.

1. Describe the encounter between the narrator and the tiger.
2. What was happening at Matla Four Forest Compartment? What was the author's view about the activity?
3. What does the author say about the biodiversity of the Sundarbans?
4. What is the significance of the Sundarbans?
5. How did the mangroves prevent more extensive damage caused by Cyclone Amphan?
6. Name the various species of plant and animal life mentioned in the extract. Classify the animals into creatures of the air, water and land.
7. Give two examples of similes from the chapter and explain what they mean.

Life Skills and Values — appreciating wildlife, balance of nature

Think and answer.

1. List the traits of the Royal Bengal tiger based on what you have read in the chapter.
2. Why do you think humans come into conflict with their environment?

21ST CENTURY Critical Thinking

Way with Words

Compound Adjectives

You have come across several compound adjectives in this chapter, such as **paddle-like** paws and **brown-winged** kingfisher.

A **compound adjective** is made up of two or more words usually written with a hyphen. It acts as a single idea.

Example: The **man-eating** tiger was hiding at the edge of the forest.
If we don't hyphenate a compound adjective, it can completely change its meaning. In the above sentence, without a hyphen, the compound adjective may mean 'the man who was eating a tiger'.

A. Rewrite these sentences using compound adjectives. One has been done for you.

1. The journey took five hours.
   It was a five-hour journey.
2. I love to eat tomatoes that are dried in the sun.
3. There was a gap of ten minutes.
4. I have a vacation of two weeks.
5. The lecture lasted an hour.
6. My memories of that holiday are bitter and sweet.
7. That dog looks dangerous.

8. Seema is always satisfied with herself.
9. The colour of the wallpaper was as blue as the sky.

Commonly Confused Words

B. Complete the paragraph by choosing the correct options from these commonly confused words.

It is hypocritical to ____________ (moan/mourn) about the ____________ (damage/injury) done to our environment out of ____________ (shear/sheer) human selfishness. We should not ____________ (presume/assume) that we will have time to make amends. We must make a ____________ (concerned/conscious) effort to change our ____________ (lifestyles/living) before it ____________ (affects/effects) our future. One of the ____________ (principal/principle) dangers is ____________ (apathy/empathy) about the ____________ (consequences/sequences) of our actions.

C. Make sentences with these expressions from the passage.

1. marked for life
2. within striking distance
3. a near halt
4. direct onslaught
5. in flesh and blood
6. heart fit to burst

Grammar in Use

Types of Adjectives

You know that adjectives are classified into four main types, based on what they say about a noun.

Adjectives of quality provide information about the shape, size, colour or condition of a noun or a pronoun. They answer the question, *what kind*.

Example: The Sundarbans is a **tropical** swamp forest.

Adjectives of quantity answer the questions *how much?* or *how many?*

Example: By the time we reached the Matla Four Forest Compartment, **all** thoughts of heaven had been forgotten.

Demonstrative adjectives (*this*, *that*, *these*, *those*) point out something about a noun or identify it. They answer the question, *which?*

Example: **This** experience leaves me marked for life.

Interrogative adjectives are used for asking questions and usually come before a noun.

Example: **Which** bird can you spot on the tree?

A. Underline the adjectives in these sentences and identify their types. There may be more than one adjective in a sentence.

1. There are ten dancers in this talented group.
2. Do you have enough food for the picnic?
3. He lost all his money due to bad loans.
4. This film seems interesting. Which day of the week are you free to watch it with me?
5. Several people were chosen for the second trip to Mars.
6. The young man has a bright future.
7. If you go that way, you will reach the old municipal building.
8. Only a few days are left for the final examinations.

TENSES

You know that tenses are classified into the present, past and future tenses, which exist in the simple, continuous, perfect and perfect continuous forms.

Look at this table which shows the different tense forms.

Tense	Simple	Continuous	Perfect
Present	*is/am/are*	*is/am/are* + verb + *-ing* form	*has/have* + verb in past tense
	It **is** three in the afternoon.	We **are moving** away from the shore.	I **have disturbed** the tigress.
Past	verb + *-ed* or past tense form	*was/were* + verb + *-ing* form	*had/had been* + verb + *-ed/* past tense of verb
	Cyclone Amphan **caused** massive devastation.	I **was shouting** harsh instructions to the boatman.	The cat was forced to do the opposite of what she **had wanted**.
Future	*will/shall*	*will/shall be* + verb + *-ing* form	*will/shall have* + verb in past tense
	The tiger **will head** straight for the far bank.	Rivers and tides **will be circulating** nutrients.	This system **shall have set up** a conflict of interest.

B. Complete the sentences with the correct forms of the given verbs.

1. Prerna __________ all morning on Sunday. (sing)
2. Vincent __________ of travelling around the world. (dream)
3. I __________ in this office for seven years. (work)
4. She __________ her lunch after the others finished theirs. (eat)
5. Food and water __________ in short supply during a drought. (be)
6. By this time next year, she __________ thirty years of service in the school. (complete)
7. They __________ (finish) the project before the teacher __________ (ask) for it.
8. Radha __________ (play) tennis regularly. She __________ (play) in a tournament right now.

C. Fill in the blanks with the simple past or past continuous forms of the verbs given in the brackets.

1. Nutrients __________ (pour) into this 'food factory' from all sides.
2. Humans __________ (be) not really welcome in the Sundarbans and life __________ (can) be very dangerous for them.
3. This utterly fragile, strange and magical ecosystem __________ (evolve) throughout the past years.
4. The air __________ (be) thick with drama as the sun __________ (begin) to set.
5. Half an hour later, we __________ (dock) at the Haldibari Camp jetty.
6. We __________ (walk) through a net-protected walkway when we suddenly __________ (hear) a loud roar.

Study Skills

Pronounce Well

You know what syllables are. Each syllable in a word is spoken with a different force or **stress**. This means that we say one syllable longer or louder than the other(s). This is called the **accented syllable**. It is usually marked with an apostrophe (').

Example: In the word **chapter**, there are two syllables: chap'/ter.

If you say the word aloud correctly, you will notice that the first syllable, **chap**, is stressed.

Look at the way the syllables have been separated in the following words and the stress marked.

be/lieve' sur'/face

Now, say the words aloud, with stress on the correct syllable.

Remember:

- A word can only have one stress.
- Only vowels (and not consonants) are stressed.

Say the following words aloud and choose the option that shows the correctly stressed syllable.

1. a. mov/ing'
   b. 'mov/ing
2. a. ti'/ger
   b. ti/ger'
3. a. per'/haps
   b. per/haps'
4. a. dis'/turb
   b. dis/turb'
5. a. re'/morse
   b. re/morse'
6. a. es'/cape
   b. es/cape'

Listening and Speaking

A. Listen to a passage about the Royal Bengal tiger and write whether these statements are true (T) or false (F). Correct the false statements.

1. The Royal Bengal tiger can only be found in tropical or subtropical forests. ☐
2. The male tigers weigh up to 300 kg, while females weigh up to 180 kg. ☐
3. Tigers prefer to live in groups. ☐

4. The animals that tigers usually hunt include small elephants and rhino calves.
5. Tigers can break their prey's spinal cord.
6. Tigers are strong enough to carry away prey up to seven times their weight.

B. You have read briefly about Project Tiger in this chapter. Do some research on it in pairs and give a short presentation in the class.

You can include information on the following points:

- why it was started
- tiger census of 2006
- how India's tiger population has risen thanks to the project
- problems, if any, surrounding the project

Pen it Down

Imagine that you are a tiger/tigress living in the Sundarbans. Write an account of a typical day in your life. You can use these points in your essay:

- hunt at night—keen eyesight
- avoid humans; prefer own company
- striped coat as camouflage
- travel many miles to look for prey
- hunt only when hungry

Self Assessment

Now I can

- read a passage about the richness of the flora and fauna in the Sundarbans.
- identify the effects of man's continuing conflict with the environment.
- use compound adjectives, revise the types of adjectives and use the different tenses.
- identify the stressed syllables in words, research and give a presentation, and write an account on a given topic.

Read More

Life of Pi: This fantasy novel by Yann Martel is about a fourteen-year-old Indian boy, Pi, who is shipwrecked in the Pacific Ocean and spends 227 days on a lifeboat with a Royal Bengal tiger called Richard Parker. It won the Man Booker Prize in 2002.

Born Free: This real-life story by Joy Adamson narrates the author and her husband's experiences of raising Elsa, an orphaned lion cub, to adulthood before releasing her into the wild in Kenya. The book was made into a popular movie.

sonnet

6

Composed upon Westminster Bridge, September 3, 1802

William Wordsworth

Let's Get Started

SUSTAINABLE DEVELOPMENT GOALS

The United Nations Sustainable Development Goal 11 highlights the need for sustainable cities with access to basic services for all. Bridges are an important part of a city as they help people move from one place to another and also connect various areas.

Learn about the famous bridges in the world. Unjumble the words to find out what types of bridges they are structurally. Then research and tag the bridges to their respective countries in a blank world map.

1. The Westminster Bridge has supportive structures in the shape of a curved arch to hold its weight. CHAR: ___________

2. The Glenfinnan Viaduct consists of a series of arches, piers, or columns supporting a long, raised railway. AVIDCTU: ___________

3. The deck of the Golden Gate Bridge is suspended by cables. SUPSENONSI: ___________

4. The Howrah Bridge is built with structures that are supported on only one end. CAVEILERNT: ___________

5. The Donghai Bridge is one of the longest sea-crossing bridges in the world. MEAB: ___________

HC **Active Participation:** Exploring uniqueness and complementarity among the various entities in nature

Reading

Have you ever come across a scene in nature that has left you spellbound? Read this poem composed by William Wordsworth one September morning in 1802, when he took a walk across London's Westminster Bridge and was captivated by the early morning sight of the city.

Earth has not anything to show more fair:
Dull would he be of soul who could pass by[1]
A sight so touching in its **majesty**:
This City now **doth**, like a **garment**, wear[2]
The beauty of the morning; silent, bare,
Ships, towers, domes, theatres, and temples lie
Open unto the fields, and to the sky;
All bright and glittering in the **smokeless** air.
Never did sun more beautifully **steep**
In his first splendour, valley, rock, or hill;
Ne'er saw I, never felt, a calm so deep!
The river **glideth** at his own sweet will:
Dear God! the very houses seem asleep;
And all that mighty heart is lying still!

Literary terms

1. This is a **hyperbole**. The poet uses it to emphasize how beautiful the city of London is to him.

2. This is an example of **personification**. Here the city, being bathed in the morning light, is being imagined as a person wearing clothes.

How does the splendid sight make the poet feel?

majesty: grandeur; splendour

doth: (archaic) does

garment: clothing

smokeless: clean, clear of any smoke or pollutants

steep: (here) immerse

glideth: (archaic) flowed smoothly

About the poet

William Wordsworth (1770–1850) was one of the most important British poets of all time. He believed that Nature was man's greatest teacher. 'Lucy Gray', 'The Ruined Cottage' and 'The Solitary Reaper' are some of his most famous poems.

Comprehension

Quick Recap

A. Answer the questions in brief.

1. What is the poet describing in the poem?
2. Which year was the poem composed in?
3. Name the city structures mentioned in the poem.
4. What are the things in nature that the poet talks about in the poem?
5. How are the first eight lines of the poem different from the next six lines? What shift in the poet's tone can you identify?

B. Answer the questions with reference to context.

1. *This City now doth, like a garment, wear*
   The beauty of the morning;
   a. Identify the figure of speech used in these lines.
   b. What is the comparison being drawn by the poet?
   c. What effect does this comparison create in the poem?
2. *All bright and glittering in the smokeless air.*
   a. What is being referred to here?
   b. Why do you think the poet uses the word 'smokeless'?
   c. Does the time of the day play a significant role in the poem? How?
3. *Dear God! the very houses seem asleep;*
   And all that mighty heart is lying still!
   a. Why do the 'houses seem asleep'?
   b. What does the poet mean by the phrase 'mighty heart'?
   c. What is the impact of the exclamatory comment, 'Dear God!'?

Life Skills and Values appreciating nature's beauty

Think and answer.

1. Mention two examples of imagery in the poem that you find appealing.

2. 'Dull would he be of soul who could pass by/A sight so touching in its majesty:' – What does the poet mean by these lines? How relevant are these lines in our everyday lives?
3. Do you feel that this poem highlights the coexistence of man and nature? Use lines from the poem to explain your answer.

HC exploring balance in natural and material orders

Way with Words

Simile and Personification

The poem creates images in our minds by using figures of speech like **similes** and **personification**. You know that in a simile we make a comparison between two things using the words *like* or *as*.

Example: This City now doth, like a garment, wear
The beauty of the morning;

Here, the poet compares the beautiful morning light enveloping the city of London to a garment wrapped around it.

A. Complete the similes with the given words.

night and day   bone   nails   log   midnight   glove   new pin

1. After travelling the whole day, the child slept like a __________, on reaching home.
2. They might be twins, but they are as different as ____________.
3. The glass slipper fit Cinderella like a ____________.
4. The new marble I added to my collection is as shiny as a ____________.
5. The trek leader was as tough as _________, and guided the team safely out of the blizzard.
6. It was as dark as ___________ inside the cave, and we could barely see anything.
7. Please give me some water. My throat is as dry as a __________.

B. You came across examples of personification in the poem. Read these lines and point out what has been personified.

1. Never did sun more beautifully steep/In his first splendour, valley, rock, or hill
2. The yellow and blue bike raced past us, screaming for attention.
3. The very houses seem asleep.
4. The bees played hide and seek with the flowers in the garden.
5. The autumn breeze brushed my cheek and blew my hat away.
6. The smell of warm apple pie welcomed him inside.
7. The flood water devoured everything in its path.
8. Time and tide wait for none.

Grammar in Use

Perfect and Perfect Continuous Tense

Read this line from the poem.
The Earth **has not shown** anything more fair to the poet.

It is in the present perfect tense.
You know that the perfect tense takes the following forms.

	present	past	future
perfect	have seen	had seen	will have seen
perfect continuous	have been seeing	had been seeing	will have been seeing

A. Complete the sentences with the given verbs, according to the instructions.

1. I ______________ a funny film yesterday. (watch, past perfect)
2. By the time you come home, I ______________ my dinner. (finish, future perfect)
3. Saima ______________ in a TV show for a year now. (act, present perfect continuous)
4. ______________ you ______________ the Taj Mahal? (see, present perfect)
5. Who ______________ my story book? (take, present perfect)
6. I ______________ for two hours, but I am still five kilometres away from the campsite. (walk, present perfect)
7. Sohini ______________ a champion badminton player before she injured her wrist in an accident. (be, past perfect)
8. Come December, I ______________ in Pune for five years. (live, future perfect continuous)

Punctuation

Look at this line from the poem.
Dear God the very houses seem asleep;
We must insert an exclamation mark after 'God' to understand the meaning of the sentence.
A wrongly-placed punctuation can change the meaning of a sentence.

Example: Let's eat Rohit.
Let's eat**,** Rohit. (with correct punctuation)

B. Insert punctuation marks in the correct places.

1. Look out Man eating tiger ahead.
2. Prithviraj Kapoor his two sons Shashi Kapoor and Raj Kapoor were all talented actors.
3. There is only one thing to do surrender, said the general, and we did it.
4. My sister carries the following items to work her lunch box her laptop and her purse.

5. Who thought wondered Tanuja that I would be a successful singer today. it all began with a newspaper advertisement for the singing stars of tomorrow competition. After winning the contest I started singing in mumbai.
6. Have some water the March Hare said in an encouraging tone alice looked all round the table, but there was nothing on it but tea. I dont see any water she remarked. There isnt any said the march hare. Then it wasnt very civil of you to offer it,' said alice angrily.

APOSTROPHE

You know that apostrophes are used for the following:

1. In place of the missing letters in shortened forms of words.
   Examples: Ne'er (Never) saw I, never felt, a calm so deep!
   Earth hasn't (has not) shown anything more fair.
2. To create possessive forms of nouns.
   Example: the poet's words

C. Rewrite the sentences by expanding the shortened words.

1. She's practising hard for the badminton match. She'd have to be at her best to defeat her opponent.
2. Haven't you finished reading this book yet? It's such a quick read.
3. They're raising funds to start a school for poor children in the locality. David's donated some money to them.
4. It'd be great if you could send out the invitations. It isn't a good idea to leave it till the last minute.
5. They'll leave for Australia tomorrow morning. Shouldn't we go and say goodbye to them?

Study Skills

Spell Check

Say these words aloud: **A**pril, br**ai**n, pr**ay**, n**ei**gh

They are all pronounced with the same **long a** vowel sound.

The **long a** is spelt in a number of ways:

1. With the letter 'a'. **Examples:** b**a**sic, **a**te
2. With the letters 'ai'. **Examples:** m**ai**l, expl**ai**n
3. With the letters 'ay'. **Examples:** s**ay**, r**ay**
4. With the letters 'ei': **Examples:** r**ei**n, sl**ei**gh

Circle the words in the grid which are pronounced with the long a.

P	A	N	G	E	L	B	Z	S	A	N	N
O	A	J	H	N	O	L	S	M	R	O	M
F	Q	I	T	G	I	J	S	K	R	I	G
B	D	D	N	A	M	M	W	P	A	Z	A
L	D	M	M	T	V	W	A	C	Y	T	L
D	I	S	P	L	A	Y	Y	D	V	N	E
M	A	W	E	I	G	H	T	M	Y	L	K
L	B	I	D	A	E	L	M	L	J	L	J
O	H	R	B	N	I	H	P	L	A	K	E
Q	Q	G	R	E	G	R	E	I	G	N	S
X	U	B	V	V	H	J	D	V	H	I	V
C	A	B	L	E	T	O	T	T	L	K	W

Listening and Speaking

A. Read this conversation between the poet and his friend, standing on the Westminster Bridge.

Poet: This bridge is so majestic, and it stretches as far as the eyes can see!

His friend: That's true. Look at its reflection in the river below. It's quite serene!

Now imagine a situation where you and your friend have come across a beautiful work of art, a monument or a scene of natural beauty. Work in pairs and enact a conversation expressing your admiration for it.

You may talk about these points:

- what the scene consists of
- how it changes during different times of the day
- how it inspires you

Useful words and phrases

- Have you seen such a...
- It fills my heart with...
- There has never been...
- How beautiful/splendid/pretty...

Stressed and Unstressed Syllables

The rhythm of a poem often depends upon the combination of stressed and unstressed syllables. Usually, important words such as nouns, verbs, adjectives and adverbs are stressed. The unstressed syllables are often prefixes, suffixes, prepositions and articles.

Look at these lines from the poem, where the underlined syllables are stressed. The remaining syllables are unstressed.

Dear <u>God</u>! the <u>ver</u>/y <u>hou</u>/ses <u>seem</u> a/<u>sleep</u>

And <u>all</u> that <u>might</u>/y <u>heart</u> is <u>ly</u>/ing <u>still</u>!

B. Read these lines from the poem carefully. Then, divide the words into syllables and underline the stressed syllables.

Never did sun more beautifully steep
In his first splendour, valley, rock, or hill;
Ne'er saw I, never felt, a calm so deep!
The river glideth at his own sweet will:

Pen it Down

A. Imagine that you have signed up for a conducted walking tour of an interesting part of your city. Write an email to a friend, inviting him/her to join you on the walk, where you would view certain historic monuments, learn about them and take photographs. Mention the city areas the tour will cover, along with the date, time and meeting place for the participants.

B. Look at this image of a modern city in the early hours of the morning. Write a paragraph on it, comparing it with the image of the city the poet has painted in the poem. You may use the following points:

- the skyline of the two cities (horizon, silhouette)
- the impact of the time of day on the two cities (wee hours of the morning, break of dawn)
- the kind of lives people might be living (hectic, routine, busy)

Self Assessment

Now I can

- read and enjoy a poem celebrating the beauty of a city in the morning light.
- identify similes and instances of personification, practise perfect and perfect continuous tenses, and revise punctuation including apostrophe.
- have a conversation, identify stressed and unstressed syllables, write an email and a paragraph on a picture.

Read More

Lines Written in Early Spring: This poem by William Wordsworth celebrates the harmony that exists in nature, and dwells on how man has failed to follow nature's peaceful example.

Glasgow: This poem by Alexander Smith presents a balanced depiction of his mixed feelings about the city of Glasgow, capturing both its positive and negative sides vividly.

7

Mary Shelley

Let's Get Started

A. In this chapter, you will read the story of the creation of the novel, *Frankenstein*. Read the following passage about the novel and fill in the blanks with the given words.

intelligent	perfect	everything	cobbled
accepted	appearance	scientist	revenge

Mary Shelley's novel is about the gifted young __________, Victor Frankenstein who brings to life a human-like creature, __________ together using the body parts of dead people. Frankenstein had hoped to create the __________ man, but his Creature is hideous. However, he is an __________ being whose deepest wish is to be loved and __________ by others. He is rejected by his maker, who is horrified by his __________, as well as by other people he meets. Enraged, he seeks __________ on his creator. Frankenstein wanted to 'play God' by creating life, but by the end of the story, he loses __________ he holds dear.

B. Do you like stories about ghosts and monsters? There are some creatures of lore which only come out at night, having a deep connection with darkness. Work in pairs and match these famous sinister beings with their places of origin.

Name	Place of Origin
1. *Babadook*: a very tall faced man with long fingers, who wears a hat	a. Transylvania
2. *Banshee*: a female spirit, known for her loud shrieking	b. Ireland
3. *Dracula*: an immortal demon who takes the shape of a bat and drinks blood	c. India
4. *Gremlin*: a mischievous creature who enjoys damaging machinery	d. Australia
5. *Nishi*: a night spirit which lures its victim by calling their names	e. England

HC **Learning and Awareness:** Exploring the relation between self-reflection and knowledge

Reading

Have you ever wondered about life, death and what comes after? Would it surprise or shock you if something dead came alive before your eyes? An 18-year-old girl did imagine such a scenario! This is the story of Mary Shelley, the creator of Frankenstein.

By the time the week was almost up, the men had already written their stories—about frightening, ghastly beings.
Oh, what do I write about? I have thought and thought, but my mind is blank! It has to be **sinister** and something never heard or thought of before, something that would shock them.
At that moment, Byron and Shelley were discussing their favourite topic: the latest scientific experiments. Mary listened.
The theory doing the rounds is that electricity might be used to resume life in the dead.
It's fascinating! It will be man's ultimate triumph! Can you imagine the power we will have over Nature if this could be achieved?
It's an interesting possibility, but doesn't it go against the very laws of Nature?
Her mind in turmoil, Mary lay down, but couldn't sleep. She heard the rumbling thunder, the howling winds, and she thought of monsters. Sleeping fitfully, she had a '**waking dream**'.
Who's that? Lord, what a terrible vision is this! Who is that pale figure? A young man! He seems to be a scientist… he is now kneeling beside the creature he has **assembled** together! Oh, but how frightful the creature is! It is turning its head... it is looking at me!
What had the men written their stories about?

FLASHBACK!
Who was Mary?
Mary came from an **illustrious** family. Her mother, Mary Wollstonecraft, was a champion of women's rights. Her father was William Godwin, a political writer. But the early death of her mother left a **void** in her heart, and loneliness was a constant presence.
Mary Wollstonecraft Godwin 27 April 1759– 10 September 1797
She would often read books, sitting before her mother's tomb.
She would often seek **solace** in the books in her father's library. Books were her closest friends.
I want to write something one day that will astound everybody!
In 1807, when she was only ten years old, she published her first poem.
MOUNSEER NONGTONGPAW
Mary did not go to school, unlike her stepsister Claire. Mary often spent her time daydreaming, her imagination providing an escape from her often challenging life at home.
At the age of 17, Mary decided to leave home. Accompanied by Claire, she embarked on an adventure with her future husband, the poet, Percy Bysshe Shelley.
The trio travelled through a war-torn France and Switzerland, and returned to England via the Dutch port of Maassluis. In May 1816, they left for Geneva, to spend the summer with the poet, Lord Byron.
When did Mary publish her first poem?

Back to the present in 1816 at Villa Diodati
It was on a dreary night of November that I saw what I had achieved in two years of toil. With great anxiety, I collected the instruments of life around me to infuse a spark of being into the lifeless thing that lay at my feet. I saw the dull yellow eyes of the creature open; it breathed hard; and its limbs jerked in uncontrolled movements. How do I describe the wretch I had created with such pains? He had yellow skin which barely covered the work of muscles and arteries beneath; his hair was lustrous black and flowing; his teeth had a pearly whiteness; and his watery eyes were set in dun-white sockets.
However, now horror and disgust filled my heart for the being. Unable to look at the creature I had created, I rushed out of the room. I tried to sleep in my room, but started up, disturbed by my dreams. By the dim and yellow light of the moon I saw the miserable monster. He was holding up the curtains of the bed, and his eyes were fixed on me. He might have spoken; one hand stretched out to hold me back, but I escaped and rushed downstairs. I took refuge in the courtyard, and passed the night miserably. In the morning, I found the house empty of the creature.
The morning after her 'waking dream', Mary knew what she wanted to write about. It was the story of young Victor Frankenstein, a scientist who brought to life a creature **cobbled together** from old body parts. What would be the dreadful consequences of his act?

When Mary read her story to the **motley** group at Diodati, Byron described it as 'a wonderful work for a girl of nineteen'.
In 1818, with Shelley's encouragement, Mary completed the novel and published it **anonymously**, with the title *Frankenstein*.
FRANKENSTEIN; OR, THE MODERN PROMETHEUS
Frankenstein was a bestseller. People's reactions to it ranged from astonishment to shock.
My goodness! What a frightful topic! But the story is so moving … Did you know that the book was written by a woman?
Indeed! And authored at such a young age! Can someone so young express such extraordinary ideas? I suspect her husband, Percy Shelley is the real author.
In nineteenth century Europe, a woman's true place was thought to be at home, as a daughter, wife or a mother. Few women wrote. Fewer women wrote of never-before-heard ideas like scientists creating new life by **reanimating** the dead.
Five years later, a recently-widowed Mary was living in London when she came to know that *Frankenstein* had been turned into a successful play, complete with a frightening monster which sprang from a concealed laboratory.
I find the play quite entertaining, despite the added elements of **spectacle**. It's a pity that the plot is not well managed. My Creature was an innocent victim. He was never meant to be evil. The music, the **pantomime**—these have altered the message considerably.
What was the title of Mary's novel?

At 25, Mary had also lost three of her children, after losing Percy in a boating accident. But she kept writing to support herself and to bring up and educate her only surviving son, Percy Florence.
Just a few more pages, Percy, till this one is finished. Then, we shall go for a walk.

She also edited and published her husband's poems, all while continuing to produce her own novels.
How did Percy Shelley die?
The Fortunes of Perkin Warbeck by Mary Shelley
Valperga
The Last Man
Lodore
Falkner

Mary died in 1851, from a suspected brain tumour, having suffered from **chronic** headaches for several years. She was 53. Mary's life as a writer had been one of **unrelenting** struggle in the face of rejection from publishers. But she was a **dogged** survivor who continued to write even though she was often forced to publish anonymously.
MARY SHELLEY
August 30 1797-
February 1 1851
Her son and daughter-in-law created a **shrine** for her at Bournemouth, where her parents were also buried, in memory of the remarkable woman who let her distinct voice be heard, and wrote what is often considered the first true science fiction novel in English literature.

spells: (here) short periods of weather events

venture: go

sinister: evil; menacing

waking dream: an experience one has while being awake that feels similar to dreaming

assembled: put together

illustrious: famous, celebrated

void: emptiness

solace: comfort

cobbled together: made or produced something roughly or quickly

motley: (here) consisting of different people

anonymously: not revealing one's identity

reanimating: bringing back to life

spectacle: a grand and impressive event or performance

pantomime: a form of entertainment characterized by farce, music, lavish sets, and jokes

chronic: lasts for a very long time

unrelenting: constant

dogged: determined

shrine: memorial

Did You Know? History

Mary Wollstonecraft was an English writer, philosopher, and passionate advocate of educational and social equality for women. During her brief career, she wrote novels, treatises, travelogues and even a history of the French Revolution. She is best known for *A Vindication of the Rights of Woman* (1792), which calls for women and men to be educated equally. She is also remembered for her contribution in shaping the art of travel writing as a literary genre.

Comprehension

Quick Recap

A. Answer these questions in brief.

1. Who were the people staying at Villa Diodati?
2. Describe the weather during the summer of 1816.
3. Who issued the challenge and what was it?
4. What were the two traits of the story Mary had wanted to write?
5. Who were Mary's parents?
6. How did Mary spend her time as a child?
7. What was the general public's reaction to Mary's novel? Why did they suspect that Percy Shelley was the real author of the book?
8. How did Mary support herself after Percy Shelley's death?

B. Answer the questions with reference to context.

1. '*Lord, what a terrible vision is this!*'
   a. Who was having the 'vision'?
   b. What led her to have the 'vision'? Why was it referred to as a 'waking dream'?
   c. What did she see in the 'waking dream'?
2. …*Mary knew what she wanted to write about.*
   a. What did Mary want to write about?
   b. When and how did Mary publish her novel?
   c. How did Lord Byron react to her story?

3. *'...these have altered the message considerably.'*
   a. Who said these words?
   b. What prompted her to say these words?
   c. What was the message that she had wanted to convey through her writing?
   d. Why did she feel that the message had been altered?

Life Skills and Values science vs nature, understanding gender inequality

Think and answer.

1. 'It's an interesting possibility...' – What was the 'possibility'? Who were discussing it, and what was Mary's doubt regarding the 'possibility'? Do you feel her concern was valid? Explain your answer.
2. What was the position of women like in nineteenth century Europe? How do you think women are treated today in your country/city? What similarities or differences can you find between the treatment during two time periods?
3. Mary defied societal norms to write and publish her works. What kind of a person do you think she was? Make a character sketch of her with examples from the story.

Way with Words

A. Match the words and phrases from the story with their meanings.

Word/Phrase	Meaning
1. hush	a. being passed from one person to another
2. spurred on	b. silence
3. doing the rounds	c. destroyed by war
4. fitfully	d. supporter of some cause or a person
5. champion	e. encouraged by
6. war-torn	f. irregularly, not continuous

Forming Antonyms with Prefixes

A common way of forming an antonym or opposite is to add prefixes like **un-** and **in-** to adjectives.
Examples: interesting – uninteresting, constant – inconstant, successful – unsuccessful
Prefixes like **dis-** are used to form the antonyms of verbs.
Examples: own – disown, assemble – disassemble, embark – disembark

B. Rewrite the following sentences using the antonyms of the underlined words. You may have to make other necessary changes. One is done for you.

1. The coach was not pleased with the team's performance in the football match.
   The coach was displeased with the team's performance in the football match.

2. The athlete did not qualify for the final round of the race.
3. The teacher said that Mala's rude behaviour was not acceptable in school.
4. Deepak was not satisfied with a third place in the race.
5. She is not reliable or trustworthy.
6. There is no need to wear formal clothes for the party.

Grammar in Use

ADJECTIVE PHRASES

An **adjective phrase** modifies the noun in the sentence.

Example: I find the play quite entertaining.

In this sentence, **play** is the noun, while **quite entertaining** is the adjective phrase.

A. Underline the adjective phrases in these sentences.

1. The man with the beard is an artist.
2. The main character in the novel was of Malaysian origin and seven feet tall.
3. The tribesmen lived in houses made of wood.
4. Batman is a superhero in a black cape who fights crime.
5. His father was a man of great wealth.
6. This craftsmanship is of the highest quality.

TRANSFORMATION OF SENTENCES WITH ADJECTIVE PHRASES

Look at these sentences.

Is *Frankenstein* a **horror** story?

Is *Frankenstein* a story **full of horrors**?

Both the sentences mean the same. In the second sentence, the adjective **horror** is replaced with the adjective phrase **full of horrors**. This is how we can transform sentences with adjective phrases.

B. Rewrite the following sentences by replacing the adjectives with adjective phrases. One is done for you.

1. Sourav found a golden pot in the ruins of the old city.
   Sourav found a pot made of gold in the ruins of the old city.
2. The boy made silly mistakes in the math test.
3. William Shakespeare was a playwright of great renown.
4. The umpire made a wise decision.
5. The grey-haired stranger was her father.
6. This mobile phone is useless as it does not charge properly anymore.

Noun Phrases

A **noun phrase** does the work of a noun, and acts as the subject or object in a sentence. It answers the questions *what* and *who*. A noun phrase can include articles, nouns, adjectives and participles in it.

Examples: **The music and the pantomime** have altered the message considerably. (noun phrase as the subject of the verb 'have altered')
In 1807, Mary published **her first poem**. (noun phrase as the object of the verb 'published')

C. Underline the noun phrases in these sentences.

1. Children love to fly kites.
2. I did not watch my favourite channel.
3. Annoying people is a bad habit.
4. The captain wanted to win the toss.
5. He refused to answer the question.
6. Cheating in examinations is unacceptable.

Study Skills

Spell Check

Underline the correct spelling in each pair of words.

1. cronic/chronic
2. occasion/occassion
3. spectackle/spectacle
4. acquaintance/aquaintance
5. arguement/argument
6. dissappointed/disappointed
7. calender/calendar
8. sinister/sinistar

Listening and Speaking

You read how Mary had a 'waking dream' which resulted in her getting ideas for her story. Have you ever had a similar dream or nightmare, which terrified you greatly? Talk about it to the class, in brief. You can use the following points:

- what you saw and heard
- why it was frightening
- the feelings of dread and anxiety
- how it affected you even after waking up

Pen it Down

Imagine that you are the secretary of the theatre club in your school. Your club plans to put up a play adaptation of Mary Shelley's *Frankenstein* during the school's Annual Day function. Write a notice inviting interested students from classes 6-8 to audition for certain roles. Mention the details of the play, and the date, time and venue for the audition.

Self Assessment

Now I can

- read and enjoy a graphic story on the life and works of Mary Shelley.
- form antonyms with prefixes, understand adjective and noun phrases, and transform sentences with adjective phrases.
- spell words correctly, speak on a topic, and write a notice.

Read More

The Strange Case of Dr Jekyll and Mr Hyde: This novella by Robert Louis Stevenson is about a London legal practitioner named Gabriel John Utterson who investigates strange occurrences between his old friend, Dr Henry Jekyll, and the evil Edward Hyde, who turn out to be the same person.

A Wrinkle in Time: This book by Madeleine L'Engle describes the fantastic journey that the Murry siblings embark on through space and time, from universe to universe, as they try to save their father, and subsequently, the world.

Research and Write

A. **The story 'Looking for Vultures' Eggs' is about a child who was not understood by the adults around him.**

Divide yourselves into three equal groups. Each group will research and discuss one of the following topics:

- how children are sometimes not understood by adults
- what adults can do to understand children better

B. **Both 'Where Tigers Swim' and 'Coromandel Fishers' are about man's interaction with the environment.**

1. You read about the devastation caused by Cyclone Amphan. Work in groups of four, and research on the impact of other cyclones like Aila and Yaas which have hit the Sundarbans in recent years. Make a comparative study on the devastation caused by these cyclones and present the facts and figures in a bar graph. You may chart the Y-axis for the number of people who lost their lives or were displaced by the cyclone. The X-axis should mention the names of the cyclones and the year each took place in.

   Point out which cyclone caused the most extensive damage and the one which had the least effect.

2. **Read the following passage. Identify the collocations that are generally used to talk about the environment.**

   Endangered species from both the plant and animal kingdoms need immediate protection if they are to survive. Shrinking habitats are upsetting our ecological balance. Global warming has brought about climate change. The situation will become more difficult due to overpopulation and the overutilisation of limited natural resources. There is a very real possibility that there will be no tropical rainforests left by 2050.

3. Find the words or phrases in the passage that mean the following:
   a. uncontrolled use of resources
   b. forests growing in regions of high temperature and rainfall
   c. animals and plants whose existence is threatened
   d. decreasing living space for animals
   e. balance of natural relationships in the environment

C. **You read that Mary Shelley's 'Frankenstein' was the first true science fiction novel in English literature. Work in groups of four. Read any one of these novels and make a fact file on it.**

a. The Time Machine, by H. G. Wells
b. The Doom Machine, by Mark Teague
c. Twenty Thousand Leagues Under the Sea, by Jules Verne

8

Grannie

Vernon Scannell

Let's Get Started

SUSTAINABLE DEVELOPMENT GOALS

3 GOOD HEALTH AND WELL-BEING

The United Nation Sustainable Development Goal 3 underlines the importance of good health and well-being of all family members. Do you know what a human right is? They are rights which all people have. They can never be taken away.

Make a list of five human rights specifically for the elderly, which you think all countries should have. Put up your list on the class soft board and then do a gallery walk of your classmates' lists. You can show your support for a right by inserting a tick mark next to it on the lists put up by your classmates.

After the activity, check the rights that have got the most 'votes' and discuss why they are important.

Right to adequate medical care

HC **Feelings:** Recognising feelings and values: affection

Reading

Are you close to your grandparents? In the busy lives we lead, we often forget to value the older generation, including our grandparents, who have showered us with unconditional love.

lavender: a fragrant flower

enfold: surround

lavishly: generously

circumstance: a set of events

seized: took hold of

hobbled: walked in an awkward way due to injury or pain

peered: looked with concentration or difficulty

Literary terms

1. This is a **simile**. The poet compares the warmth of his grandmother's smile to that of a shawl in winter.

2. This is a **metaphor**. Here, the poet compares his grandmother to a mountain, who stood like a shield, protecting him from his fears.

3. These are **run-on lines** where the meaning of one line flows into the next.

What did the grandmother do when the narrator was good and bad?

In this poem, set during World War II, the poet's grandmother reminds him of the innocence of his childhood and his once-uncomplicated life.

I stayed with her when I was six then went
To live elsewhere when I was eight years old.
For ages I remembered her faint scent
Of **lavender**, the way she'd never scold

No matter what I'd done, and most of all
The way her smile seemed, somehow, to **enfold**
My whole world like a warm, protective shawl.[1]

I knew that I was safe when she was near,
She was so tall, so wide, so large, she would
Stand mountainous between me and my fear,[2]
Yet oh, so gentle, and she understood
Every hope and dream I ever had.
She praised me **lavishly** when I was good,
But never punished me when I was bad.

Years later war broke out and I became
A soldier and was wounded while in France.
Back home in hospital, still very lame,
I realised suddenly that **circumstance**
Had brought me close to that small town where she
Was living still.[3] And so I **seized** the chance
To write and ask if she could visit me.

She came. And I still vividly recall
The shock that I received when she appeared
That dark cold day. Huge grannie was so small!
A tiny, frail old lady. It was weird.
She **hobbled** through the ward to where I lay
And drew quite close and, hesitating, **peered**.
And then she smiled: and love lit up the day.

About the poet

Vernon Scannell (1922–2007) was one of the most respected British poets of the 20th century. He was, at one time, a professional boxer and an accountant. He fought in World War II and his poems such as 'Walking Wounded', draw on his war experiences.

Comprehension

Quick Recap

A. Answer the questions in a few lines.

1. How long did the speaker live with his grandmother?
2. Mention a visual memory the speaker had of his grandmother and another related to smell.
3. Give two examples of run-on lines in the poem.
4. Explain the line, 'and love lit up the day.' What does it say about the speaker's relationship with his grandmother?

B. Answer the questions with reference to context.

1. *She was so tall, so wide, so large, she would*
   Stand mountainous between me and my fear.
   a. Who is the speaker in these lines?
   b. Who is 'she'? Why was her being 'tall' and 'large' important to the speaker?
   c. What, according to the speaker, did 'she' do even though she was tall and large?
2. *I realised suddenly that circumstance*
   Had brought me close to that small town where she
   Was living still.
   a. Which country was the speaker in at the time? What was his occupation?
   b. What circumstance had brought the speaker to his grandmother's town?
   c. What did he do when he found himself in the same town as her?
3. *And I still vividly recall*
   The shock that I received when she appeared ...
   a. What was the shock that the speaker received?
   b. Why was it a shock for him?
   c. What did 'she' do when 'she' appeared?

Life Skills and Values

importance of family

Think and answer.

1. Why did the poet's grandmother hesitate at first when she saw him?
2. Do you think the poet had lost touch with his grandmother over the years? Mention the lines that give this impression.

21ST CENTURY Critical Thinking

Way with Words

Emotive Language

Emotive language is the use of words in such a way that they to appeal to people's emotions. It is also used to convince people about something.

Examples: She was so tall, so wide, so large, she would/Stand mountainous between me and my fear. (**emotive language**)
She was a large woman. She stopped me from feeling afraid. (**non-emotive language**)

A. Rewrite these sentences using emotive words or phrases. One is done for you.

1. The boy ran past me with an older boy running behind him.
   The boy fled past me with a bully chasing him.
2. Mr Roberts was killed by a thief for Rs 500.
3. Let us feed that dog.
4. Miss Sims has a headache.
5. Kavya burnt her hand.

B. Identify examples of emotive language used in the poem.

Grammar in Use

Question Tags

You know that **question tags** are short questions at the end of statements. They are used to confirm whether something is true or to encourage a reply.
Remember the following rules for using question tags.

- A positive statement is followed by a negative question tag and vice versa.
  Example: Grannie **is** quite frail, **isn't** she?
- The subject of the sentence and that of the question tag should be the same. If the subject of the sentence is a noun, the subject of the tag should be a pronoun of the same gender.
  Example: **The poet** loved his grandmother, didn't **he**?
- A statement with a helping verb is followed by a question tag with the negative form of the helping verb. Example: Grannie should **scold** the naughty boy, **shouldn't** she?

A. Match the sentences with the correct question tags.

A	B
1. She knows her dialogues,	a. didn't they?
2. They went home,	b. mustn't we?
3. Roy ate a hearty breakfast,	c. should I?
4. I shouldn't be sharing this,	d. didn't he?
5. We must work together,	e. haven't they?
6. They have come,	f. doesn't she?

Comparison of Adjectives

You have learned that adjectives have three degrees of comparison: positive, comparative and superlative.

Look at the degrees of comparison for the following adjectives from the poem.

Positive	Comparative	Superlative
gentle	gentler	gentlest
tiny	tinier	tiniest
protective	more protective	most protective

B. Complete the paragraph using the correct form of the given adjectives.

At eighteen, I was the __________ (young) boy in my platoon. All the others were at least a few years __________ (old). Among them, I found Joseph the __________ (fascinating). He was the __________ (swift) when it came to picking up new drills and he was also the __________ (well-read) than any of us. But he had a single flaw. 'This is __________ (troublesome) than I imagined. The lad's afraid of spiders!' I overheard our sergeant exclaim one day. Spiders? I couldn't think of anything __________ (funny). __________ (smart), __________ (handsome) than any of us, the __________ (capable) Joseph scared of creepie crawlies? This had to be told to the others.

Study Skills

Pronounce Well

We often confuse the sounds of the letters **v** and **w** with each other.

Example: We often use the /v/ sound for the word, **west** and the /w/ sound for the word, **very**.

Note that for the **/w/** sound, we put our lips forward and make a round shape.
For the **/v/** sound, we put the lower lip slightly behind or against the upper teeth.
The **/v/** sound is voiced, which means that the vocal cords vibrate when it is produced.

A. Now, say these words aloud, clearly pronouncing the letter with which they begin.

wounded	world	weird	warm	awaiting	ward
visit	vividly	vest	vociferous	lavishly	vacate

B. Work in pairs. Take turns to read these sentences aloud, with your partner, ensuring that you pronounce the /v/ and /w/ words correctly.

1. We had to attend a wedding during the summer vacation.
2. When a volcano erupts, the weather is also affected.
3. The wicked and vain queen was punished by the witch at the end of the story.

Listening and Speaking

A. Although the poem has run-on lines, similar to everyday speech, it also has a clear rhyme scheme. Identify it and write the words that rhyme in each stanza.

B. With smaller families and faster lifestyles, are old age homes a necessary evil in our society? Organise a debate in class on the topic. Some students should speak in favour of the topic, and some should speak against it. You can include the following points in the debate:

For the topic:

- People travel away from home for jobs
- No one to take care of aged parents
- Old age homes take care of daily needs and provide company

Against the topic:

- Responsibility of children to care for parents
- Age brings wisdom with it
- Older people often keep a family closely knit

Pen it Down

Imagine that the city council is organizing an event to honour veterans of a recent war who have returned to their country. Make a poster advertising the event and inviting community members to participate. Remember to mention a list of planned events, and the date, time, and venue of the event.

Self Assessment

Now I can

- read a poem about the lasting love between a grandmother and a grandson.
- understand the use of run-on lines and emotive language.
- revise question tags and practise comparison of adjectives.
- identify rhyme scheme, debate on a topic and make a poster.

9 Grandpa Learns to Read and Write

Michael Morpurgo

Let's Get Started

The United Nations Sustainable Development Goal 4 discusses the importance of education for all. The coronavirus pandemic that started in 2020 affected the education of students in several ways. Many students from economically underprivileged backgrounds were forced to stop going to school.

Imagine that you have taken up a tutoring project to help out fellow students from underprivileged backgrounds. You have to plan a 'language week' for the students. Make a list of language activities and exercises for the week on the given topics.

Topic	Activities
My neighbourhood and friends	
My favourite subject	
My country	

List three ways in which adult education may help those who are past the usual school or college-going age.

1. ____________________

2. ____________________

3. ____________________

Feelings: Contribution in others' studies

Reading

Do you think knowledge can be gained only from books? The following extract, taken from the novel, **Farm Boy**, *is about an old English farmer who has managed his farm all his life despite being unable to read and write. But in old age, he feels a longing for the world of books.*

This extract begins with him asking for help from his grandson, who reluctantly agrees to teach him.

He reached out suddenly and took me by the arm. 'Well, will you?'
I still hadn't a clue what he was asking me.

'Will you stay here for a few months? You could give us a hand out on the farm. I'd pay you, mind, proper man's wages. And maybe . . .'

He was looking down at his hands, picking at his knuckles. 'And maybe, you could teach me. I'd learn quick.'

'Teach you what, Grandpa?' I said.

'I can't read,' he **mumbled**. 'And I can't write either.' There were tears in his eyes. 'You got to teach me, lad. You got to.'

'But you went to school,' I said.

'Till I was thirteen and I wasn't bad either. Then I missed a year of school with scarlet fever. And when I got better, I wanted to be out on the farm all I could. I'd fetch in the cows. I'd feed Joey in his stable and old Zoey too. It was near enough a two-mile walk to school after that. I was late most mornings, and I was always dropping off to sleep in Mr Burton's lessons and he didn't like that; so then I got a **wigging**.

And sometimes, if the brown **trout** were rising down on the Ockment, I'd bunk off school anyway. Harvest times, too. Father and Mother couldn't have managed without me, 'specially at harvest time. But I was happy enough to do it. You ask me where I'd rather be, in Mr Burton's writing lesson at school or cleaning out the pens? Pens any day. Honest. And I could read all the words I'd need. I could write a bit, too.

Trouble was that when I left school, I forgot even the little learning I had learnt. No cause to practise much, see? Then, your grandmother comes along, and she can read and write well enough for both of us. So I never bothered with it after that, until she told me she'd teach me. But we left it too late, didn't we?'

He sighed and sat back in his chair.

'I want to learn so I can write just like I can speak, so I can read an Agatha Christie book from cover to cover. Well?'

'I don't know, Grandpa,' I said. 'I've never taught anyone anything. And besides, I was thinking of going to Australia for a while, after Christmas, when I've got some money saved up.'

'Tell you what we'll do. You stay here till after Christmas, till the New Year, say. I'll do it in four months, easy.'

I must have made a doubting face.

Why didn't Grandpa need to practise reading and writing after he got married?

mumbled: spoke quietly, in an unclear way

wigging: (informal) scolding

trout: a common freshwater fish

'I'm betting you one hundred pounds that if you teach me . . . let's say three hours a day till Christmas, I'll be able to read an Agatha Christie book all on my own, cover to cover; and what's more, I'll write you out a bit of a story of my own, too. So you'll have a hundred pounds more to take with you to Australia.'

We got out the paper and pencil there and then, sat down at the kitchen table and began.

It turned out to be a lot more than three hours a day. Grandpa stopped only to cook, to eat, to walk up the lane at dusk to shut the chickens up and to sleep. The moment I came in from feeding the cows or checking the sheep, he'd be sitting there at the kitchen table with his pencil and his books, waiting.

He'd barely give me time to wash my hands. He learnt all his reading from newspapers. He liked the large print and the photographs helped him to guess a word sometimes when he couldn't quite make it out.

Any new word he came across he'd write down in his book. That way, I thought, he could practise his reading and writing at the same time. He found the writing harder. He said his fingers wouldn't do what he told them. Mostly he'd find ways to laugh off his failures; but from time to time, when things didn't go right, he would become angry and **morose**, and then I'd leave him to get on by himself.

After a while, I could see the newspapers weren't helping. He'd sit silent through a meal, **dwelling on** some dreadful story he'd just struggled so hard to read. One evening, after he'd read a piece about yet another **savagery** in Bosnia, I saw there were tears in his eyes.

'Doesn't it ever stop?' he said. 'I can remember Father telling me that there'd be no more wars, not after this one. It shames me. It shames all of us. What's the good in reading, if that's all there is to read about?'

Then a **jumble sale** up in Iddesleigh Village Hall produced unexpected treasures: a copy of *Animal Farm* and *Travels with a Donkey*, and a dozen *Tintin* books; but best of all, a dictionary and a magnifying glass. After that, his reading seemed to come on in leaps and bounds. His writing was slower, though. He would **print** each letter very **deliberately**, pressing down too hard on the paper and often breaking his pencil in the process.

morose: in a bad mood

dwelling on: thinking a lot about something

savagery: cruel and violent behaviour

jumble sale: a sale of old or used items

print: (here) write

deliberately: slowly and with effort

What distressing news did Grandpa read about in the newspaper?

Did You Know? History

The Bosnian War (1992–1995) was the most devastating war in Europe since World War II. Fought between Bosnia and Herzegovina, it cost the lives of around 100,000 people.

But he never let up, not for a single day. Some nights he'd stay up till midnight; and I'd be dead on my feet and longing for bed.

On Christmas Eve at midnight, he took me up the lane to the barn. He switched on the light. The cows on one side lay in their straw, blinking at us; and on the other side the sheep eyed us lazily.

Grandpa sat down on a bale of straw, patted the straw beside him and told me to sit. He took a book from his coat pocket.

'I've got a surprise for you,' he said. Then he began. '*Death on the Nile* by Agatha Christie. Chapter One.'

He read slowly, stumbling every now and again, his eyebrows meeting in a frown of **frustration** whenever he did. When he'd finished the chapter, he closed the book and looked at me, a smile of wild **exhilaration** in his eyes.

'You'll get two chapters a day till I've done,' he said. And so I did, sometimes three, and by the end, by New Year, he wasn't reading the words, he was reading the story.

A week or so later, I found myself on the train from Eggesford Junction to Exeter. I was on my way home, then off to Australia sometime in February. I should have been looking forward to it, but I was not. I had been a farm boy for only a few months and had loved every smelly, backbreaking moment of it.

I had no real desire to travel anymore, nor to go to college either. I had hated leaving Grandpa all alone down at Burrow. He had waved me off rather abruptly, a quick pat on the head. 'Off you go. Miss your train else,' he'd said.

My rucksack tumbled over at my feet. As I picked it up, I saw a white envelope sticking out of its side pocket. I pulled it out. There were ten ten-pound notes inside. The bet! I'd forgotten all about it.

There was a note with it. It read: 'I hope you like my story. I wrote it for you just to show you I could. It's about the old Fordson tractor at the back of the barn and it's about Joey and it's about me. Thanks a million for teaching me. God bless. Grandpa.'

frustration: annoyance and impatience

exhilaration: happiness and excitement

What was Grandpa doing by New Year?

Did You Know? G.K.

The books which the narrator finds are classics of western literature. George Orwell's *Animal Farm* is a modern fable about a group of animals which throws out the humans from their farm.

Travels with a Donkey in the Cevennes is a travel book by Robert Louis Stevenson about his walking tour through a mountainous area of France.

About the author

Michael Morpurgo (1943–) is a much-loved English author of children's fiction. He joined the army and also tried his hand at school teaching before finding success as a writer of stories for children. His well known works include *Little Foxes, Tom's Sausage Lion* and *Billy the Kid.*

Did You Know? G.K.

Agatha Christie was an English writer best remembered for her two characters, the detectives Hercule Poirot and Miss Marple. *Death on the Nile* is a crime thriller featuring Poirot, set in Egypt.

Comprehension

Quick Recap

A. Answer the questions in a few lines.

1. Where did Grandpa live as a child? How far was his school from his home?
2. Why and when did Grandpa's parents need him on the farm?
3. Why would Grandpa get a 'wigging'?
4. Why were there tears in Grandpa's eyes after he read a newspaper report about Bosnia?
5. What kind of effort did Grandpa put into his work? What were the challenges that he faced?
6. What treasures did the jumble sale produce? How did they speed up Grandpa's learning?

B. Answer the questions with reference to context.

1. *'Will you stay here for a few months? ... I'd pay you, mind, proper man's wages.'*
   a. Who is the speaker? Whom was he talking to?
   b. Why did he want to pay 'proper man's wages' to the person spoken to?
   c. Why was the speaker picking at his knuckles while he said these words?
2. *On Christmas Eve at midnight, he ... patted the straw beside him and told me to sit.*
   a. Where was the narrator?
   b. What did the person referred to as 'he' do next? Why was it a surprise for the narrator?
   c. Why do you think he took the narrator to that particular place and nowhere else?
3. *I had no real desire to travel anymore, nor to go to college either.*
   a. Who is the speaker? Where was he at the time?
   b. Why did he have no desire to travel anymore? What were his future plans at the time?
   c. What did Grandpa give him before he left?

Life Skills and Values family ties, determination

Think and answer.

1. What kind of a relationship do you think Grandpa had with his wife?

   HC Evaluating assumptions about relationships

2. Would you consider Grandpa's effort praiseworthy? Why?
3. What appeals to you about the note written by Grandpa? Give reasons for your answer.

Way with Words

A. Complete the crossword using the clues. (Hint: All the words are to be found in the story.)

Across

2. British currency
4. where two or more roads or railway lines meet
5. a quantity of valuable objects, such as gems and money
7. take the trouble to do something
9. location of the most destructive conflict in Europe since World War II

Down

1. bring one's eyebrows together when one is thinking, angry or worried
3. a flat paper with a flap, used to enclose a document or a letter
6. a period of learning or teaching
8. collective noun for 'straw'
10. a river in Egypt

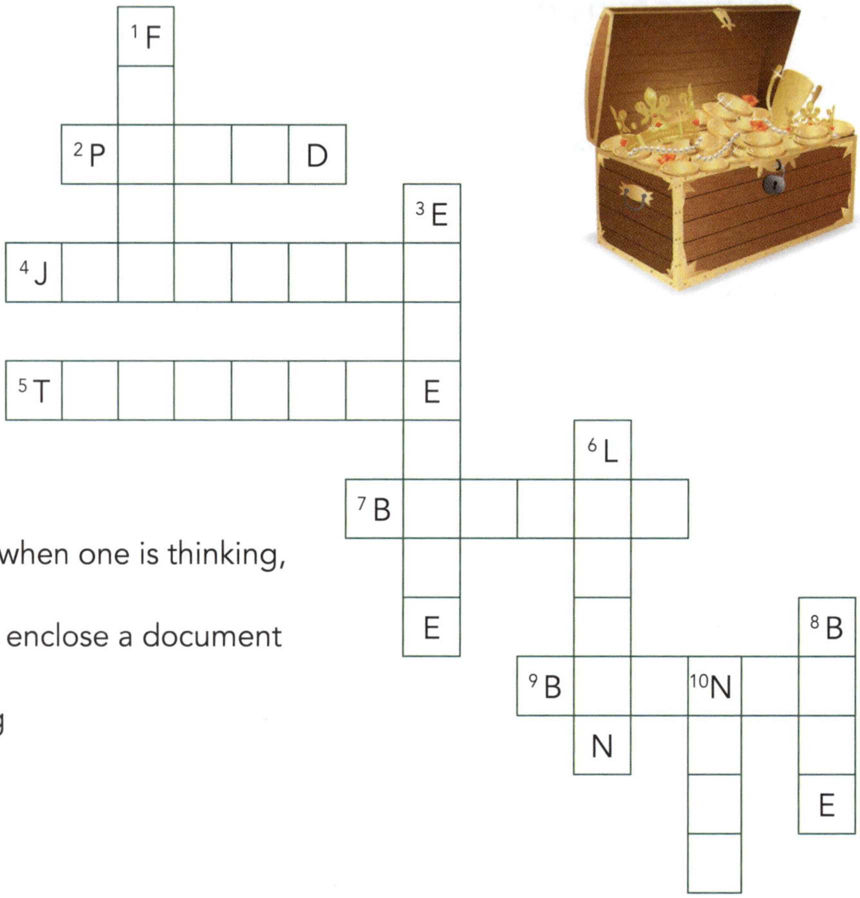

Expressions Related to Studying

B. Look at the expressions in bold in the following sentences. They are all related to studying. Choose the option that best matches the meaning.

1. I was so nervous before my history exam that when I got the question paper, my mind **went blank**.
   a. I became confused. b. I became upset. c. I couldn't remember anything.
2. He seemed to **breeze through** his exams even though he did not study more than three hours a day.
   a. fail b. succeed easily c. to not be serious about studies
3. Due to a sudden illness, she **fell behind** in her studies and needed extra help from the teachers.
   a. to slow down in progress b. forgot all she knew c. made mistakes

4. You should **know** the chapters **inside out** if you want to be fully prepared for the oral exam.
   a. memorise b. know very well c. find new information
5. Rajesh had to **drop out of** school to support his family when his father passed away.
   a. take up another subject b. leave school or college, without completing your studies
   c. make excuses

Grammar in Use

Prepositions and Prepositional Phrases

You know that **prepositions** are words that come before a noun or a pronoun and describe its relationship to another word.

Look at this table which shows the different types of prepositions and how they are used in sentences.

Type of Preposition	Purpose	Example
Time	gives information about the time when the action in the sentence takes place	Mother couldn't have managed without me, 'specially **at** harvest time. Some nights he'd stay up **till** midnight.
Place	shows the position of the person, place, animal or thing referred to by the noun	You could give us a hand out **on** the farm. Grandpa patted the straw **beside** him.
Movement	shows the movement to and from a place	Any new word he came **across** he'd write down in his book. Then, your grandmother comes **along**, and she can read and write well enough for both of us.
Direction	shows the direction which is to be taken	He took me **up** the lane to the barn. Grandpa sat **down** on a bale of straw.

A. Complete the sentences with the given prepositions.

on among in into with of off along

1. She disposed ________________ the old cans.
2. The shirt was kept ________________ the shelf.
3. The pond abounds ________________ fish.
4. I ran ________________ an old friend the other day.
5. He deals ________________ people very courteously.
6. Do you know the name ________________ that girl?
7. She got ________________ well with everyone at school.
8. Distribute these sweets ________________ the needy.

Prepositional phrases are easy to detect. They begin with a preposition and usually include a noun, pronoun or clause. They do the work of an adjective or adverb in a sentence.

Examples: I had been a farm boy **for only a few months**.
This story is **about Joey**.

B. Complete the sentences with these prepositional phrases.

at the top of	under the weather	in defence of	on the brink of
by means of	in keeping with	in exchange for	in the garb of

1. The spy came to the party ________________ a business tycoon.
2. She screamed in anger ________________ her voice.
3. She spoke up ________________ her friend who was absent.
4. She was a little ________________ after getting wet in the rain.
5. They let the prisoner go ________________ a heavy ransom.
6. We celebrated all festivals ________________ the traditions of our country.
7. He got to the top of the mountain ________________ a strong rope.
8. The two countries were ________________ war.

Study Skills

Spell Check

Plurals of Foreign Words

The plurals of words that have come into English from foreign languages such as Latin or Greek often have two spellings: the foreign spelling and the English one. For some words, only one of the two is used, while for others, both can be used.

Look at the plural forms of these words that came into English from Latin.

Word	Latin plural	English plural
alga	algae	–
arena	–	arenas
cactus	cacti	cactuses
curriculum	curricula	curriculums

Write the Latin and English plural forms of these words.

1. index
2. stadium
3. thesaurus
4. formula
5. gymnasium
6. millennium
7. aquarium
8. antenna
9. nucleus

Listening and Speaking

Listen to a passage about a girl remembering her grandmother. Then, complete the sentences with words or phrases from the passage.

1. Grannie was one of the ____________________.
2. She would carry her old, ____________ chair to her large lawn.
3. She ____________ with the ____________, ____________, and ____________ passing by.
4. The cook made ____________ for ____________.
5. At night, Grannie would ____________________.
6. The narrator had permission to ____________________.
7. Grannie never gave the narrator the ____________________.

Pen it Down

Imagine that your grandmother is a famous children's author. You recently visited a book fair where you met someone who considered her his favourite author. Write a letter to your grandmother describing the experience of meeting and discussing her books with him. You can use the following points:

- how you both met, and his surprise upon realising who you were
- discussing your grandmother's books with him
- your impression about the person

Self Assessment

Now I can

- read and appreciate a story about a grandson teaching his grandfather to read.
- use expressions related to studying, prepositions and prepositional phrases.
- identify English words of Latin origin, listen to a passage and complete sentences, and write an informal letter.

Read More

War Horse: This novel by Michael Morpurgo is a touching tale about the relationship between a boy and a horse, set against the backdrop of World War I.

The Evolution of Calpurnia Tate: Set in 1899 in Texas, USA, this story by Jacqueline Kelly is about a young girl, Calpurnia, who develops a close relationship with her irritable grandfather, a naturalist, as she explores the rich animal and plant life around her house.

10

Dar es Salaam to Nairobi by Ford Prefect

Roald Dahl

Let's Get Started

A. Is travelling solo more preferable or travelling with others? Divide your class into two groups, with one supporting the cause of solo travel and one preferring to travel with friends or family. List out the arguments in favour of each and then take a class vote on which mode of travel is the general choice.

B. Match the names of these famous travellers with the places they travelled to.

Name of the Traveller	Places of Travel
1. Ibn Battuta	a. India, and sacred Buddhist sites in Central, South and Southeast Asia
2. Marco Polo	b. India and other sacred Buddhist sites in South Asia (during the reign of Harshavardhana)
3. Hiuen Tsang	c. Indian subcontinent (in 1017)
4. Megasthenes	d. China, Persia, India, Japan and other Asian countries in and around the Silk Road
5. Fa Hien	e. Central, Southeast and South Asia, China, and the Iberian Peninsula
6. Al Biruni	f. India (in 303 BCE, during the reign of Chandragupta Maurya)

HC **Active Participation:** Exploring uniqueness and complementarity among various entities in nature

Reading

Have you ever been to Africa? It was 1939 and World War II had just begun. A young Roald Dahl, working in Africa for Shell Oil Company in Dar es Salam, Tanzania (then called Tanganiyaka), set out in his old car to join the Royal Air Force (RAF). His destination was the city of Nairobi in Kenya. This passage from his autobiographical book, **Going Solo,**

is about his journey and the animals and people he encountered on the way.

In November 1939, when the war was two months old, I told the Shell Company that I wanted to join up and help in the fight against Bwana Hitler, and they released me with their blessing. In a wonderfully **magnanimous** gesture, they told me that they would continue to pay my salary into the bank wherever I might happen to be in the world, and for as long as the war lasted and I remained alive. I thanked them very much indeed and got into my ancient little Ford Prefect and set off on the 600-mile journey from Dar es Salaam to Nairobi to **enlist** in the RAF.

When one is quite alone on a lengthy and slightly **hazardous** journey like this, every sensation of pleasure and fear is enormously **intensified**, and several incidents from that strange two-day safari up through central Africa in my little black Ford have remained clear in my memory.

A frequent and always wonderful sight was the astonishing number of giraffes that I passed on the first day. They were usually in groups of three or four, often with a baby alongside, and they never ceased to **enthral** me. They were surprisingly tame. I would see them ahead of me nibbling green leaves from the tops of acacia trees by the side of the road. Whenever I came upon them, I would stop the car and get out and walk slowly towards them, shouting **inane** but cheery greetings up into the sky where their small heads were waving about on their long long necks. I often amazed myself by the way I behaved when I was certain that there were no other human beings within fifty miles. All my **inhibitions** would disappear and I would shout, 'Hello, giraffes! Hello! Hello! Hello! How are you today?' And the giraffes would incline their heads very slightly and stare down at me with **languorous demure** expressions, but they never ran away. I found it **exhilarating** to be able to walk freely among such huge, graceful wild creatures and talk to them as I wished.

magnanimous: generous
enlist: join the armed forces
hazardous: dangerous
intensified: greatly increased
enthral: hold one's attention
inane: silly, meaningless
inhibitions: shyness
languorous: lazy
demure: shy
exhilarating: exciting

Wordwise

The word 'bwana' means 'boss' or 'master' in the African language, Swahili. It comes from the Arabic word, *abuna*, meaning 'our father'.

Where was the narrator going and why?

ruts: deep narrow marks made in the ground by a vehicle

current: continuously flowing water

astern: behind

serenity: peace

Where did the narrator meet the cobra?

The road northwards through Tanganyika was narrow and often deeply rutted, and once I saw a very large thick greenish-brown cobra gliding slowly over the **ruts** in the road about thirty yards ahead of me. It was seven or eight feet long and was holding its flat spoon-shaped head six inches up in the air and well clear of the dusty road. I stopped the car smartly so as not to run it over and, to be truthful, I was so frightened that I went quickly into reverse and kept backing away until the fearsome thing had disappeared into the undergrowth. I never lost my fear of snakes all the time I was in the tropics. They gave me the shivers.

At the Wami river, the natives put my car on a raft and six strong men on the opposite bank started to pull me across the hundred yards or so of water with a rope, chanting as they pulled. The river was running swiftly and in midstream the slim raft upon which my car and I were balanced began to get carried downriver by the **current**. The six strong men chanted louder and pulled harder. I sat helpless in the car watching the crocodiles swimming around the raft, and the crocodiles stared up at me with their cruel black eyes. I was bobbing about on that river for over an hour, but in the end the six strong men won their battle with the currents and pulled me across. 'That will be three shillings, bwana,' they said, laughing.

Only once did I see any elephant. I saw a big tusker and his cow and their one baby moving slowly forward in line **astern** about fifty yards from the road on the edge of the forest. I stopped the car to watch them, but I did not get out. The elephants never saw me and I was able to stay gazing at them for quite a while. A great sense of peace and **serenity** seemed to surround these massive, slow-moving, gentle beasts. Their skin hung loose over their bodies like suits they had inherited from larger ancestors, with the trousers ridiculously baggy. Like the giraffes, they were vegetarians and did not have to hunt or kill in order to survive in the jungle, and no other wild beast would ever dare to threaten them. Only the foul humans in the shape of an occasional big game hunter or an ivory poacher were to be feared, but this small elephant family did not look as though they had yet met any of these horrors. They seemed to be leading a life of absolute contentment. They are better off than me, I told myself, and a good deal wiser. I myself am, at this moment, on my way to kill Germans or to be killed by them, but those elephants have no thought of murder in their minds.

Who were the only threats to the elephants?

At the frontier between Tanganyika and Kenya, there was a wooden gate across the road with an old shack alongside it, and in command of this great outpost of Customs and Immigration[1] was an ancient and toothless black man who told me he had been there for thirty seven years. He gave me a cup of tea and said he was sorry he did not have any sugar to put into it. I asked him if he wished to see my passport but he shook his head and said all passports looked the same to him. In any event, he added, smiling secretly, he could not read without spectacles and he did not possess any.

Outside the Customs shack, a group of enormous Masai tribesmen holding spears were crowding round my car. They stared at me curiously and patted the car with their hands, but we were unable to understand each other's language.

A little later on, I was bumping along on a particularly narrow bit of road through some very thick jungle when all of a sudden the sun went down and in ten minutes, darkness descended over the jungle land. My headlamps were very dim. It would have been foolish to push on through the night. So I parked just off the road in a scrubby patch of thorn trees to wait for the dawn, and I sat in the car with the window down. I sat there listening to the jungle noises all around me and I was not afraid. A car is good protection against almost any wild animal. I had with me a sandwich with hard cheese inside it and I ate that. Then I wound up the two windows, leaving just a half-inch gap at the top of each and got into the back seat and curled up and went to sleep.

I reached Nairobi at about three o'clock the next afternoon and drove straight to the aerodrome where the small RAF headquarters was situated. There I was given a medical examination by an **affable** English doctor who remarked that six feet six inches was not the ideal height for a flier of aeroplanes.

'Does that mean you can't pass me for flying duties?' I asked him fearfully.

'Funnily enough,' he said, 'there is no mention of a height limit in my instructions, so I can pass you with a clear **conscience**. Good luck, my boy.'

Literary term

1. This is an example of **irony**. The wooden gate beside the old shack managed by a man with poor eyesight was exactly the opposite of how a great outpost of Customs and Immigration should have been.

Did You Know? Geography

The Masai are a semi-Nomadic African tribe with a reputation as fearsome warriors. They herd cattle and live in the African Great Lakes region.

affable: friendly

conscience: a moral sense of right or wrong

On what grounds was the narrator passed for flying duties?

About the author

Roald Dahl (1916–1990) was one of the greatest children's writers of the twentieth century. Some of his best known books are *Charlie and the Chocolate Factory* and *Fantastic Mr Fox*. During World War II, his RAF plane was shot down over the Libyan desert. Dahl later wrote about the incident, which became his first published story. He also wrote dark short stories such as 'Man from the South'.

Comprehension

Quick Recap

A. Explain these lines with reference to context.

1. *When one is quite alone on a lengthy and slightly hazardous journey like this, every sensation of pleasure and fear is enormously intensified.*
2. *'That will be three shillings, bwana,' they said, laughing.*
3. *They are better off than me, I told myself, and a good deal wiser.*

B. Answer the questions.

1. What was the 'magnanimous gesture' shown to the narrator by the Shell Company?
2. Describe the narrator's encounter with the giraffes. Why did he call them 'tame'?
3. Describe the cobra that the narrator met along the way. How did he react to it?
4. How did the narrator describe the elephant family he saw passing by?
5. How did the old man at the frontier treat the narrator? How was it different from the usual behaviour of a person at a Customs and Immigration outpost?
6. What did the narrator do after it became dark in the jungle?
7. Why did the narrator fear that he might not be selected for flying duties?

Life Skills and Values — importance of peace, humour

Think and answer.

1. Give two examples where the narrator contrasts the peace in the animal world with the war and unrest in his own.

   HC Exploring complementarity between animal and human order

2. Who were the various African people the narrator met during his journey?
3. Why do you think the narrator wanted to join the war effort even though he seemed to prefer peace to violence?
4. Which parts of the account do you find the most humorous? Give three examples.

Way with Words

Onomatopoeia

The narrator mentions listening to 'jungle noises' at night. You know that words which are used to describe a sound are called **onomatopoeic words**.

A. Complete the sentences using the onomatopoeic words in the box.

slammed	gurgling	chirping	squeaked	rattled	sizzled

1. The ________________ of the crickets filled the heart of the forest.
2. As the fire ________________ and burned higher, it warmed the weary travellers and kept the animals away.
3. The windows of the old wooden cabin ________________ in the wind every night.
4. I woke up to the sound of the ________________ brook which flowed past our hotel in the hills.
5. Matilda ________________ the door shut and left with an angry look on her face.
6. The old couch ________________ when the man sat on it.

B. Complete the crossword using the clues given. All the words are from the story.

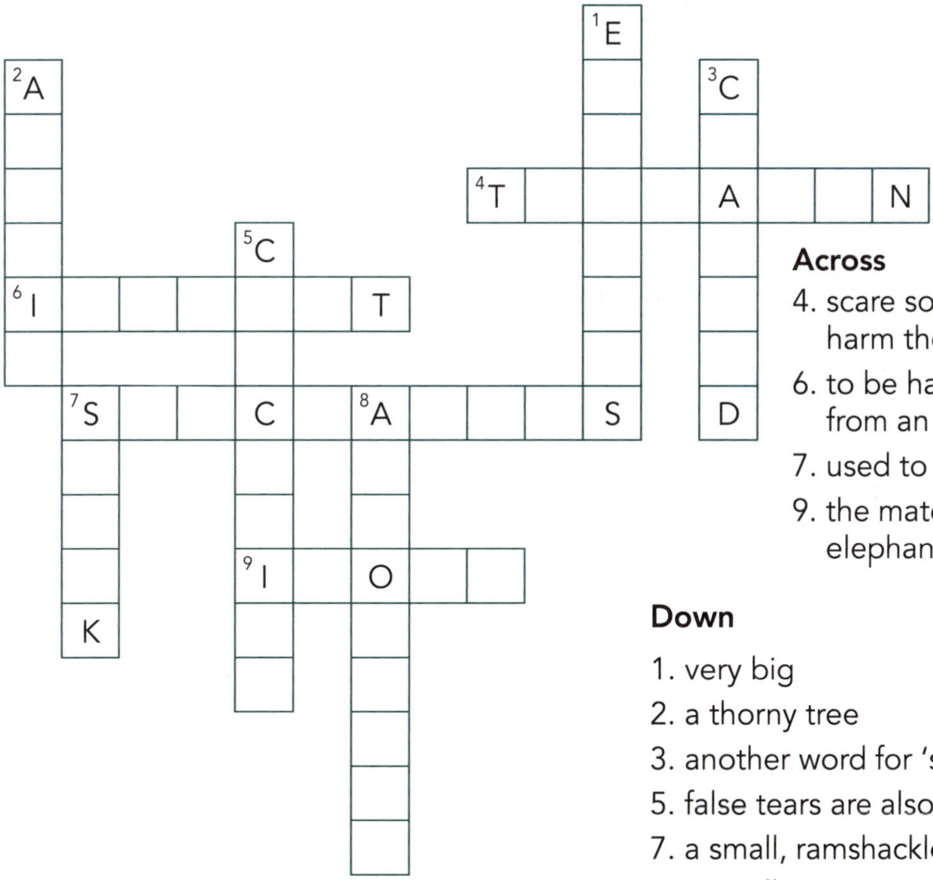

Across

4. scare someone saying you would harm them
6. to be handed down something from an earlier generation
7. used to improve eyesight
9. the material you get from elephant tusks

Down

1. very big
2. a thorny tree
3. another word for 'sang'
5. false tears are also known as ________ tears
7. a small, ramshackle hut
8. a small airport

Grammar in Use

INFINITIVES

Look at these sentences.

I **reached** Nairobi at about three o'clock yesterday.

We **will be reaching** Nairobi at about three o'clock tomorrow.

The form of the verb **reach** depends on the tense, and the number and person of the noun. Such verbs are finite verbs.

However, there are many verbs whose form do not depend on these factors. They are of three types: infinitives, gerunds and participles. These are non-finite verbs. We will discuss infinitives and gerunds in this chapter.

Infinitives are formed by the addition of **to** before the base form of a verb.

Examples: I wanted **to join** the army.
They continued **to pay** my salary.

An infinitive without the preceding **to** is called a **bare infinitive**.

The bare infinitive is used in the following ways.

1. As the main verb with other helping verbs.
   Example: I would **see** them ahead of me nibbling green leaves.
2. With verbs such as *let, need, make, bid, hear, see, watch, know* and *feel.*
   Example: Let me **volunteer** for flying duties.
3. With the phrases *had better, would rather, would sooner than* and *rather than.*
   Example: I had better **stop** for the night.
4. With *than* and *but* when they mean 'except'.
   Example: The foul humans did nothing but **cause** harm to the elephants.

A. Fill in the blanks using the infinitive forms of the given words. You may not need to add 'to' in some cases.

1. I am going ________________ (study) in a prestigious business school.
2. She need not ________________ (lie) about her qualifications.
3. It proved difficult for me ________________ (drive) the car without enough fuel.
4. It is no fun ________________ (look) after so many children in kindergarten.
5. It is unwise ________________ (waste) an opportunity like that.
6. She can ________________ (speak) louder than this.

TRANSFORMATION OF SENTENCES USING INFINITIVES

We can change complex sentences to simple sentences by using infinitives.

Example: The Masai tribesmen were excited when they saw my car. (complex)
The Masai tribesmen were excited **to see** my car. (simple)

B. Rewrite these sentences using infinitives. One is done for you.

1. We were excited when we heard of the picnic.
   We were excited ***to hear*** *of the picnic.*
2. Neil Armstrong was the first man who walked on the moon.
3. I was sad when I heard of her illness.
4. The pilot was the first man who parachuted out of the plane.
5. I found it exhilarating when I was able to walk freely among the wild creatures.
6. Mr Gordon was the only man who came forward as a witness to the crime.
7. The robber escaped from the police station so that he could avoid punishment for his crimes.
8. We were shocked when we saw the newspaper headlines.
9. You will have to work hard if you want to pass the test.

GERUNDS

Gerunds are verbs that act like nouns. They take the **-ing** form of the verb. Like nouns, they can act as the subject of a sentence.

Examples: **Swimming** is a good form of exercise.
Listening to music is her favourite pastime.

C. Complete the sentences with the gerund form of the given verbs.

1. I apologise for ____________________ your plans. (upset)
2. He is sure of ____________________ the award this year. (win)
3. Vijay was scolded by his teacher for ____________________ in the test. (cheat)
4. She delayed ____________________ us the bad news. (give)
5. She was praised for ____________________ a beautiful model of an artesian well. (make)
6. Akbar rewarded Birbal for ____________________ the riddle. (solve)

Study Skills

Use Your Dictionary

There are several expressions in the English language that include names of animals, in which there is no direct relation between the creature and the meaning of the expressions.

Some such expressions are given below. Use a dictionary to find their meanings. Then, use them in sentences of your own.

1. red herring
2. eager beaver
3. dark horse
4. black sheep
5. guinea pig
6. clothes horse

Listening and Speaking

Listen to a passage about a mysterious disappearance and answer the questions.

1. Who were the people who had disappeared?
2. Where had these people gone? What, according to the speaker, happened to them?
3. Why was the window kept open every evening till dusk?
4. Who do you think the speaker is? Which song did she mention in her account?
5. Why did the open window make the speaker uneasy?

Pen it Down

Imagine that you had gone on a visit to an animal sanctuary on the outskirts of your city, where you found that poachers had killed a protected animal. Write a letter to the editor of your local newspaper protesting against the incident and suggesting measures to prevent such an unfortunate incident from taking place again.

21ST CENTURY Media Literacy

You can include the following points in your letter:

- negligence of forest officials
- not enough forest guards
- strong punishment for poachers to stop future incidents

Self Assessment

Now I can

- read an interesting description of the natural world, set against the backdrop of war.
- appreciate the use of humour and irony in the passage.
- use onomatopoeic words, learn about infinitives, bare infinitives and gerunds, and write a letter to the editor of a newspaper.

Read More

Boy: This book by Roald Dahl is about his growing up years, from infancy to childhood and teenage, including his school days in a boarding school in England. He writes about nearly losing his nose in an automobile accident, his love for sweets and enjoying free samples of Cadbury's chocolate bars.

The Innocents Abroad: This travelogue by Mark Twain is about the author's cruise on a ship from the USA to Jerusalem. During the voyage, he travelled across the Atlantic Ocean to cities like Paris and Rome.

11

Humour

Uncle Alfred's Long Jump

Gareth Owen

Let's Get Started

A. Match the different forms of humour with their definitions.

Form of humour	Definition
1. farce	shows exaggerated incidents of physical harm
2. improv	shows incidents that are too ridiculous to be true
3. stand-up	creates a skit or tells unplanned jokes in the moment or on the spot
4. slapstick	entertains an audience with jokes and humorous stories

B. Read about the following situations. In groups of four, plan and enact a five-minute skit to bring out the humour in any one of these situations.

- A girl is in a hurry to go to a party and ends up wearing shoes in different colours
- A mother complains about her lazy children not realizing that they are making her a surprise birthday cake
- A police station gets robbed
- A child makes excuses so that she can skip school, without realizing that it's Saturday

HC **Learning and Awareness:** Evaluating our assumptions about happiness

Reading

There are often a few members in our families who say and do things that we consider eccentric. Do you have such a relative? What strange things does he/she do? Read a poem about a man

paced out: measured out the distance by taking steps

Jehovah's Witnesses: a Christian denomination with many beliefs that are different from mainstream Christianity

St Bernard: a large, powerful breed of dogs

trudged: walked in a heavy-footed way

Did You Know? G.K.

Mary Rand was a British athlete. She was the first British woman to win an Olympic gold medal. She won it in the 1964 Summer Olympics held in Tokyo.

What was the distance covered by Mary Rand, according to Auntie Hilda?

who ends up with broken bones because of his eccentric behaviour.

When Mary Rand
Won the Olympic Long Jump,
My Auntie Hilda
Paced out the distance
On the pavement outside her house.
'Look at that!'
She shouted challengingly
At the dustman, the milkman, the grocer,
Two **Jehovah's Witnesses**
And a male **St Bernard**
Who happened to be passing.

'A girl, a girl did that;
If you men are so clever
Let's see what you can do.'
Nobody took up the challenge
Until Uncle Alfred **trudged** home
Tired from the office
Asking for tea.
'Our Mary did that!'
Said Auntie Hilda proudly
Pointing from the lamppost
To the rosebush by her gate.
'You men are so clever,
Let's see how near
That rosebush you end up.'

His honour and manhood at stake,[1]
Uncle Alfred put down his **bowler**,
His briefcase and his **brolly**
And launched himself
Into a fifty yard run-up.
'End up at that rosebush,'
He puffed mockingly,
'I'll show you where I'll end up.'
His take off from the lamppost
Was a thing of beauty,
But where he ended up
Was in The Royal **Infirmary**
With both legs in plaster.
'Some kind of record!'[2]
He said proudly to the bone specialist;
While through long nights
In a ward full of coughs and snoring
He dreamed about the washing line
And of how to improve
His high jump technique.

Where did Uncle Alfred's attempt land him?

Literary terms

1. This is an example of **hyperbole**. The poet exaggerates the situation, showing that Uncle Alfred could take a small issue very seriously.

2. This is an example of **irony**. Uncle Alfred's accident was not a record at all, but a failed attempt, in which he ended up with his legs in a plaster cast.

bowler: a round and hard hat with a narrow brim

brolly: umbrella

infirmary: hospital

About the poet

Gareth Owen (1936–) is an English writer, actor and broadcaster. He has worked as a factory worker, bookseller, gardener, a school teacher and a teacher of drama. Some of his famous works are *Say Cheese!*, *Mr Chips and the Silver Chicken* and *Ruby and the Dragon*.

Comprehension

Quick Recap

A. Answer the questions in a few lines.

1. Why did Auntie Hilda challenge everyone she came across to equal Mary Rand's Olympic record?
2. Whom did she finally challenge to equal Mary's record?
3. Give an example of hyperbole used in the poem, other than the one mentioned. Explain it in your own words.
4. Explain the use of irony in the lines, 'He dreamed about the washing line/And of how to improve/His high jump technique.'

B. Answer the questions with reference to context.

1. *His honour and manhood at stake,/Uncle Alfred put down his bowler*
   His briefcase and his brolly ...
   a. Who is Uncle Alfred? In what way was his honour and manhood at stake?
   b. What was his condition when he returned home?
   c. What did he do after taking up the challenge to defend his 'honour and manhood'?
   d. Describe his attempt to take on the challenge. Was he successful?
2. *'Some kind of record!' He said proudly to the bone specialist;*
   a. What record did the speaker set?
   b. Whose record was he referring to in the context of his own?
   c. Where did the conversation take place? Describe the place.
   d. What did the speaker dream about afterwards?

Life Skills and Values humour, being a sport

Think and answer.

1. Why do you think Uncle Alfred accepted the challenge readily and even talked about his broken bones with pride after he was injured?
2. Point out a few elements in the poem that make it comic.

Way with Words

IRONY

A. Read these sentences and explain why they are ironic.

1. The car is moving as fast as a bullock cart.
2. Fantastic! Now I have another day's hard work to look forward to.
3. The *Titanic*, which was advertised as the 'unsinkable ship', sank on its first voyage.
4. 'What a palatial room this is!' she exclaimed, looking around at the bare walls.
5. My old dog, Bouncer, is as excitable as a wet carpet.

PROVERBS

Proverbs are short, well-known sayings, which state a general truth or a piece of advice.

This poem illustrates two proverbs.

1. Look before you leap. (You shouldn't do anything without thinking of the consequences.)
2. Fools rush in where angels fear to tread. (Foolish people attempt to do things that wiser people would avoid.)

B. Match the proverbs with their meanings.

Proverb	Meaning
1. Birds of a feather flock together.	a. Things that are offered for free have a hidden cost.
2. It's no use crying over spilt milk.	b. Don't harm the person who helps you.
3. Don't bite the hand that feeds you.	c. People of the same sort are usually found together.
4. Beauty lies in the eye of the beholder.	d. We should not worry about a situation that can't be changed.
5. There's no such thing as a free lunch.	e. What one person finds beautiful might not seem admirable to another.

Grammar in Use

Coordinating and Subordinating Conjunctions

Coordinating conjunctions join two sentences or clauses of equal importance. They are usually single words.

Some common coordinating conjunctions are **and**, **but**, **or**, **for**, **yet**, **neither**, **so** and **still**.

Examples: Uncle Alfred put down his briefcase **and** launched himself.
Uncle Alfred's jump was good **but** he ended up in the hospital.

A. Join these sentences with suitable coordinating conjunctions. One is done for you.

1. He is a bright student. He is extremely nervous.
   He is a bright student, ***but*** *he is extremely nervous.*
2. He wanted to paint the pot red. He did not have red paint. He had to paint the pot green.
3. I was very upset. I kept quiet.
4. Jane is planning a picnic. Mary is planning a picnic.
5. She did not do her job efficiently. She was dismissed.
6. Study hard. You will fail.
7. He came from a poor family. He rose to the top of his profession.
8. I requested for only a day's leave. I was refused.

Conjunctions that connect a main clause with a dependent clause are called **subordinating conjunctions**.

Some common subordinating conjunctions are **while**, **as**, **because**, **since**, **until**, **although**, **even though**, **as soon as** and **so that**.

Examples: **If** you men are so clever, let's see what you can do.
I'll show you **where** I end up.

B. Choose the most appropriate coordinating or subordinating conjunction to complete the sentences.

1. I need to study well __________ (because/so that) I can pass the test.
2. __________ (If/Although) he was the best actor in the group, he did not get the role.
3. They had said the film was good, __________ (since/so) I watched it.
4. He is liked by all because he is kind __________ (or/and) helpful.
5. We will cross the bridge __________ (when/though) we come to it.
6. I don't know __________ (where/as) I can buy new headphones.
7. He cannot come with us, __________ (or/nor) can he reach the venue by himself.

Indefinite Pronouns

We use **indefinite pronouns** to refer to people or things without saying exactly who or what they are.

Examples: **Nobody** took up Auntie Hilda's challenge until Uncle Alfred returned home.
I can't see **anything** when I step outside in this foggy weather.

C. Fill in the blanks with suitable indefinite pronouns.

everyone anyone something everything nobody anything

1. ______________ in the buffet looks delicious.
2. Your milk appears to have ______________ floating on it.
3. The politician didn't say ______________ sensible in his speech.
4. She is a marvellous person. She helped ______________ during the training.
5. I can't recognise ______________ in the photos.
6. ______________ remembered where they had last seen Tommy.

Study Skills

Pronounce Well

You know that in English, we often don't pronounce all the letters in a word.
Examples: **h**onour, s**c**ene, hym**n**, dou**b**t, whis**t**le (the letters in bold are silent in these words)

Write these words in the correct column depending on the silent letter they contain.

debt	symptom	empty	heir	subtle	knell	malign
bristle	rhetoric	moisten	almond	knuckle	campaign	palm

silent b	silent p	silent h	silent t	silent l	silent k	silent g

Listening and Speaking

A. Listen to a passage about a surprising incident and answer the questions.

1. What did Aunt Mithila believe herself to be?
2. What would she try on people?
3. Who was the woman in blue? Where was she going?
4. What was Aunt Mithila's warning to her?
5. What happened a day later?
6. Why do you think the narrator stayed away from Aunt Mithila?

B. Do you think that people who claim to have the power to see into the future are telling the truth? Have a class discussion on the subject.

21ST CENTURY Information Literacy

Pen it Down

Imagine that you are a special correspondent for a daily newspaper. You witnessed Uncle Alfred's 'memorable feat'. Write a news report, describing what happened and trying to find an explanation for Uncle Alfred's act. You should write it as a funny incident, highlighting the absurd behaviour of an ordinary office-goer immediately after Mary Rand's win. Remember to include the reactions of Uncle Alfred, Aunt Hilda and any other person who may have watched the jump. Give your report a catchy headline.

21ST CENTURY Media Literacy

Self Assessment

Now I can

- enjoy a humorous poem about the underlying competitiveness in people.
- learn proverbs, revise coordinating and subordinating conjunctions and use indefinite pronouns.
- participate in a class discussion and write a news report.

Read More

Uncle Podger Hangs a Picture: This story by Jerome K. Jerome recounts the comic commotion that unfolds when fussy but inefficient Uncle Podger decides to hang a picture on the wall.

Dear Examiner: This poem by Gareth Owen is a witty account of a young examinee who, when faced with a difficult examination paper, thinks of an unexpected way to avoid being declared a failure.

12

The Invisible Man

H. G. Wells

Let's Get Started

Read this paragraph on science fiction, its origins, components and famous writers. Fill in the blanks with words from the box.

Arthur C. Clarke	fiction	travel	Frank Herbert	William Gibson	Isaac Asimov
Sci-fi	technology	exploration	life	futuristic	Forrest J. Ackerman

'Science fiction' is a term which was first used in 1958 by ____________. Science fiction or ____________ as it is known, is a genre of ____________ which talks of themes of space ____________, time ____________ and extra terrestrial ____________. This type of writing talks of imaginative and ____________ concepts based on advanced science and ____________. Some famous science fiction works are *Dune* by ____________, *The Foundation* trilogy by ____________, *Neuromancer* by ____________ and *2001: Space Odyssey* by ____________.

Learning and Awareness: Evaluating our assumptions and preconditioning about life and situations around us

Reading

If you were given the power to become invisible, how would you use it?* The Invisible Man *is about a scientist who discovers a way to become invisible. Initially excited about a life free of rules, he quickly realises the difficulties of being invisible. This passage describes his first experience of venturing into the crowded streets of London as an invisible man.

In Oxford Street

In going downstairs the first time, I found an unexpected difficulty because I could not see my feet; I stumbled twice and there was an **unaccustomed** clumsiness in gripping the **bolt**. By not looking down, however, I managed to walk on the level passably well.

My mood, I say, was one of **exaltation**. I felt as a seeing man might do, with padded feet and noiseless clothes, in a city of the blind. I experienced a wild impulse to **jest**, to startle people, to clap men on the back, fling people's hats astray and generally **revel** in my extraordinary advantage.

But hardly had I emerged upon Great Portland Street, when I heard a clashing noise and was hit violently behind, and turning, saw a man carrying a basket of **soda water siphons** and looking in amazement at his burden. Although the blow had really hurt me, I found something so irresistible in his astonishment that I laughed aloud. 'The devil's in the basket,' I said and twisted it out of his hand. He let go of it and I swung the whole weight into the air.

But a fool of a cabman, standing outside a public house, made a sudden rush for it and his extended hand hit me under the ear painfully. I let the basket down with a smash on the cabman. Then, with shouts and the clatter of feet about me, people coming out of shops, vehicles pulling up, I realised what I had done. Cursing my **folly**, I backed against a shop window and prepared to escape the confusion. I pushed the butcher boy, who luckily did not turn to see the nothingness that **shoved** him aside, and dodged behind the cabman's four-wheeler. I hurried straight across the road and hardly seeing which way I went, plunged into the afternoon **throng** of Oxford Street.

unaccustomed: unfamiliar

bolt: a wooden or metal bar used to fasten a door

exaltation: great joy

jest: joke

revel: take great pleasure

soda water siphons: bottles with a device that could be pressed to pour carbonated or soda water

folly: stupidity

shoved: pushed forcefully

throng: crowd

Where did the cabman hit the narrator?

sallied forth: set out

scrape: trouble

Salvation Army: a Christian charitable organisation which has a partly military structure

resonance: echo

gaping: staring

Suddenly, a bright idea came into my head. I ran around and got into the cab. And so, shivering, scared, sniffing with the first intimations of a cold, and with the bruises in the small of my back growing, I rode slowly along Oxford Street and past Tottenham Court Road. My mood was very different from that in which I had **sallied forth** ten minutes ago. This invisibility indeed! The one thought that possessed me was—how was I to get out of the **scrape** I was in.

We crawled past Mudie's and there a tall woman hailed my cab, and I sprang out just in time to escape her. I headed to Bloomsbury Square, intending to strike north past the Museum and get into the quiet district. At the northward corner of the square, a little white dog ran out of the Pharmaceutical Society's offices and made for me, nose down.

I had never realised it before, but the nose is to the mind of a dog what the eye is to the mind of a seeing man. The brute began barking and leaping, showing clearly that he was aware of me. I crossed Great Russell Street, glancing over my shoulder, and went some way ahead before I realised what I was running towards.

I heard a blare of music and looking along the street saw a number of people coming out of Russell Square, and the banner of the **Salvation Army** in front. Such a crowd I could not hope to go through. Deciding on the spur of the moment, I ran up the white steps of a house facing the museum railings and stood there until the crowd passed. Happily, the dog stopped at the noise of the band too, hesitated and turned tail.

On came the band. Thud, thud, thud, came the drum with a vibrating **resonance** and for the moment I did not notice two urchins stopping at the railings by me.

'See 'em,' said one. 'See what?' said the other. 'Why—them footmarks—bare. Like what you makes in mud.'

I looked down and saw the youngsters had stopped and were **gaping** at the muddy footmarks I had left behind on the newly whitened steps. 'There's a barefoot man gone up them steps,' said one. 'And he ain't never come down again. And his foot was bleeding.'

The thick of the crowd had already passed. 'Looky there, Ted,' said the younger of the detectives, with the sharpness of surprise in his voice, and pointed straight to my feet. I looked down and saw at once the hint of their outline sketched in splashes of mud. For a moment I was paralysed.

What did the urchins observe in the snow?

'Why, it's just like the ghost of a foot, ain't it?' exclaimed the elder. He hesitated and advanced with outstretched hand. In another moment, he would have touched me. I took a step, the boy started back with an exclamation and with a rapid movement I swung myself over into the porch of the next house. But the smaller boy was sharp-eyed enough to follow the movement. He was shouting out that the feet had gone over the wall.

eddy: (here) disturbance
interrogation: questioning
unaccountable: unexplained

They rushed round and saw my new footmarks flash into being on the lower step and upon the pavement. 'What's up?' asked someone. 'Feet! Look! Feet running!' There was an **eddy** of surprise and **interrogation**. In another moment I was rushing headlong round the circuit of Russell Square, with six or seven astonished people following my footmarks.

How many people started following the narrator's footmarks?

My back had now become very stiff and sore, my tonsils were painful from the cabman's fingers and the skin of my neck had been scratched by his nails; and I was lame from a little cut on one foot. I saw in time a blind man approaching me, and fled limping, for I feared his subtle intuitions. Once or twice accidental collisions occurred and I left people amazed, with **unaccountable** curses ringing in their ears. Across the square, a thin veil of slowly falling flakes of snow was coming down. I had caught a cold and I could not avoid an occasional sneeze. And every dog that came in sight, with its pointing nose and curious sniffing, was a terror to me.

Then came men and boys running, shouting as they ran. It was a fire. They ran in the direction of my lodging, and looking back down a street I saw a mass of black smoke streaming up above the roofs and telephone wires. It was my lodging burning; my clothes, my apparatus, all my resources indeed. I had burnt my boats—if ever a man did! The place was blazing.

The Invisible Man paused and thought. Kemp glanced nervously out of the window. 'Yes?' he said. 'Go on.'

Wordwise

'Burning one's boats' means a commitment to a course of action that cannot be changed. It may have originated from the Spanish conquest of Mexico in 1519, when the commander, Hernán Cortés, ordered his ships to be sunk (mistakenly referred to as 'burning' in a later account) to stop his soldiers from deserting.

About the author

H.G. Wells (1866–1946) is considered to be the father of modern science fiction. Though trained as a scientist, he also wrote on history and politics and was outspoken about social inequality and the prevention of war. His novels describe a future, many of whose aspects are a reality today.

Comprehension

Quick Recap

A. Answer the questions in a few lines.

1. Why did the Invisible Man find it difficult to go downstairs?
2. What was the first mishap that he had to deal with?
3. What bright idea came into his head as a way of escaping his situation?
4. Name the various London streets and buildings mentioned in the story.
5. Make a list of the people and creatures the Invisible Man runs away from in the course of the story.

B. Answer the questions with reference to context.

1. *My mood, I say, was one of exaltation. I felt as a seeing man might do, with padded feet and noiseless clothes, in a city of the blind.*
   a. Who is the speaker in these lines? Who is he speaking to?
   b. Why was the speaker in a mood of exaltation?
   c. What did he want to do at that moment?
   d. Explain the line, 'I felt ... blind' in your own words.
2. *At the northward corner of the Square, a little white dog ran out of the Pharmaceutical Society's offices and made for me, nose down.*
   a. Where was the speaker when he saw the dog?
   b. How did the dog behave? Why was it an issue for the speaker?
   c. What problem did the speaker face next?
   d. How was the speaker's mood different from the way it was at the beginning of the passage?
3. *'There's a barefoot man gone up them steps,' said one. 'And he ain't never come down again. And his foot was bleeding.'*
   a. Who is the speaker in these lines? Who is he talking about?
   b. What did the speaker see, to make him say these lines? What made him conclude that 'he' had not come down the stairs?
   c. What did the speaker draw his friend's attention to next?
   d. How was 'he' close to being found out by the speaker and his friend? What did 'he' do to escape them?

4. *I had burnt my boats—if ever a man did!*
   a. Explain these lines.
   b. What did the speaker see that made him say these words?
   c. Describe the physical and mental condition of the speaker at that time.

Life Skills and Values pursuit of science, pitfalls of being overambitious

Think and answer.

1. The Invisible Man thinks that invisibility would free him from rules. Do you agree? Give reasons for your answer.
2. The Invisible Man loses everything by the end of the passage, including his scientific equipment. Do you feel sympathy for his fate? Why/Why not?

HC Understanding what knowing entails

Way with Words

Figurative Language

Figurative language is the use of words in an imaginative way to state more than bare facts.

Example: We **crawled** past Mudie's. Here, 'to crawl' means 'to move very slowly'.

A. Explain these phrases from the story, with reference to the words in bold.

1. **intimations** of a cold
2. **ghost** of a foot
3. **eddy** of surprise and interrogation
4. a thin **veil** of slowly falling flakes of snow
5. the **nothingness** that shoved him aside
6. **strike** north
7. **plunged** into the afternoon throng

Nominalisation

Nominalisation is the formation of nouns from verbs and adjectives.

Example: revolve → revolution

B. Rewrite these sentences by converting the words in bold into nouns. One is done for you.

1. The Earth **revolves** around the Sun. This creates the seasons.
   *The **revolution** of the Earth around the Sun creates the seasons.*
2. The man looked at the boy, **amazed** by his skill with the football.

3. Not looking which way he was going, Rajesh **collided** with a moving vehicle.
4. The policemen decided to **interrogate** the thief in his own house.
5. Kemp was **nervous** about the Invisible Man's presence in his home.
6. Kishori did not **hesitate** to ask for a promotion.

Grammar in Use

Present and Past Participles

You have studied finite and non-finite verbs in an earlier chapter. Participles are a type of non-finite verbs.

Present participles are formed by adding *-ing* to the base form of the verbs. They refer to incomplete actions or states of being.

Examples: I felt as a **seeing** man might do, in a city of the blind.
Lila watched the **smiling** baby in its mother's lap.

Past participles are formed by adding *-ed*, *-en*, *-d*, *-t* or *-n* to the base form of the verbs. They refer to actions that have been completed in the past but whose effects are still present.

Examples: His **extended** hand hit me under the ear painfully.
Tired after a hard day's work, the man lay down on the bed.

A. Complete the sentences with the participle form of the given verbs. State the type of participle being used.

1. ______________ children need adequate nourishment. (grow)
2. His announcement was greeted with ______________ expressions all around. (shock)
3. The ______________ trekkers were glad to reach the base camp. (exhaust)
4. I just finished a ______________ book on Alexander the Great. (fascinate)
5. We sat by a clear pool with ______________ water. (sparkle)
6. The ______________ puppy needs to be taken for a walk. (whine)
7. The ______________ chair needs to be repaired soon. (break)

Active and Passive Voice

You know that in a sentence which is in the **active voice**, the subject is the doer of the action.
Example: **A tall woman** *hailed* my cab. (Here, **a tall woman**, the subject, is the doer of the action.)

In a sentence which is in the **passive voice**, the subject is acted upon.
Example: **My cab** *was hailed* by a tall woman. (Here, the subject, **my cab**, is the thing on which the action is done.)

Remember that only the sentences which have an object can be changed to passive.

Look at the changes that take place when a sentence is changed from the active to the passive voice.

Active to passive

- If the doer of the action is implied, understood or unknown, it is not mentioned in the passive sentence.
- We add *by* before the doer of the action, which was the subject earlier.
- Sometimes, the personal pronoun also changes its form in the passive.
- We use the verb *be* and the past participle form of the verb.

B. Change the voice in these sentences, without altering their meaning.

1. The bad wolf was chased away by the sheep dog.
2. Who broke this vase?
3. Excessive rains might destroy the harvest this year.
4. By whom are you taught karate?
5. The press photographers crowded the entrance to the theatre.
6. Violence against women should be stopped.
7. The mansion was decorated with streamers.
8. They believe that God exists.
9. Who created this work of art?

Study Skills

Use Your Dictionary

You know that dictionaries, in addition to word meanings, also provide information about pronunciation, parts of speech and examples explaining word usage. Advanced dictionaries also give grammatical information, which includes if the word is singular or plural, and degrees of comparison.

Look at the dictionary entry for the word 'blind'.

headword — part of speech — pronunciation

blind[2]/blaind/***noun***

a piece of cloth or other material that you can pull down over a window to cover it: — meaning

Susan pulled the blinds up to let the bright sunlight into the room. — example sentence

A. Find the entry for the word exaltation in an advanced dictionary and write the following details about the word.

- headword
- meaning
- pronunciation
- part of speech
- example sentence

B. Make up a fictional word, and create a dictionary entry for it.

Listening and Speaking

Listen to a conversation about a lady requesting another person for help. Then, in pairs, enact a conversation where the Invisible Man asks Kemp for help.

You can use these phrases in your conversation:

- I'd be very grateful if …
- If it is not too much trouble …
- I have another favour to ask of you …

Pen it Down

Do you think science is a blessing or a curse? Can you think of any advances in science that could have been helpful for people, but were used in harmful ways?

Research and write an essay on the topic, giving examples of scientific discoveries and advances that were beneficial as well as those that were harmful for people.

Self Assessment

Now I can

- read a story about how science can be both a blessing and a curse.
- enjoy the use of suspense in the story.
- learn about figurative language, use present and past participles, and revise active and passive voice.
- converse on a given topic and research and write an essay.

Read More

The Time Machine: This classic novel by H. G. Wells describes the adventures of a man who invents a time machine and travels to the future. There, he sees Earth in various stages of degeneration, including a time period in which human beings have become divided into the lazy Eloi and the brutish Morlocks.

The War of the Worlds: This novel, also by Wells, narrates the story of an invasion of Earth by Martians. Armed with 'Heat Rays' and three-legged fighting machines, they lay Victorian London and its surrounding areas to waste before succumbing to germs, against which they had no immunity.

Research and Write

A. 'Grannie', 'Grandpa Learns to Read and Write' and 'Uncle Alfred's Long Jump' are about relatives in the immediate or extended family.

Draw your own family tree, tracing your roots as far back as possible. You can ask your parents or relatives for help. Add photographs of your family. Share your tree with the class.

ART INTEGRATION

B. 'Dar es Salaam to Nairobi by Ford Prefect' celebrates the spirit of exploration and adventure.

1. Look at the words below that we use to describe places. Match them with their meanings.

tranquil	bustling	isolated	breathtaking
picturesque	ancient	cosmopolitan	far-flung

a. extremely beautiful or exciting
b. remote and distant
c. historic and old
d. a mix of cultures
e. pretty, striking and vivid
f. calm and peaceful
g. fast paced and hectic
h. uninhabited

2. How well do you know the city you live in? Work with a partner, and make an information chart on your city.

You can research and write about these points:

- the sights and sounds of your city
- the important buildings, famous landmarks and modes of transport
- the variety of food that is available
- the different types of people who stay here, and their festivals
- what sets your city apart from others

You can also add photographs to highlight the different points.

C. 'The Invisible Man' is a science fiction story. Write a review of a science fiction film that you have seen recently. Rate the performance by the actors and comment on the director's handling of the script. Discuss the use of special effects, the action sequences, music and other technical elements.

Keep the following points in mind for your review:

- Support every point with an example.
- Analyse the story and characters. (Was the plot realistic? Were the characters believable?)
- Could anything have been done to make the film better?

Remember not to give away the key elements of the plot!

13

Art and Culture

The Model Millionaire

Oscar Wilde

Let's Get Started

Match the following pictures with the artists. The brief information given on the artists will help you answer correctly.

1. 
2. 
3. 

a. **Manjit Bawa**: This artist's subjects include figures of deities, animals and nature. His art upholds the idea of co-existence between man and animals.

b. **Nandalal Bose**: This artist was known for his 'Indian style' of paintings. He painted scenes from Indian mythologies, women, and village life, often using European and Japanese artistic techniques.

c. **Amrita Sher-Gil**: This artist used intense colours to vividly portray the many moods and occupations of the daily life of Indian women in the 1930s.

Now, choose any one of these three artists and find out how their work reflected their life and experiences. Work in groups and share your findings with the class.

HC **Feelings:** Participating in society and helping in maintaining systems

Reading

Have you ever helped someone without expecting anything in return? Read this story about a young man who offers alms to a beggar out of pity. His act of kindness is richly rewarded and changes his life.

Unless one is wealthy, it is no use being a charming fellow. Love is the **privilege** of the rich and not for the unemployed. The poor should be practical. These are the great truths of modern life which Hughie Erskine never realised.

Poor Hughie! He never said an ill-natured thing in his life. He was good-looking with crisp brown hair, a clear-cut face and grey eyes. He was popular and had every ability except that of making money.

His father had left him nothing more than his sword and a *History of the Peninsular War* in fifteen volumes. Hughie lived on £200 a year that an old aunt allowed him. He had tried everything to earn money. He had gone on the **Stock Exchange** for six months. He had been a tea merchant for a little longer. Ultimately, he became nothing more than a delightful, useless young man with a perfect face and no profession.[1]

But he was in love. The girl he loved was Laura Merton, the daughter of a retired Colonel. They were the most handsome couple in London and had not a penny between them. The Colonel would not hear of any engagement.

'Come to me, my boy, when you have £10,000 of your own and we will see about it,' he used to say. Hughie looked very glum on those days.

One morning, he dropped in to see his friend, Alan Trevor, a painter. He was a rough fellow with a **freckled** face and a red **ragged** beard. However, when he took up the brush, he was a real master and his pictures were in great demand. He liked Hughie as much for his **buoyant** spirits as his generous **reckless** nature.

What had Hughie's father left him?

When Hughie came in, he found Trevor putting the finishing touches to a life-size portrait of a beggar. The beggar himself was standing on a

privilege: a special right

Stock Exchange: a place where shares in companies are bought and sold

freckled: having small, brownish spots on the skin, caused by the sun

ragged: rough and uneven

buoyant: cheerful and optimistic

reckless: not worrying about the consequences of one's actions

Literary term

1. This is an **euphemism**. It is an indirect way of saying that Hughie was unemployed.

raised platform in a corner of the studio. He was an old man with a face like wrinkled **parchment** and a **piteous** expression. Over his shoulders was a **tattered**, coarse brown cloak and his thick boots were patched. With one hand he leant on a rough stick, while with the other he held out his battered hat for alms.

'What an amazing model!' whispered Hughie, as he shook hands with his friend.

'I should think so!' shouted Trevor at the top of his voice, 'Such beggars are not to be met with every day. My stars! What an **etching** Rembrandt would have made of him!'

'How miserable he looks!' said Hughie, 'But I suppose, to you painters, his face is his fortune?'

'Certainly,' replied Trevor, 'you don't want a beggar to look happy, do you?'

'How much does a model get for sitting?' asked Hughie.

'A shilling an hour.'

'And how much do you get for your picture, Alan?'

'Oh, for this I get two thousand guineas.'

'Well, I think the model should have a percentage,' cried Hughie, 'they work quite as hard as you do.'

'Nonsense! Why, look at the trouble of laying on the paint alone, and standing all day long at one's easel! It's all very well, Hughie, for you to talk, but there are moments when Art is almost like manual labour. But you mustn't chatter; I'm very busy.'

After some time, the servant came in and told Trevor that the frame-maker wanted to speak to him.

The old beggar sat down to rest for a moment on a wooden bench behind him. He looked so lonely and wretched that Hughie could not help pitying him. He felt in his pockets to see what money he had. All he could find was a sovereign and some coppers. 'He wants it more than I do,' he thought to himself, 'but it means no **hansoms** for a fortnight.'

He walked across the studio and slipped the sovereign into the beggar's hand.

The old man **started** and smiled faintly. 'Thank you, sir,' he said, 'thank you.'

parchment: a type of stiff paper

piteous: causing one to feel pity

tattered: torn and in poor condition

etching: a picture printed using a metal plate that has the image cut into it

hansoms: horse-drawn carriages

started: moved suddenly out of surprise

How much did a model get for sitting?

Did You Know? **History**

Rembrandt was a 17th-century Dutch painter, considered one of the greatest in Europe. He was best known for his portraits and scenes from *The Bible*. He experimented with the use of light and shadow in his paintings.

Wordwise

The word **'sovereign'** usually means a supreme ruler or monarch. In the story, it refers to a British gold coin that was in use at the time. It equals one pound.

Then Trevor arrived and Hughie took his leave.

That night, he strolled into the Palette Club about eleven o'clock and found Trevor sitting by himself.

'Well, Alan, did you get the picture finished?' he asked.

'Finished and framed!' answered Trevor; 'By the by, that old model you saw is quite devoted to you. I had to tell him all about you—who you are, where you live, what your income is—'

'Alan,' cried Hughie, 'I shall probably find him waiting for me when I go home. But the poor wretch! I wish I could do something for him. I have heaps of old clothes at home—do you think he would want any of them? His rags were falling to bits.'

'But he looks splendid in them,' said Trevor. 'I wouldn't paint him in a frock coat for anything. However, I'll tell him of your offer.'

sulkily: in a bad-tempered way

'Alan,' said Hughie, 'you painters are a heartless lot.'

'Our business is to show the world as we see it, not to make it better,' replied Trevor, 'And now tell me how Laura is. The old model wanted to know about her.'

What private affairs of Hughie had Alan discussed with the beggar?

'You talked to him about her?' said Hughie.

'Certainly I did. He knows all about the colonel, the lovely Laura and the £10,000.'

'You told that old beggar all my private affairs?' cried Hughie, looking very angry.

'My dear boy,' said Trevor, smiling, 'that old beggar, as you call him, is one of the richest men in Europe. He could buy all London tomorrow. He has a house in every capital and dines off gold plates.'

'What on earth do you mean?' exclaimed Hughie.

'The old man was Baron Hausberg,' said Trevor, 'He is a great friend of mine and asked me to paint him as a beggar. It's a millionaire's fantasy! I must say he made a magnificent figure in his rags, or rather, my rags—they are an old suit I got in Spain.'

'Baron Hausberg!' cried Hughie in dismay. 'Good heavens! I gave him a sovereign!'

Trevor burst into a roar of laughter.

'You might have told me,' said Hughie **sulkily**, 'and not let me make such a fool of myself.'

'Well, to begin with,' said Trevor, 'it never entered my mind that you went about distributing alms in that reckless way. Besides, I didn't know whether Hausberg would like his name mentioned.'

Literary term

2. This is a **pun** on the word, 'model'. In the first instance, it refers to a person who is hired to be painted or photographed. In the second, it means someone who is considered the best example of something.

What was written on the envelope?

'What a fool he must think me!' said Hughie.

He walked home that evening, feeling very unhappy and leaving Alan Trevor in fits of laughter.

The next morning, an old gentleman came to Hughie's house. 'I have come from Baron Hausberg,' he said.

'Please offer him my sincerest apologies,' stammered Hughie.

'The Baron,' said the gentleman, with a smile, 'has sent this letter.' He handed Hughie a sealed envelope.

On the outside was written, 'A wedding present to Hugh Erskine and Laura Merton, from an old beggar'. Inside was a cheque for £10,000.

When Hughie and Laura were married, Alan Trevor was the best-man, and the Baron made a speech at the wedding breakfast.

'Millionaire models,' remarked Alan, 'are rare enough; but model[2] millionaires are rarer still!'

About the author

Oscar Wilde (1854–1900) was an Irish author, dramatist and essayist. The novel, *The Picture of Dorian Grey* and the play, *The Importance of being Earnest* are among his most famous works. He also wrote several short stories for children, like 'The Selfish Giant' and 'The Nightingale and the Prince', which are popular even today.

Comprehension

Quick Recap

A. Answer the questions with reference to context.

1. *'Come to me, my boy, when you have £10,000 of your own, and we will see about it'.*
   a. Who said these words and to whom?
   b. What does 'it' refer to?
   c. Why did the 'boy' need to have £10,000?

2. *'How miserable he looks!' said Hughie, 'But I suppose, to you painters, his face is his fortune?'*
   a. Who is being referred to in these lines? Describe his appearance.
   b. Why was his face his fortune?
   c. Who was Hughie speaking to? What was this person doing at the time?
   d. What was his reply to Hughie's question?

3. *'You might have told me,' said Hughie sulkily, 'and not let me make such a fool of myself.'*
   a. Who is Hughie speaking to?
   b. What had this person just told him?
   c. Why did Hughie feel that he had made a fool of himself?

B. Answer the questions.

1. Who was Hughie Erskine? What were the 'great truths of modern life' that he never understood?
2. How had Hughie tried to earn money?
3. How did Alan Trevor's appearance contrast with his work as a painter?
4. What did Hughie do when he saw the beggar? What was the latter's reaction?
5. How did Hughie want to help the beggar further?
6. Point out a simile in the story and explain it.
7. Explain the line,'Millionaire models are rare enough; but model millionaires are rarer still!'

Life Skills and Values — kindness, reduced inequalities

Think and answer.

1. Hughie suggests that models must get a percentage of the earnings of the painter. What does it say about the kind of person he is?
2. Does the proverb 'appearances can be deceptive' apply to this story? Give reasons for your answer.
3. Do you agree that Baron Hausberg was a 'model millionaire'? Explain your answer.

HC **Feelings:** generosity

Way with Words

A. Complete the sentences with these words from the story. Change the form where necessary.

strolled	stammered	devoted	battered	patched

1. The raindrops ________________ the tin roof of the shack.
2. My father goes for a ________________ in the park after dinner.
3. There are blue ________________ on your shirt where the colour has run.
4. The ________________ dog wouldn't leave her master's bedside throughout his illness.
5. Renu was so nervous during the oral exam that she began to ________________, even though she knew the answer.

B. Write the antonyms of these words from the story.

1. charming 2. private 3. coarse

4. old-fashioned 5. generous 6. manual
7. crisp 8. raised 9. sincere

Look at this sentence from the story.

Ultimately, he became nothing more than a delightful, useless young man with a **perfect** face and no profession.

C. The word perfect has various meanings. Match the following meanings with the usage of the word in these sentences.

free of mistakes	exact and accurate	of excellent quality
making something as good as possible	the best of its kind	

1. This painting is a perfect example of Rembrandt's style.
2. He was busy perfecting his bowling technique before the team selections began.
3. You have to make perfect copies of these documents before you submit them at the office.
4. The perfect crime is where the criminal is never discovered.
5. The kebabs are perfect; they are neither too soft nor too spicy.

Grammar in Use

Modals

Modals or modal verbs are a type of auxiliary or helping verbs.

Depending on the context, they express the following: necessity, ability, possibility, advice, permission, suggestion, future action and request.

The most commonly used modals are **can**, **could**, **may**, **might**, **will**, **ought to**, **shall**, **should**, **must**, **need**.

Examples:

1. We **must** brush our teeth daily. (necessity)
2. I **can** play the piano. (ability)
3. I **may** eat that ice cream at night. (possibility)
4. You **should** always be punctual about school timings. (advice)
5. **May** I have another slice of cake? (seeking permission)
6. You **may** have another slice of cake. (giving permission)
7. **Could** you please hand me the serving spoons? (request)
8. Heena **will** travel abroad next year. (future action)

A. Write what the modals in these sentences express. One is done for you.

1. The roads are unsafe. You must drive carefully. *advice*
2. Can you explain the problem to me?

3. May I have some water, please?
4. We might go to Sikkim for the summer holidays.
5. You may have to meet the teacher before leaving.
6. I will finish my syllabus on time this year.
7. Could you pick your sister up from the crèche on your way home?
8. We can overcome any hurdle if we have faith.

TRANSFORMATION OF SENTENCES USING *IF* AND *UNLESS*

The words **if** and **unless** are used to suggest that a condition must be met for something to happen. The clause with **if** or **unless** is the subordinate clause and includes the condition, while the main clause includes the result of the condition. With **if**, the main clause is always positive, and with **unless**, it is always negative.

Examples: **Unless** one is wealthy, it is no use being a charming fellow.
The food won't cook **if** you don't stir it from time to time.

Notice that in sentences with **if** and **unless**, we use the present tense to talk about something that will happen in the future.

Examples: **If** Hughie has the money, he can marry Laura.
Hughie cannot marry Laura **unless** he has the money.

B. Rewrite the following sentences according to the instructions. Be careful not to change the meaning.

1. If you love the subject, you should take it up for further studies. (Begin: Unless...)
2. Unless you try out the dress, you will never know if it fits you. (Begin: If...)
3. Don't make a promise if you do not intend to keep it. (Begin: Make...)
4. Harry won't fight Voldemort unless he is forced to. (Begin: If...)
5. The brook will run dry if you do not heed the warning. (Begin: Unless...)
6. If you know the truth, speak up. (Begin: Unless...)
7. Unless we insist, they will not keep the area clean. (Begin: If...)

Study Skills

Pronounce Well

The letter **g** has several different pronunciations depending on the letters that come after it. Look at the various pronunciations.

1. with a hard **g**. **Examples:** grand, figure
2. with a soft **g** or **/j/** sound. **Examples:** page, giraffe
3. **g** is silent when followed by certain consonants. **Examples:** high, foreign

Write the following words in the correct columns depending on the pronunciation of the letter g.

legal	privilege	design	growth	barrage	gentle
delightful	begin	sign	weight	Hausberg	apologies

soft g	hard g	silent g

Listening and Speaking

In the story, when Hughie Erskine realises that he had given a sovereign to a millionaire, he exclaims, 'Good Heavens!' in surprise.

Listen to some conversations where people express their astonishment. Then, in pairs, enact an imaginary conversation between Hughie Erskine and Laura Merton when he tells her about mistakenly giving alms to Baron Hausberg and the latter's generous gift to him.

You can use the following phrases in your conversation:

- I don't believe it!
- Are you serious?
- That's amazing/ extraordinary!
- You don't say!
- Who would have thought?

Pen it Down

Imagine you are a millionaire. Write a diary entry describing a typical day in your life.

You can include the following points in your entry:

- personal butler to attend to all needs
- day spent in business meetings
- attending a charitable event to donate a large sum of money
- day ends with taking a flight to a foreign country to finalise a business agreement

Self Assessment

Now I can

- read and understand a story about how kindness can bring unexpected rewards.
- use antonyms, understand the usage of modals and practise transformation of sentences using *if* and *unless*.
- practise conversations on expressing surprise and write a diary entry.

Read More

The Canterville Ghost: This humorous story by Oscar Wilde is about a ghost who finds it impossible to frighten an American family that moves into a haunted mansion once owned by him.

The Nightingale and the Rose: This story, also by Wilde, is about a nightingale who gives up its life to create a red rose for a young man. He gives it to his professor's daughter but when she rejects him, he throws the rose away, unable to understand its value.

14

The Human Seasons

John Keats

Let's Get Started

A. What are the different stages in the life of a person?

Collect pictures from your family album to create a sequence of your life from the time you were a baby till now. You may even choose the photos of a parent tracing the different stages of their lives.

Share this sequence with your class, discussing your experiences while creating this unique project.

B. Which is your favourite season? Collect images of your favourite season and list the features that you like the most about it. Does this season remind you of any stage in the life of man? Discuss your findings with the class.

HC **Active Participation:** Exploring complementarity among the various entities in nature

Reading

Which stage in life do you think is the most enjoyable? Read a poem that suggests that

human life has four distinct phases or seasons. Each phase has its unique value.

Four seasons fill the **measure** of the year;
There are four seasons in the mind of man:
He has his **lusty** spring,[1] when **fancy** clear
Takes in all beauty with an easy span:
He has his summer, when luxuriously
Spring's honeyed cud of youthful thought he loves
To **ruminate**, and by such dreaming high
Is nearest unto heaven: quiet **coves**
His soul has in its autumn, when his wings
He **furleth** close; contented so to look
On mists in idleness—to let fair things
Pass by unheeded as a threshold brook.
He has his winter too of pale **misfeature**,
Or else he would forego his **mortal** nature.

measure: capacity or extent
lusty: vigorous, robust
fancy: imagination
ruminate: think seriously
coves: sheltered places
furleth: furled or rolled up
misfeature: becoming misshapen
mortal: subject to death

Literary term

1. This is a **metaphor**. Spring is imagined as an energetic young man.

About the poet

John Keats (1795–1821) was an English Romantic poet. His poetry is known for its vivid imagery and for celebrating the beauty of nature and the human mind. His best-known poems are 'Ode to a Nightingale', 'To Autumn' and 'Ode on a Grecian Urn'. He died of tuberculosis at the young age of twenty-five.

What are the four seasons in a year compared with?

Comprehension

Quick Recap

A. Answer the questions in a few lines.

1. How much is the measure of a year?
2. What does man do in his 'spring'?
3. What is every person's mortal nature?

B. Answer the questions with reference to context.

1. *He has his summer, when luxuriously*
   Spring's honeyed cud of youthful thought he loves
   a. Who is being referred to as 'he' in these lines?
   b. What happens when he has his summer?
   c. Why are his youthful thoughts referred to as 'honeyed cud'? What figure of speech is it?

2. *His soul has in its autumn, when his wings*
   He furleth close; contented so to look
   On mists in idleness
   a. Why does he close his wings in autumn? What is he being compared to here?
   b. What does he do in autumn?
   c. What is he happy to ignore at this stage of his life?

3. *He has his winter, too of pale misfeature,*
   Or else he would forego his mortal nature.
   a. What does 'pale misfeature' mean?
   b. Which stage of his life does 'winter' refer to?
   c. Why would he 'forego his mortal nature' if his life did not have a 'winter'?

Life Skills and Values appreciating stages of life, understanding Nature

Think and answer.

1. How are the different stages in the life of a human being similar to the seasons?
2. Explain the imagery associated with each season. Mention the adjectives used by the poet to describe each of them.
3. Do you think it is important to experience each of the four seasons of life? Give reasons for your answer.
4. Suggest another title for the poem and explain your choice.

Way with Words

Idioms Related to Nature

We often use words related to nature in a figurative way.

Examples: He **breezed in** and sat down for dinner, forgetting that his parents had been waiting for him for a long time. (moved in a cheerful and confident way)
Her **breezy** manner charmed everyone. (pleasant)

A. Choose the correct meaning of the underlined idioms.

1. The little girl was a ray of sunshine to her ailing grandmother.
   a. She brought joy and happiness.
   b. She was quick and energetic.
   c. She was noisy and troublesome.

2. For Tamojoy, deciding whether to study science or commerce was like being caught between a rock and a hard place.
   a. The decision upset and overwhelmed him.
   b. He had to choose between two equally difficult options.
   c. He did not know which option was good and which was bad.
3. Sarah often makes a mountain out of a molehill and gets people's attention.
   a. She invents a problem. b. She pretends to be ill.
   c. She makes a problem seem bigger than it is.
4. If you have faith in yourself, you can weather any storm.
   a. You can overcome any problem. b. You can find a solution.
   c. You can help others around you.
5. Sachin's was the lone voice in the wilderness when he tried to bring about changes in the way the company was being run.
   a. He was the only person expressing a particular opinion, which people understood later to be correct.
   b. He expressed an unpopular opinion. c. He created an unpleasant situation.

WORD MEANINGS

B. Write the meaning of these words from the poem, as they have been used in the following sentences.

1. The cow **ruminated** quietly in its shed.
2. You must **season** the food well before serving.
3. He wore a **fancy** tie with a design of the world map across it.
4. We must take strict **measures** to stop thefts in our locality.

Grammar in Use

MAIN AND SUBORDINATE CLAUSES

You know that a **clause** is a group of words that forms part of a sentence and has a finite verb in it.

Example: His soul has in its autumn, when his wings/He furleth close

In this sentence, 'His soul has in its autumn' is the main clause because it can stand on its own in the sentence. It has a subject (**His soul**) and a finite verb (**has**).

The clause 'when his wings/He furleth close' is the dependent or subordinate clause because it does not make complete sense by itself and relies on the main clause for meaning.

A **main clause** has a subject and a finite verb and makes complete sense by itself.
A **subordinate clause** also has a finite verb and a subject. However, it depends on the main clause for its meaning, and provides more information about the main clause.

Underline the main clause and circle the subordinate clause in each sentence.

1. That he will be elected is a known fact.
2. This is the house that Jack built.
3. The audience wondered what was being said on stage.
4. The school, which is near my house, is being whitewashed.
5. I want to reach home before it gets too hot.
6. I exercise every day so that I stay fit.
7. She ran as if she had seen a ghost.
8. Mary had a little lamb whose fleece was white as snow.

Study Skills

Pronounce Well

In English, the letters **th** can be pronounced in three different ways.

1. With a soft **th**. **Examples:** thank, thought, thigh
2. With a hard **th**. **Examples:** therefore, together, though
3. With the **/t/** sound. **Examples:** Thailand, Thames

A. Say these sentences aloud. Circle the hard th- words, underline the soft th- words and tick those with a /t/ sound.

1. After many weeks, my mother and my thirteen cousins went out in the thawing snow. They bought the groceries, but forgot the thyme.
2. The athlete and the author talked about the marathon at great length and then went their separate ways.
3. Thomas' maths test went badly. He has to rethink his strategy for the biology theory paper.

You must have noticed that we pronounce the letter **c** at the beginning of words in two ways.

1. With a /**k**/ sound. **Examples:** cart, caution, carbon
2. With an /**s**/ sound. **Examples:** cereal, certainty, cellar

B. Write the following words in the correct columns.

caterpillar, cycle, cacophony, cease, comedy, cinema, cosmetic, cedar

/k/ sound	/s/ sound

Listening and Speaking

You have learnt that the tone of speech often decides the meaning of a sentence. Intonation or the rise and fall in speech has two main patterns: **falling intonation** and **rising intonation.**

Read the following sentences aloud.

1. When does the movie <u>fin</u>ish? (↓)
2. Are you <u>hung</u>ry? (↑)

In the first sentence, the voice falls on the stressed syllable in the last word. This is falling intonation. It is often used with **wh-** questions, commands and statements.

In the second sentence, the voice rises at the end of a sentence. This is rising intonation. It is common in **yes/no** questions.

In poetry, as in everyday speech, we use rising and falling intonation.

Listen to the first two stanzas of William Wordsworth's poem, 'Daffodils' and do the following.

1. Underline the stressed syllables.

2. Mark the words that have rising intonation with an upward arrow (↑) and those that show falling intonation with a downward arrow (↓). The first two lines are done for you.

I <u>wand</u>er'd <u>lone</u>ly as a <u>cloud</u> (↓)
That <u>floats</u> on <u>high</u> o'er <u>vales</u> and <u>hills</u>, (↓)
When all at once I saw a crowd,
A host of golden daffodils,
Beside the lake, beneath the trees
Fluttering and dancing in the breeze.

Continuous as the stars that shine
And twinkle on the milky way,
They stretch'd in never-ending line
Along the margin of a bay:
Ten thousand saw I at a glance
Tossing their heads in sprightly dance.

Pen it Down

In Keats' poem, life has been compared to the four seasons. Write a short poem explaining life through another symbol or metaphor. You could think of life as a painting, a journey or a garden to be cultivated.

21ST CENTURY Creativity

Self Assessment

Now I can

- understand the parallels between the four seasons and the four stages of human life.
- identify idioms related to nature, and understand the differences between main and subordinate clauses.
- differentiate between rising and falling intonation and write a poem on a given topic.

Read More

The Seven Ages of Man: This excerpt from William Shakespeare's play, *As You Like It*, compares human life to a play in which people are the actors. It talks about the seven ages of man's life, each having its own distinct features.

Dreams: This poem by Langston Hughes asks people to hold on to their dreams. He goes on to compare a life without dreams to a broken-winged bird that cannot fly.

short story

15 Miss Smith and the Black Pearl

Maureen Lee

Let's Get Started

SUSTAINABLE DEVELOPMENT GOALS — REDUCED INEQUALITIES

ART INTEGRATION

The United Nations Sustainable Development Goal 10 discusses how people migrate to places where they can safely pursue opportunities together.

Read this passage about a unique migration movement that transformed an entire community. Fill in the blanks with the words from the box.

slavery	discrimination	cultural	community	instilled	intellectuals	vehicle	jazz

From the 1920 to the 1940s, the Harlem Renaissance was an important ____________ period for the African American ____________. Harlem, a New York City neighbourhood, became the centre of activity for black artists, musicians, ____________ and writers. They had migrated from various parts of America to seek a new identity free from ____________ and poverty. Through their work, they expressed pride in their racial identity and spoke against prejudice and ____________ based on race. The Harlem Renaissance included poetry and prose, painting and sculpture, ____________ and swing, opera and dance. The movement ____________ in African Americans a new spirit of self-determination and provided a foundation for the Civil Rights Movement of the 1950s and 1960s. In doing so, it validated the belief that art could be a ____________ to improve the lives of the discriminated.

HC **Feelings:** Recognizing feelings and values: guidance and care

Reading

Do you think that talent is God-given? Or, does it need to be perfected through hard work?

Read a story about a poor boy with an exceptional gift and a teacher who recognized it and pushed him to excel.

Excitement **coursed** like a fever through the narrow century-old corridors of Penrose Road School the day they heard James Ogori was coming back to see the end-of-term concert.

James Ogori was their ideal. He was living proof that even if you came from an area described as a '**sociologist's** nightmare' such as Penrose Road, you could make it. Success was not an impossible dream, but was waiting for anyone, whether black, white, brown or yellow, if they wanted it enough.

Who was Miss Smith?

James owed it all to Miss Smith. He'd said that on television on more than one occasion when he was being interviewed.

There weren't any specialist teachers at Penrose Road School. Miss Smith was Class XI's Form Teacher. **Painstakingly**, she **imparted** the mysteries of spelling and sums, and taught them how to draw and read stories. She also took the whole school for musical movement and drama. It was then that Miss Smith came into her own.

In her black **leotard** and tights, she stood before the rows of children on the creaking boards of the hall, like a tiny **beacon**,[1] back arched, arms outstretched and willed, **coaxed**, practically hypnotised them to dance.

And they responded. They hung their arms out like branches in a wind, kicked their legs, swung their hips and forgot they would not be eating lunch and Mum wouldn't be home till eight o'clock that night when the factory shift finished.

What did it matter if they couldn't remember their three times table or thought 'cough' ended with an 'f'? They moved to the music on Miss Smith's record player and pretended they were butterflies or gazelles or whatever she wanted them to be.

James Ogori was nine when he came to Penrose Road School and it was obvious straight away that he was special. There was more zest in his movements, more rhythm in his steps. It wasn't just with his body that he was dancing, but with his mind and heart too.

The better you were, the more demanding Miss Smith was. Her brown-gray hair was cropped short; her skin was waxy and colourless. But her eyes were bright, cornflower blue and they glared at James Ogori, willing him to do the impossible.

Literary term

1. This is a **simile**. Just as a beacon guides people on a dark road, Miss Smith too showed her students the way forward by bringing out the best in them.

coursed: flowed

sociologist: someone who formally studies the way society is organised

painstakingly: carefully

imparted: passed on knowledge to others

leotard: a one-piece garment worn by dancers

beacon: a light placed in order to guide vehicles or to act as a signal

coaxed: persuaded by speaking gently

And sometimes it seemed he very nearly did, leaping to fantastic heights, taking unbelievable strides.

When he danced, bare from the waist up, he would glisten with oily perspiration and someone said he looked like a black pearl. The name stuck.

Miss Smith had Mrs Ogori come to the school and asked if James could be sent to dancing lessons. But with four sons and a husband to support, Mrs Ogori couldn't raise an extra shilling. So Miss Smith herself paid to send James to a good dancing school on Saturday mornings.

At first, the posh students in their **immaculate** clothes and special shoes laughed at James Ogori in his shorts and bare feet. But they didn't laugh when they saw him dance.

Like everyone else, when he turned eleven, the Black Pearl had to leave Penrose Road School and go to **Comprehensive** School. That year, they did *West Side Story* for the end-of-term concert and James played the leader of the Puerto Rican gang.

Why did Miss Smith pay for James' dance lessons?

You'd have thought his performance was a sort of 'thank you' to Miss Smith. He danced like magic and the glittery dust of that magic touched the rest of the cast too. They danced and sang like stars.

Mrs Ogori shed more than a few tears when she saw her son dance and sing so beautifully; her husband felt an **unaccustomed** lump of pride in his throat.

Only Miss Smith calmly thanked the audience for coming and refused to let anybody take a bow by themselves. But the children knew Miss Smith and could tell she was pleased with them.

Did You Know? G.K.

West Side Story is a musical drama inspired by Shakespeare's *Romeo and Juliet*. It is set in New York and is about the rivalry between two teenage street gangs.

There was never another end-of-term concert like *West Side Story*.

James did his five years at the Comprehensive and his dad pleaded with him to go on to university. But firmly, James refused.

immaculate: neat and tidy

Comprehensive: (here) public school

unaccustomed: unfamiliar

Mrs Ogori went to see Miss Smith. 'He wants to go to London and on the stage,' she said, frightened for her baby.

James had never gone back to see Miss Smith, but she was not the slightest bit hurt. He would come one day, in his own good time.

Now she answered Mrs Ogori. 'He will never let you down. Let him go to London if that's what he wants. It's what he was born for.'

In London, James was quickly picked out of the **chorus line** of some second-rate show and given a solo part. Then, he got a larger part in a better show, until at nineteen he was cast in a revival of *West Side Story*, in the very same role that he'd played in school years ago.

He was on his way to the top. A famous songwriter had written a rock version of *Othello* specially for James Ogori. It was a tremendous success in London. The show had gone to New York where James had been **feted** and adored.

Someone had **resurrected** the nickname and there he was on the cover of smart magazines and Sunday colour supplements, 'The Black Pearl' **blazoned** underneath.

Now, decided Miss Smith, he will come and see me. He's reached the very top of his career. There is talk of more ambitious shows and films, but he will never be greater than he is today.

Did You Know? G.K.

Othello is a tragedy by William Shakespeare.

Godspell is a musical created by Stephen Schwartz, based on a book by John-Michael Tebelak.

It was no surprise when the headmaster told her one morning, 'I've had a letter from James Ogori—well, from his agent, actually. He's coming back for the end-of-term concert.'

This year it was *Godspell* and Miss Smith told everyone that on no account must they be nervous because of James Ogori.

During the show, James sat in front with his mother. Mr Ogori had come too, along with one of the brothers who was James's manager.

What did the headmaster receive?

When the headmaster came onto the stage and gestured to their guest to join them, everyone cheered and clapped. James came onto the stage holding something glittery in his hands. He went up to Miss Smith and slipped it over her head. It was a fragile chain on which hung a delicate shell and nestling inside it—a black pearl.

She looked down at the jewel. She was **greyer**, more lined. Her ex-pupil towered above her, slim and powerful. He held out his arms.

chorus line: a group of performers who sing and dance in a musical show

feted: praised

resurrected: revived

blazoned: decorated with a design or words

greyer: (here) older

'They're going to dance!' someone murmured.

But as James moved her gently backwards, she whispered urgently, 'No!'

He looked startled. There was a note of near desperation in her voice.

'Miss Smith,' he said quietly so only she could hear, 'one of the ambitions of my life has been to dance with you. I was never good enough till now.'

Miss Smith gave a rare smile, but it was tinged with anxiety. There was no alternative now. She had to tell him. The audience was silent, wondering what was being said up there.

'I can't dance, James,' she whispered hoarsely. 'I've got two left feet. I'm clumsy, uncoordinated. All I can do is make other people dance.'

She watched him, waiting for disappointment. But James Ogori gave a huge grin. Laughing, he picked Miss Smith up and carried her to the stage piano where he sat her.

'I love you, Miss Smith,' he whispered, as he moved on to the stage to dance.

What was one of James' ambitions in life?

Did You Know? G.K.

'Black Pearl' was the name given to former Brazilian footballer Pele, considered to be one of the greatest footballers of all time.

About the author

Maureen Lee (1932-2020) was a British author who wrote over one hundred and fifty short stories. She also published historical romance novels, most of which are set in Liverpool, England. *Dancing in the Dark*, *Mother of Pearl*, and *Amy's Diary* are some of the novels written by her.

Comprehension

Quick Recap

A. Answer the questions.

1. Explain the term 'sociologist's nightmare'. Why was Penrose Road School described as such?
2. Describe Miss Smith's appearance.
3. What made Miss Smith believe that James Ogori was gifted?

4. How did James get the name 'Black Pearl'?
5. What role did Miss Smith play in honing James' talent?
6. When did Miss Smith think that James Ogori would return to see her? What made her believe so?
7. What did James Ogori gift Miss Smith? What did the gift stand for?
8. What startling revelation did Miss Smith make to James Ogori?
9. Give two examples of similes used in the story and explain them.

B. Answer the questions with reference to context.

1. *What did it matter if they couldn't remember their three times table or thought 'cough' ended with an 'f'?*
   a. Who are being referred to as 'they'? What did 'they' do in Miss Smith's musical movement class?
   b. How did Miss Smith encourage them? What else did she teach them?
   c. What do you know about their home lives?
   d. What does the quoted line say about their education?
2. *There was never another end-of-term concert like* West Side Story.
   a. When was the concert being referred to here held?
   b. Who did James Ogori play in the concert?
   c. What was special about the concert?
   d. What was the reaction of James' parents?
3. *'He will never let you down. Let him go to London if that's what he wants. It's what he was born for.'*
   a. Who is speaking and to whom in these lines?
   b. In response to what statement did she say these lines?
   c. What did 'he' want to do in London?
   d. What kind of success did he have in the city?
4. *Miss Smith told everyone that on no account must they be nervous because of James Ogori.*
   a. Where was James Ogori going to come and on what occasion?
   b. How did Miss Smith come to know of his arrival?
   c. Why would 'everyone' be nervous because of him?
   d. What did 'everyone' perform for the occasion?

Life Skills and Values teacher-student bond, looking beyond one's race

Think and answer.

1. What are the qualities that made Miss Smith a special kind of teacher?
2. How could Miss Smith be a good dance teacher even though she could not dance herself?
3. What does James' reaction to his teacher's confession tell us about him?

21st Century Critical Thinking

HC **Feelings:** gratitude and respect

Way with Words

Multiple Meanings of *Good*

Look at these sentences.

Miss Smith herself paid to send James to a **good** dancing school. (high quality)
He would come one day, in his own **good** time. (suitable)

The adjective **good** has various meanings depending on the context.

A. Choose the correct meaning of good for these sentences. One is done for you.

delicious | skilled | morally upright | dependable | kind | long | happy

1. She took her mind off work and got a **good** night's sleep. *long*
2. A **good** friend is one who stands by you through difficult times.
3. Madhu has always been **good** with computers. There is no code she cannot break.
4. It is **good** of you to come and visit me at the hospital.
5. The **good** food and pleasant company at the party made everyone feel very **good**.
6. My grandmother was a **good** woman who always tried to help those in need.

Homographs

Homographs are words that are spelt the same, but have different meanings and are sometimes pronounced differently.

Examples: take a **bow** (rhymes with 'now')
bow tie (rhymes with 'low')

B. Underline the homographs in these sentences. Then, write the word given in brackets which rhymes with each homograph.

1. The boy I live with has performed live on stage. (give/dive)
2. Can you lead us away from the harmful lead paint on the walls? (seed/head)
3. The blessed saint blessed his faithful followers. (ragged/dressed)
4. A minute is a minute unit of time. (flute/linnet)
5. When she saw the tear in her favourite dress, she burst into tears. (pear/near)

C. Make sentences with these words and phrases from the story.

1. impart
2. plead with
3. inspiration
4. feted
5. hypnotised
6. let someone down
7. revival
8 have two left feet

Grammar in Use

Simple, Compound and Complex Sentences

Look at this sentence.

James owed it all to Miss Smith.

It has a subject (**James**) and a verb (**owed**).

A **simple sentence** is one which contains only one finite verb and one independent clause.

Now, look at this sentence.

She imparted the mysteries of spelling and sums, and taught them how to draw and read stories.

It contains the following clauses:

1. she imparted the mysteries of spelling and sums
2. she taught them how to draw and read stories

Both clauses have a verb and a subject. They make complete sense by themselves and are joined by the coordinating conjunction 'and'.

Sentences that contain two or more independent clauses joined by coordinating conjunctions are called **compound sentences.**

Finally, look at this sentence.

James Ogori was nine when he came to Penrose Road School.

'James Ogori was nine' is the main clause since it expresses complete meaning by itself and can stand on its own. The subordinate clause is 'he came to Penrose Road School' since it does not make complete sense and, therefore, cannot stand on its own. They are joined by the subordinating conjunction 'when'.

A **complex sentence** is one which contains one main clause and one or more subordinate clauses. The clauses are joined using subordinate conjunctions or relative pronouns.

A. Write whether the following sentences are simple (S), compound (C) or complex (CO) sentences. Underline the independent clauses in the compound and complex sentences.

1. Raj invited us for his birthday party and all of us attended it. ☐
2. My mother smiled brightly at me. ☐
3. If everyone agrees, we will plan the picnic for Sunday. ☐
4. Anju said she might get her brother a gift or take him out for a film. ☐
5. Mrs Sen, who taught us geography, retired last April. ☐
6. Sid doesn't need a new bike, nor does he need another vacation. ☐
7. Who took the last cookie from the jar? ☐
8. I want to go to Seema's house, but it's raining cats and dogs. ☐
9. Although Mala was sick, she came for football practice. ☐

Transformation of Sentences

Look at these sentences.

The Black Pearl had to leave Penrose Road School. He had to go to Comprehensive School.
The Black Pearl had to leave Penrose Road School **and** go to Comprehensive School.

The two simple sentences have been joined to form a compound sentence by using the coordinating conjunction **and**. Simple sentences can be joined by using coordinating as well as correlative conjunctions to form compound sentences.

Now, look at these sentences.
Mrs Ogori saw her son dance so beautifully. She shed more than a few tears.
Mrs Ogori shed more than a few tears **when** she saw her son dance so beautifully.
The two simple sentences have been joined to form a complex sentence by using the subordinating conjunction **when**.
To join two simple sentences into a complex one, we can also convert one of them into a subordinate clause, while the other is used as the main clause in the sentence.

Examples: James was coming to see Miss Smith. It was no surprise. (simple)
<u>That James was coming to see Miss Smith</u> was no surprise. (complex)
The show had gone to New York. James had been feted there. (simple)
The show had gone to New York <u>where James had been feted</u>. (complex)

B. Combine the following simple sentences to form compound and complex sentences.

1. John Keats was a talented poet. He died at a young age.
2. I have informed the authorities. They have taken action.
3. I was very hungry after school. I went to a nearby shop to buy a cupcake.
4. John admitted hesitantly. He was guilty.
5. Subhash does not like cricket. Subhash does not like watching films.
6. He should not have sweets. He has them every day on his way home.
7. The tiger is wounded. The tiger is in pain.
8. The soldier was hurt. He was waiting to be rescued.

Adjective Clause

Subordinate clauses are of three main types: **adjective clause**, **noun clause** and **adverb clause**. They are classified depending on the function they perform. We will discuss the adjective clause in this chapter.

An **adjective clause** performs the function of an adjective in a sentence. It modifies the noun in the main clause. It begins with a relative pronoun (**who**, **whom**, **whose**, **that**, **which**) or **when**, **where** or **why**.

An adjective clause answers the questions *who?* or *which?* in relation to the noun it qualifies, and it is always placed close to the noun it describes.

Example: The day <u>that James Ogori came to see her</u> was Miss Smith's happiest.

In this sentence, 'that James Ogori came to see her', tells us more about the noun, 'day' in the main clause.

C. Underline the adjective clauses in these sentences and mention the nouns they qualify.

1. The mansion, which is situated on the banks of the river, was built by a *zamindar*.
2. He would come on the day that he was ready.
3. Miss Smith gave a rare smile, which was tinged with anxiety.
4. The Mughal dynasty, which was in power for about 400 years, built some of the most magnificent monuments in India.
5. This is the site where the new hotel is going to be built.
6. The boy, who is wearing pink pyjamas, is the new boarder.

D. Complete the following sentences with adjective clauses.

1. That is the book ...
2. She is the girl ...
3. They are the people ...
4. The students ... were rewarded.
5. Indians ... are praiseworthy.
6. The man ... is a famous author.

Study Skills

Use Your Dictionary

You know that an **abbreviation** is a shortened form of a word.

Examples: Mr (mister), AC (air conditioner), MP (Member of Parliament)

A. Using your dictionary, write the full forms of the abbreviations in Column A. Then, match them with the place where you would find them being used in Column B.

Abbreviations	Used in
1. CFC	a. on an academic certificate
2. BP	b. on a letter or an envelope
3. B.Sc.	c. on an aerosol can
4. C/O	d. on a tombstone
5. RIP	e. on a medical certificate

An **acronym** is an abbreviation formed with the first letters of a group of words. It can be pronounced as a word.

Examples: NATO (North Atlantic Treaty Organization)
UNICEF (United Nations International Children's Emergency Fund)

B. Consult your dictionary to find the full forms of the following acronyms.

1. laser 2. scuba 3. FAQ 4. radar 5. ASAP 6. RAM

Listening and Speaking

Listen to a conversation in which a teacher encourages a new student to develop his talent. Then, in pairs, write and enact an imaginary conversation between Miss Smith and James Ogori when they meet for the first time. You can use some of the phrases you hear during the conversation.

HC **Recognizing feelings and values:** guidance

Pen it Down

Do you have a favourite teacher? What are the qualities that make him or her your favourite? Imagining yourself as an adult, write a letter to your favourite teacher from your future self.

21st Century Creativity

You can include the following points in your letter:

- what you did after completing school
- the values and skills you learned from your teacher
- a memorable incident related to your teacher

Self Assessment

Now I can

- read a story about how a teacher helps a boy from an underprivileged background to follow his dreams.
- identify homographs, practise transformation of simple, compound and complex sentences, and use adjective clauses.
- distinguish abbreviations from acronyms, converse on a given topic, and write a letter.

Read More

The Miracle Worker: This play by William Gibson is based on the scholar and political activist, Helen Keller's autobiography, *The Story of My Life*. It portrays the relationship between the blind and deaf Keller and her teacher, Anne Sullivan.

To Sir, with Love: This autobiographical novel by E. R. Braithwaite is about an idealistic young teacher who strikes a chord with a group of rowdy students from underprivileged backgrounds through his novel approach to teaching.

Women in Sports

16
Unbreakable

M. C. Mary Kom

SUSTAINABLE DEVELOPMENT GOALS
5 GENDER EQUALITY

Let's Get Started

The United Nations Sustainable Development Goal 5 underlines the need to empower women and girls, and ensure their equal rights. We should start by breaking some myths attached to our homes and society.

Look at the pictures of a few such myths, and then read the related facts. Draw pictures to show your understanding of the facts. Then discuss in class ways to bring about these changes in your own families and communities.

ART INTEGRATION

MYTH: Only women should do household work.

FACT: Men and women should share household chores equally.

MYTH: Football is a man's sport, women are not strong enough for it.

FACT: Equal opportunities help develop talents regardless of gender.

MYTH: Girls should not go out at night alone.

FACT: Public spaces are meant for everyone.

HC **Feelings:** Feeling of confidence and usefulness due to participation

Reading

Mary Kom was born into great poverty in a village in Manipur. Through determination and a passion for boxing, she has become the best-known Indian woman boxer. In the Tokyo 2020 Olympics, she made her final appearance, as a member of the Indian boxing team. This extract, from her autobiography,* Unbreakable, *describes her attempt at winning the gold medal at the 2012 London Olympics. What do you think went through her mind as she fought her opponents?

At the Olympics. July 2012

I was on a flight to London. For years, I had dreamt of this moment; for months, I had thought of nothing else. Yet I did not fully know what to expect. I called my husband and sons. Onler, as always, spoke words of encouragement. My sons demanded to know where I was, then commanded me to come back soon with lots of goodies. I closed my eyes and prayed.

As the plane took off, I thought of Rengpa and Nainai. They might not understand what it was all about now, but when they grew up, they would know why their mother was missing in action so often in their childhood years.

At Heathrow, I felt as if I were a **matador** facing an angry bull. There were posters advertising the Games everywhere and I could feel my stomach fluttering with anticipation.

Charles was waiting for me in Liverpool. It was a relief to see his familiar face. We had planned on reaching early so that I could **acclimatise** to the British climate. While I was training, the local kids would often come to watch me. I felt **buoyed** by their excitement.

We practised at a boxing gym where Charles had arranged for **sparring** partners for me. By this stage, I needed to be comfortable sparring with anyone. I also mentally calculated my moves according to the opponents I thought I would meet.

Charles himself had come to be a father figure to me. While his technique and skills have improved me as a boxer tremendously, it is his love that I will always carry in my heart.

The days before the Olympics were devoted to training and rest. Even calls from my family were restricted to keep me free from stress. I spent time in prayer and meditation.

My physiotherapist, Dr Nikhil Latey, lifted my **morale** by

matador: bull fighter

acclimatise: become used to a new climate

buoyed: made to feel confident

sparring: boxing training without actually exchanging heavy blows

morale: self-confidence

Wordwise

'Matador', literally meaning 'killer' in Spanish, comes from the word, *matar*, which means 'to 'to kill'.

What did Mary's sons say to her?

Did You Know? G.K.

Bullfighting is a dangerous and cruel sport, in which a matador fights and kills a bull as part of a traditional public form of entertainment.

notches: levels

quelled: overcame

mantra: (here) motivational chant

hooks: short, hard blows, given with the elbows bent

stamina: strength that helps one do something over a long period

adrenalin: a hormone that increases blood circulation and boosts physical activity

predicted: said that something would happen in the future

many **notches** when he told me that I recovered faster from injuries than any athlete he'd come across.

A few days before the women's boxing events were to begin, I moved to the Olympic Games Village to stay with the Indian contingent. A day before my first bout, my husband and mother arrived in London. The very sight of them set my spirit soaring, as I prepared for the fight. I was ready for action.

When was Mary's first bout?

I also called my father. 'Apa, please pray for me. I have to play today.'

He assured me, 'Don't worry, I'm always praying for you. Sanahen, I am confident you will not come back empty-handed.'

My first bout on 5 August was against Karolina Michalczuk of Poland. It was a special day for me—the birthday of my twins. I was convinced that nothing would go wrong. I **quelled** my nervousness at the vastness of the stage—this was the Olympics, after all. I asked myself why I needed to be afraid. My opponents, like me, would have two hands, two feet and two eyes. As before every other bout, I repeated my magic **mantra**: 'I must win this bout, I must win, I must win.' With that silent prayer, I turned to my opponent.

She turned out to be very strong. It was like hitting a concrete wall. Caught unawares, at one point, I lost my footing and fell. But she lacked technique. I used skill and tactics, and drew upon my experience of facing such strong but raw boxers to counter her attacks. I flung **hooks** at her head and emptied every bit of reserve **stamina** I had. I won the bout decisively: 19-4. I declared to the Indian media there that this first win was a gift to my sons. It was the first hurdle crossed.

During the bouts, I could hear my supporters shouting, 'Mary Kom, Mary Kom'. It set my **adrenalin** flowing.

I had reached the semifinals. Yes, I wanted gold. But if nothing else, I would return home with a bronze medal. Like my father had **predicted**, I wouldn't return empty-handed.

With only a day of rest, I was up against Adams on 8 August. Adams had beaten me in the qualifiers. She was bigger and stronger than me, having worked her way down from a higher weight category to fight in the 51 kg class.

I knew that she had the advantage of height. Her reach was much better than mine. Being the shorter, smaller boxer, I did most of the attacking but try as I might, I could not get close enough to hit. Mentally, I was in good spirits and not afraid to face her. But physically, I wasn't in my best form. The first bout against Karolina had taken a toll on me. My body felt tight and stiff. My movements and my feet were slower than usual. I fought desperately, but she won 11-6. I was devastated but I also knew that I couldn't have tried harder, that I had left no stone unturned. I had given it my best. I had been honest with myself. I couldn't have done more.

ovation: applause

expended: spent money, time and energy on someone

podium: stage

When was Mary's next match and who was the opponent?

As I left the hall, the spectators gave me a standing **ovation**. I was humbled and moved. I knew that I would always remember these three bouts. But the curtains had come down on my Olympic run.

I really was sorry. After all the effort that had been **expended** on me, I felt I owed the country more than a bronze. I called my father and broke down on the phone. He was quiet for a while, then said, 'Look, my daughter, the gold is not your birthright. God gave you what you deserve. I am very happy you got an Olympic medal. Don't be discouraged. There will be other times. Be thankful for what you got.'

My coach, Charles, seconded that. He told the media later, 'I've watched that match several times and I can honestly say that Mary was the better fighter. Adams won because she fought defensively and did not pick a physical fight. Mary played the eventual gold medallist and didn't get a scratch on her.' This was balm to my soul.

Standing on the **podium** for the medal ceremony, my heart was almost bursting with pain. How I yearned for the gold and for the Indian national anthem to be played! I tried to smile for all the world to see, but couldn't help feeling that I had let my country down. But I consoled myself thinking that I would try again the next time.

The fact is that it took me days to realise that I was now an Olympic medallist—every sportsperson's dream. Suddenly, it felt like all the media attention was on me. It was more than I had expected or imagined.

As I flew back to India with Onler and my mother Anu, I thought of the many times I had walked out, leaving my sons behind, holding my chin up. It was worth the sacrifice, though, for I was returning with an Olympic medal. Some day, my boys will be old enough to understand, and I hope that they will be proud of me.

About the author

M. C. Mary Kom (1983–) is a six-time winner of the World Amateur Boxing Championship and is the only female Indian boxer to have qualified for the 2012 Olympics. She is also the only boxer to win eight World Championship medals. She was awarded the Padma Bhushan in 2013 and the Padma Vibhushan, in 2020.

Comprehension

Quick Recap

A. Answer the questions in a few lines.

1. What had Mary Kom dreamt of for many years?
2. By what name did Mary address her husband? What were the names of her children?
3. How did Mary feel about Charles?
4. What did Mary's physiotherapist tell her?
5. What reasons did Mary Kom give for losing the bout against Adams?
6. Mention two similes used in the passage and explain them.
7. What did Mary think as she flew back to India?

B. Answer the questions with reference to context.

1. *Charles was waiting for me in Liverpool. It was a relief to see his familiar face.*
   a. Who was Charles? Why was it a relief for Mary to see him?
   b. Why had they planned on reaching early?
   c. Who came to see Mary while she trained? How did Mary feel about their arrival?
   d. What kind of physical and mental preparation did Mary undertake?
2. *My first bout on 5 August was against Karolina Michalczuk of Poland. It was a special day for me ... I was convinced that nothing would go wrong.*
   a. Why was 5 August a special day for Mary?
   b. Why was she nervous? How did she quell her nervousness?
   c. What did Karolina lack during the fight? What did Mary use to defeat her?
   d. How did she commemorate the day before the Indian media?
3. *Standing on the podium for the medal ceremony, my heart was almost bursting with pain.*
   a. Which medal ceremony is being referred to here? What did Mary receive there?
   b. Why was Mary's heart bursting with pain?
   c. What advice had her father given her earlier?
   d. What was her coach's opinion about her performance?

Life Skills and Values sportsmanship, family support

Think and answer.

1. How does the story show Mary Kom to be 'unbreakable'?
2. Do you think Mary's family was supportive of her career? Substantiate your answer with examples from the passage.
3. How do we know that Mary was a loving mother?

HC **Feelings:** affection

Way with Words

A. Complete the sentences with these phrases from the passage. You may have to change the form of some of the words.

missing in action	like a father figure	curtains came down	draw upon experience
take a toll	leave no stone unturned	holding chin up	balm to the soul

1. Our team lost by a narrow margin, but we left the field ____________.
2. His bad eating habits have ____________ on his health.
3. My father ____________ as a former chef to invent new recipes.
4. India's cricket team ____________ in its preparations for the world championship.
5. Listening to her little daughter's voice was like a ____________ for Shalini after a long day at work.
6. Sahil is frequently absent from school and was ____________ during the picnic too.
7. Mahatma Gandhi was ____________ to Jawaharlal Nehru.
8. The ____________ on Mr Shah's diamond business the day he lost his investments in the stock market.

Expressions Related to Sports

B. There are several expressions we use commonly that have their origin in various sports. Match these expressions with the sport.

Expression	Sport
1. race against time	a. boxing
2. the ball is in your court	b. swimming
3. pack a punch	c. cricket
4. keep one's head above water	d. golf
5. be on a sticky wicket	e. wrestling
6. bite the dust	f. athletics
7. tee-off	g. tennis

Grammar in Use

Noun Clause

You know that there are three types of subordinate clauses: noun clauses, adverb clauses and adjective clauses. You studied the adjective clause in the last chapter. In this chapter, we will discuss the two other types of clauses.

A noun clause is a subordinate clause that performs the function of a noun in a sentence. It can be the subject, the object or the complement of the verb. It is introduced by the word *that*, and relative pronouns like *what*, *why*, and others.

Noun clauses also start with words like *how, whatever, when, where, if, whether, which, whichever, who, whoever, whom*, and *whomever.*

Examples: It is certain that India will qualify for the finals in this tournament.
That she would win a medal was a promise she made to herself.

In the first sentence, the noun clause is the object. In the second one, it is the subject of the sentence. In some cases, the noun clause may come before the main clause.

A. Underline the main clause and circle the noun clause in each sentence.

1. I am sure that he will answer the questions truthfully.
2. She wondered why nobody was her friend.
3. That he is guilty is known to everyone.
4. I know why Shweta didn't come to school on Monday.
5. Scientists predict that we are heading for drastic climate changes.
6. Ruby forgot that she had dance classes after school.
7. I don't understand why you are not getting enough sleep.
8. Where the monk lives is a mystery.

Adverb Clause

An **adverb clause** is a subordinate clause that performs the function of an adverb. It modifies a verb, an adjective or another adverb.

There are four main types: adverb clauses of place, time, manner and reason.

An **adverb clause of place** tells us *where* the action was performed.
Examples: The lamb followed Mary wherever she went.
Do not go blindly where you are led.

An **adverb clause of time** tells us *when* the action was performed.
Examples: The doctor arrived as soon as the nurse messaged him.
She will come after we have finished lunch.

An **adverb clause of manner** tells us *how* the action was performed.

Examples: He ran as if he had seen a ghost.

She danced the way a princess would.

An **adverb clause of reason** tells us *why* the action was performed.

Examples: We did not go for the picnic because it had started raining.

She spoke up for her friend as she believed in her innocence.

B. Underline the adverb clauses in these sentences and state their types. Circle the main clauses.

1. We came back after finishing our meal at the restaurant.
2. Olympic silver medallist Ravi Dahiya started wrestling seriously after he turned ten.
3. She sang as beautifully as Begum Akhtar.
4. The soldiers went where their commander asked them to.
5. He walked as if he had a stone tied to his leg.
6. Since she was hungry, she decided to make herself a quick snack.
7. There was chaos when the lockdown was announced.
8. Can you tell me where I can buy a bouquet of flowers?

Study Skills

Use Your Dictionary

English has borrowed words from many languages. Words of Greek origin are easy to recognize because of the way in which they are spelt.

The /f/ sound is spelt with **ph-**. **Examples:** philosophy, phase

The /k/ sound is spelt with **ch-**. **Examples:** chorus, character

There is a silent 'p' in words that start with the /s/ sound. **Examples:** psychology, psychic

A. Use your dictionary to find three words with each of the above spellings and write what they mean.

B. The word photo is of Greek origin. Use your dictionary to find out five words that include the word photo and write what they mean.

Listening and Speaking

Listen to a conversation between a cricketer and an interviewer after the former scores a century in a match.

Then, work in pairs to enact an interview with a sportsperson representing another sport.

You can use the following points:

- difficulties faced during a tournament/match
- the turning point in the match
- whether anything could have been done differently/better

Pen it Down

Look at this picture and write two paragraphs on it.

You can include the following points :

- what the picture signifies
- which sport is being shown, and how it can be made more popular
- the presence of women in sports and why they should be encouraged
- people's awareness about both the sport and the achievements of the sportswoman

Self Assessment

Now I can

- admire the spirit of sportsmanship and the courage of the author.
- appreciate the sacrifices made when working towards a goal.
- use expressions related to sports, and identify noun and adverb clauses.
- pronounce words of Greek origin correctly, enact an interview, and write a composition on a picture.

Read More

Koni: This book by Moti Nandi is about Koni, a talented swimmer, who lives in the slums. Her coach pushes her to overcome the odds and win a swimming competition.

The Loneliness of the Long Distance Runner: This story by Alan Sillitoe is about a poor English teenager, who is sent to a prison school after he robs a bakery. He seeks comfort in his talent for long-distance running.

ramatic
nologue

17

At the Theatre: To the Lady Behind Me

A. P. Herbert

Let's Get Started

ART INTEGRATION

A. Match the different styles of theatre to their names correctly. Use the clues given to help you with the answers. Then research and find out the countries from which each kind of theatre originates.

1. 	a. **Pantomime** – a comedy show using music and movements rather than words to tell a story
2. 	b. **Noh** – one of the oldest forms of theatre which uses masks, costumes and various props in a dance-based performance
3. 	c. **Opera** – a kind of theatre in which music takes centre-stage and some of the dramatic roles are played by singers
4. 	d. **Kathakali** – a form of theatre that uses elaborately colourful make-up, costumes and face masks and tells stories form Hindu mythology

B. Read this brief review of a play. Identify the words/phrases that comment on

- the scenery/background
- the actors and the clothes worn by them
- the organisation and guidance given
- the illusions and technology used
- the overall response

We went to see a new production of The Lion King *last night. The sets were innovative, the special effects were stunning, and the costumes looked spectacular. Every member of the cast played their parts well under the masterful guidance of the director. The audience gave a standing ovation and the newspapers carried rave reviews.*

HC **Learning and Awareness:** Evaluating our assumptions and about life and situations around us

Reading

Have you watched a film in a hall where someone gave away the plot through their loud comments? How did you feel? Read a poem about a similar incident, in which the speaker uses a polite tone to express his anger.

Dear Madam, you have seen this play;
I never saw it till today.
You know the details of the plot,
But, let me tell you, I do not.
The author seeks to keep from me
The murderer's identity,
And you are not a friend of his
If you keep shouting who it is.
The actors in their funny way
Have several funny things to say,
But they do not amuse me more
If you have said them just before;
The **merit** of the drama lies,
I understand, in some surprise;
But the surprise must now be small
Since you have just **foretold** it all.
The lady you have brought with you
Is, I **infer**, a **half-wit** too,
But I can understand the piece
Without assistance from your niece.[1]
In short, dear woman, it would suit
Me just as well if you were **mute**;
In fact, to make my meaning plain,
I trust you will not speak again.
And—may I add one human touch?—
Don't breathe upon my neck so much.

merit: the quality that deserves praise

foretold: said what would happen later

infer: conclude

half-wit: idiot

mute: silent

Who is called a half-wit?

Literary term

1. This is an example of **irony**. The speaker seems to be saying politely that he does not need the niece's help. But he is actually very angry and wants the niece to stop talking.

About the poet

A. P. Herbert (1890–1971) was an English novelist and playwright who was known for his humorous writings. He often used satire as a tool in his works. *Ballad of the Broadbrows* and *Less Nonsense!* are some of the popular books written by him.

Comprehension

Quick Recap

A. Answer the questions in a few lines.

1. Why was the speaker annoyed?
2. What kind of play was the speaker watching? Write the three elements that it consisted of.
3. Why was the speaker annoyed with the niece?
4. What were the two things that the speaker asked the lady to do?
5. Where was the speaker sitting, with respect to the talkative lady? How do you know?

B. Answer the questions with reference to context.

1. *Dear Madam, you have seen this play;/I never saw it till today.*
   a. Who do you think the speaker is? Who is being addressed as 'Madam'?
   b. How was the speaker aware that she knew the details of the plot?
   c. Why did the speaker say later that the lady was not a friend of the author of the play?
2. *The merit of the drama lies,/I understand, in some surprise;*
   a. In what did the 'merit of the drama' lie?
   b. How did the lady's actions affect the merit of the drama?
   c. Explain the irony in these lines.

Life Skills and Values — irony, social etiquette

Think and answer.

1. What kind of a person do you think the speaker is?
2. How is the tone of the speaker different from what he is actually saying?
3. Is there a change or increase in the degree of emotion in the poem? When does it occur?
4. Describe the lady and her niece. Do you think their behaviour is appropriate for the place they are in?

21st Century Social Skills

Way with Words

Idioms with *Play*

The word 'play' refers to a dramatic performance in the poem. It is also used idiomatically very often.

A. Match these idioms with play with their meanings.

Idiom	Meaning
1. play for time •	• a. try to defeat someone by tricking them to make a mistake
2. play at something •	• b. do something dangerous or risky
3. play with fire •	• c. pretend
4. play it cool •	• d. keep calm and not show emotion
5. play cat and mouse with •	• e. delay the result of an activity to gain advantage

Collective Nouns

In the poem, the play is also referred to as a 'piece'. This word is also used as a collective noun, such as *a piece of cake*, *a piece of advice* and *a piece of furniture*.

B. Complete the sentences with the collective nouns given in the box.

bulb	clump	wealth
cast	department	lump

1. Anna offered a ______________ of sugar to the horse.
2. The captured spy provided the investigators with a ______________ of information.
3. Add a ______________ of garlic to the curry before taking it off the flame.
4. The ______________ of experienced actors put up an excellent show.
5. The frightened rabbit ran into a ______________ of bushes.
6. The ______________ of education is developing a new policy for underprivileged children.

Grammar in Use

Adverb Phrases

You know that phrases are groups of words that form part of a sentence but do not make complete sense by themselves.

Adverb phrases, like adverbs, modify or describe verbs. They answer the questions *how, where, when, how often* and *why* something happened.

Examples: The audience watched the play **with great amusement.**
The poet had not seen the play **till that day.**

A. Underline the adverb phrases in these sentences.

1. After the game, the king and the pawn go into the same box.
2. You cannot go anywhere near the house after sundown.

3. He always sings on a lower scale.
4. He fired his gun without thinking of the consequences.
5. He will be back in office after the end of the match.
6. The princess lay on a velvet bed.

Transformation of Sentences with Adverb Phrases

Look at these sentences.

The actors said their lines **funnily**.

The actors said their lines **in a funny manner**.

Both the sentences mean the same. In the second sentence, the adverb **funnily** is replaced with the adverb phrase **in a funny manner**. This is how we can transform sentences with adverb phrases.

B. Replace the adverb phrases in these sentences with adverbs that mean the same.

1. She got out of bed in a sleepy manner.
2. Amar waited in silence for the sun to come up.
3. Do you know anyone who is free at this moment to take up the project?
4. At the end of a long day, Samuel walked home in a tired way.
5. It was at this spot that I had the accident.
6. The captain of the team gave his speech with confidence.

Transformation of Simple, Complex and Compound Sentences

You know that there are three types of sentences depending on the number and type of clauses in them. These are the simple, compound and complex sentences.

We can interchange simple and compound sentences in these ways:

- by adding a coordinating conjunction

Example: I trust you not to speak again. <simple>
I trust you **and** hope you will not speak again. <compound>

- by using infinitives

Example: The author plans **and** hides the murderer's identity from me. <compound>
The author plans **to hide** the murderer's identity from me. <simple>

- by using **having** + past participle

Example: The poet had already heard the plot and there was no surprise left. <compound>
Having heard the plot already, there was no surprise left for the poet. <simple>

We can interchange simple and complex sentences in these ways:

- by using non-finite verbs

Example: You are not a friend of his **if you keep shouting**. <complex>
You are not a friend of his **to keep** shouting. <simple>

- by changing one of the phrases into a clause

Example: You know the **details of the plot**. <simple>
You know **what the details of the plot are**. <complex>

- using **so... that**

Example: The lady should stay mute for the poet to enjoy the play. <simple>
The lady should stay mute **so that** the poet might enjoy the play. <complex>

We can interchange complex and compound sentences in these ways:

- by changing the coordinating conjunction to a subordinating conjunction

Example: You have seen this play, **but** I never saw it till today. <compound>
You have seen this play, **however** I have not till today. <complex>

- by changing the subordinate clause to a main clause

Example: **If you have said them just before**, they do not amuse me more. <complex>
They do not amuse me more **for you have just said them before**. <compound>

C. Rewrite the following sentences according to the instructions given in the brackets.

1. He was too excited to speak clearly. (rewrite without using 'too').
2. He was guilty and thought of running away. (rewrite without using 'and')
3. He like my suggestion for the project. (rewrite using 'suggested')
4. I spotted a beautiful lake in the middle of the valley. (rewrite using 'which')
5. The senators were biased and refused to agree with the speaker's point of view. (rewrite using 'enough')
6. Being down with fever, he could not go for the final match. (rewrite without the participle)
7. If you do not hurry, you will miss the flight. (rewrite without using 'if')
8. Rani believes that magical beings exist. (rewrite using 'existence')

Study Skills

Pronounce Well

Homophones are words with the same pronunciation, but which differ in meaning and may differ in spelling. **Homographs** are words with the same spelling, but with different meanings and pronunciations.

Look at the words in bold in each pair of sentences and say whether they are homophones or homographs.

1. We need more **flour** for the cake.
   Did you know about the carnivorous **flower** called the Venus Fly Trap?
2. The United States Congress meets in the **Capitol** Hill in Washington D.C.
   The **capital** of Brazil is Brasilia.
3. The ship is **close** to the harbour.
   Close the door to the laboratory, unless you want the passage to be filled with chemical fumes.
4. Remember to **wind** up the grandfather clock today.
   The answer, my friend, is blowing in the **wind**.
5. Clancy **moped** for days after she broke her favourite doll.
   In the 90s, my sister would ride to college on her red **moped**.

Listening and Speaking

A. Listen to the well-known humorous poem, 'You Are Old, Father William' by Lewis Carroll and complete the sentences.

1. In his youth, Father William had feared that ____________________. But now, he stood on his head again and again because ____________________.
2. Father William was extremely ____________________. But he had ____________________, which helped him do back somersaults even though he was old.
3. Father William was so weak that he could only eat ______. Yet he finished ____________________. The muscular strength of his jaw came from ____________________.
4. Father William could also balance an ____________________.
5. Father William asked his son not to ____________________. He warned that he would ____________________ if he did not leave.

B. Enact the poem in pairs, with one person playing Father William, and the other, his son.

Pen it Down

Describe an incident involving an annoying person you encountered one day. Remember to use humour to enliven your account. You can use the following points:

- how the person annoyed you
- how you dealt with the situation
- whether you learned anything from the encounter

Self Assessment

Now I can

- understand how a dramatic monologue reveals information about the speaker and listener in an indirect way.
- use collective nouns, understand adverb phrases and transform sentences using them, and also transform simple, compound and complex sentences.
- enact a poem and write a descriptive account.

Read More

The Owl and the Pussycat: This nonsense poem by Edward Lear is about an owl and a pussycat who journey to sea and marry in the land where 'the Bong tree grows'.

The Walrus and the Carpenter: In this satirical poem by Lewis Carroll, a walrus and a carpenter trick a group of oysters into taking a walk with them, only to eat them up afterwards.

18

Twelfth Night

William Shakespeare

Let's Get Started

Natural disasters like earthquakes, cyclones and floods leave unspeakable devastation in their trail. But they also culminate in new beginnings – when people pick up the pieces of their lives and make a fresh start. This is a sure testimony of the triumph of the human spirit.

Work in groups of four and carry out a survey in your immediate social environment. Ask any two individuals if they have faced such an event and how they managed to come out of it by starting anew. Your questionnaire may consist of the following points:

1. Name, age, occupation
2. Emergency/crisis faced – year, location, what happened
3. How the crisis was dealt with
4. Factors which aided their efforts
5. Factors which hindered their efforts

Once you have gathered the data, prepare a fact sheet which details all your findings. Present your fact sheet in class and discuss the important points.

HC **Learning and Awareness:** Understanding our desire for clarity and prosperity

Reading

Do you keep trying in the face of failure or do you give up soon? Act 1 Scene 1 of the play Twelfth Night *introduces the readers to Duke Orsino who thinks that he is very much in love with the Countess Olivia. He constantly tries to win the lady's heart, unfazed by her repeated rejections. In the next few scenes, Orsino meets Viola, in the guise of Cesario, who is the victim of a shipwreck. Cesario sets out to help Orsino win Olivia's heart, but in the process, leads to some unforeseen and*

entertaining complications. These scenes introduce some of the central characters of the play and lay the ground for the events to follow.

Characters

Viola, a shipwrecked young woman, disguised as a page named *Cesario*
A Sea Captain, a friend to Viola
Duke Orsino, Duke of Illyria
Valentine and Curio, gentlemen attending on the Duke
Olivia, a wealthy countess
Maria, Olivia's gentlewoman
Sailors
Attendants

Act 1, Scene 2
The seacoast

Enter ***Viola****, a Captain, and Sailors*

Viola What country, friends, is this?

Captain This is **Illyria**, lady.

Viola And what should I do in Illyria?
My brother he is in **Elysium**.
Perchance he is not drown'd: what think you, sailors?

Captain It is perchance that you yourself were saved.

Viola O my poor brother! and so perchance may he be.

Captain True, madam: and, to comfort you with chance,
Assure yourself, after our ship did split,
When you and those poor number saved with you
Hung on our driving boat, I saw your brother,
Most **provident** in peril, bind himself,
Courage and hope both teaching him the practise,
To a strong mast that lived upon the sea;
Where, like Arion on the dolphin's back[1],
I saw him hold acquaintance with the waves
So long as I could see.

Viola For saying so, there's gold:
Mine own escape unfoldeth to my hope,
Whereto thy speech serves for authority,
The like of him. Know'st thou this country?

Captain Ay, madam, well; for I was bred and born
Not three hours' travel from this very place.

Viola Who governs here?

Captain A noble duke, in nature as in name.

Viola What is the name?

Captain Orsino.

Literary term

1. This is an example of an **allusion**. It is a reference to Arion who was a Greek musician. He was thrown into the sea by pirates, but was saved by a dolphin who was charmed by his singing.

Illyria: ancient realm on the eastern coast of the Adriatic Sea

Elysium: (in Greek mythology) the place where the blessed live on after death

perchance: perhaps

provident: capable of foresight

Viola Orsino! I have heard my father name him:
He was a bachelor then.

Captain And so is now, or was so very **late**;
For but a month ago I went from hence,
And then 'twas fresh in murmur,—as, you know,
What great ones do the less will **prattle** of,—
That he did seek the love of fair Olivia.

Viola What's she?

Captain A virtuous maid, the daughter of a count
That died some twelvemonth since, then leaving her
In the protection of his son, her brother,
Who shortly also died: for whose dear love,
They say, she hath **abjured** the company
And sight of men.

Viola O that I served that lady
And might not be delivered to the world,
Till I had made mine own occasion **mellow**,
What my estate is!

Captain That were hard to **compass**;
Because she will admit no kind of suit,
No, not the duke's.

Viola There is a fair behaviour in thee, captain;
And though that nature with a **beauteous wall**
Doth oft close in **pollution**, yet of thee
I will believe thou hast a mind that suits
With this thy fair and outward character.
I prithee, and I'll pay thee **bounteously**,
Conceal me what I am, and be my aid
For such disguise as haply shall become
The form of my **intent**. I'll serve this duke:
Thou shall present me as an eunuch to him:
It may be worth thy pains; for I can sing
And speak to him in many sorts of music
That will allow me very worth his service.
What else may hap to time I will commit;
Only **shape** thou thy silence to my wit.

Captain Be you his eunuch, and your mute I'll be:
When my tongue blabs, then let mine eyes not see.

Viola I thank thee: lead me on.

Act 1, Scene 4

Duke Orsino's palace

Enter Valentine, Duke Orsino's attendant and Viola in man's attire

Valentine If the duke continue these favours towards you,
Cesario, you are like to be much advanced:
he hath known you but three days, and already you are no stranger.

Viola You either fear his humour or my negligence, that you call in question the continuance of his love.

Is he **inconstant**, sir, in his favours?

Valentine No, believe me.

Viola I thank you. Here comes the count.

Enter Duke Orsino, Curio, and Attendants

Duke Orsino Who saw Cesario, ho?

---

late: (here) recently
prattle: chatter
abjured: renounced
mellow: (here) better
compass: manage
beauteous wall: (here) outward appearance
pollution: (here) poisonous substances
bounteously: generously
intent: purpose
shape: fit, adapt
inconstant: fickle

Viola On your **attendance**, my lord; here.

Duke Orsino Stand you a while aloof, Cesario,
Thou know'st no less but all; I have **unclasp'd**
To thee the book even of my secret soul:
Therefore, good youth, address thy **gait** unto her;
Be not denied access, stand at her doors,
And tell them, there thy fixed foot shall grow
Till thou have audience.

Viola Sure, my noble lord,
If she be so abandon'd to her sorrow
As it is spoke, she never will admit me.

Duke Orsino Be **clamorous** and leap all **civil bounds**
Rather than make **unprofited** return.

Viola Say I do speak with her, my lord, what then?

Duke Orsino O, then unfold the passion of my love,
Surprise her with **discourse** of my dear faith:
It shall become thee well to act my woes;
She will **attend** it better in thy youth
Than in a **nuncio**'s of more grave aspect.

Viola I think not so, my lord.

Duke Orsino Dear lad, believe it;
For they shall yet **belie** thy happy years,
That say thou art a man: **Diana**'s lip
Is not more smooth and rubious; thy small pipe
Is as the maiden's organ, shrill and sound,
And all is **semblative** a woman's part.
I know thy **constellation** is right apt
For this affair. Some four or five attend him;
All, if you will; for I myself am best
When least in company. Prosper well in this,
And thou shalt live as freely as thy lord,
To call his fortunes thine.

Viola I'll do my best
To woo your lady:

Aside

Yet, a barful **strife**!
Whoe'er I woo, myself would be his wife.

Exeunt

Act 1, Scene 5

Olivia's house

...

(Viola visits Olivia's house, disguised as Cesario. She is refused entry at the gates, but is obstinate and refuses to leave until shown inside.)

attendance: at your service
unclaps'd: opened
gait: bearing
clamorous: noisy
civil bounds: good manners
unprofited: without any gains
discourse: language; account
attend it: pay better attention
nuncio: messenger, representative
belie: misrepresent
Diana: Goddess of the moon, huntress and protector of women
semblative: resembling
constellation: (here) character
strife: strong disagreement

Olivia Let him approach.

(to her gentlewoman, Maria)
Give me my veil: come, throw it o'er my face.
We'll once more hear Orsino's **embassy**.

Enter Viola, and Attendants

Viola The honourable lady of the house, which is she?

Olivia Speak to me; I shall answer for her. **Whence** came you, sir?

Viola I can say little more than I have studied, and that
question's out of my part. Good gentle one, give me
modest assurance if you be the lady of the house,
that I may proceed in my speech.

Olivia Are you a comedian?

Viola No, my **profound** heart: and yet, by the very fangs
of malice I swear, I am not that I play. Are you
the lady of the house?

Olivia If I do not **usurp** myself, I am.

Viola Most certain, if you are she, you do usurp
yourself; for what is yours to bestow is not yours
to reserve. But this is from my commission: I will
on with my speech in your praise, and then show
you the heart of my message.

Olivia Come to what is important in't: I forgive you the praise.

Viola Alas, I took great pains to study it, and 'tis poetical.

Olivia It is the more like to be **feigned**: I pray you,
keep it in. I heard you were **saucy** at my gates,
and allowed your approach rather to
wonder at you than to hear you. If you be
not mad, be gone; if you have reason, be
brief: 'tis not that time of
moon with me to make one in so skipping
a dialogue. Sure, you have some **hideous**
matter to deliver, when the courtesy of it is
so fearful. Speak your **office**.

Viola It alone concerns your ear. I bring no **overture** of
war, no **taxation** of **homage**: I hold the olive
in my hand; my words are as fun of peace as
matter.

Olivia Yet you began rudely. What are you? What would you?

Viola

The rudeness that hath appeared in me have I
learned from my entertainment. What
I am, and what I would, are as secret as
maidenhead; to your ears, **divinity**, to any
other's, **profanation**.

Olivia Give us the place alone: we will hear this divinity.

Exeunt Maria and Attendants

Now, sir, what is your text?

---

embassy: (here) agent
whence: from where
profound: deep
usurp: wrongfully take
commission: instruction
feigned: untrue
saucy: rude
hideous: ugly, revolting
office: (here) business
overture: declaration
taxation: imposition
homage: respect
divinity: like a holy message
profanation: an act of sacrilege

Viola Most sweet lady,—

Olivia A comfortable **doctrine**, and much may be said of it.
Where lies your text?

Viola In Orsino's bosom.

Olivia In his bosom! In what chapter of his bosom?

Viola To answer by the method, in the first of his heart.

Olivia O, I have read it: it is **heresy**. Have you no more to say?

Viola Good madam, let me see your face.

Olivia You are now out of your text: but we will draw the curtain and show you the picture.
Look you, sir, such a one I was this present: is't not well done?

Unveiling

Viola Excellently done, if God did all.

Olivia 'Tis in grain, sir; 'twill **endure** wind and weather.

Viola 'Tis beauty truly **blent**, whose red and white
Nature's own sweet and cunning hand laid on:
Lady, you are the cruell'st she alive,
If you will lead these **graces** to the grave
And leave the world no copy.

Olivia ... Were you sent hither to praise me?

Viola I see you what you are, you are too proud;
But, if you were the devil, you are fair.
My lord and master loves you: O, such love
Could be but **recompensed**, though you were crown'd
The **nonpareil** of beauty!

Olivia How does he love me?

Viola With adorations, fertile tears,
With ... sighs of fire[2].

Olivia Your lord does know my mind; I cannot love him:
Yet I suppose him virtuous, know him noble,
Of great estate, of fresh and stainless youth;
In voices well **divulged**, free, learn'd and valiant;
And in dimension and the shape of nature
A gracious person: but yet I cannot love him;
He might have took his answer long ago.

(Though Viola, dressed as Cesario, had come to persuade Olivia to respond to Duke Orsino's love for her, the scene ends with Olivia realising that she has, in fact, fallen in love with Cesario instead.)

doctrine: inspiring speech

heresy: belief or action that people think is wrong

endure: survive

blent: blended

graces: charms

recompensed: rewarded

nonpareil: peerless example

divulged: told

Literary term

2. This is an example of **hyperbole**. It shows how much Duke Orsino loves Olivia.

About the author

William Shakespeare (1564–1616) was an English playwright who is considered to be one of the greatest dramatists of all time. He wrote about 38 plays and 154 sonnets. His works have greatly influenced the English language and are performed around the world. His plays show a deep understanding of human nature. *Macbeth*, *King Lear* and *Romeo and Juliet* are among his best known plays.

Comprehension

Quick Recap

A. Answer the questions in a few lines.

1. Where did Viola and the captain land?
2. What did the captain say about Orsino to Viola?
3. Why would Viola not get employment with Olivia?
4. How did she plan to stay on in Illyria with the captain's help?
5. Why did Orsino feel that Olivia would pay more attention to Cesario than other messengers?
6. What did Olivia show Viola? What was the latter's reaction to it?

B. Answer the questions with reference to context.

1. *For saying so, there's gold:*
   Mine own escape unfoldeth to my hope,
   a. Who said these words and to whom?
   b. What prompted the speaker to reward the listener with gold?
   c. Explain what is meant by the phrase '*Mine own escape unfoldeth to my hope*'.
2. *I have unclasp'd*
   To thee the book even of my secret soul;
   a. Who said these words and to whom?
   b. Explain in your own words what the speaker meant by these lines.
   c. What specific instructions did he then give the listener?
3. *It is the more like to be feigned: I pray you,*
   keep it in. I heard you were saucy at my gates,
   a. Who is the speaker? What does she estimate to be 'feigned'?
   b. Who had been 'saucy' at her gates? Why had the person still been allowed to approach the speaker?
   c. What did the speaker ask the listener to do next?

Life Skills and Values understanding feelings, adaptability

Think and answer.

1. Make a character analysis of Viola, highlighting the qualities that help her survive even after being shipwrecked and losing her brother.
2. Why do you think the Duke trusted and confided in Cesario in such a short span of time? What was Cesario's role in this?
3. What estimate do you form of Duke Orsino's character? Do you believe he is really in love with Olivia?

HC Evaluating assumptions about relationships

Way with Words

Archaic Words

There are several words in the play which are in archaic English.
Examples: thee (you), **unfoldeth** (unfold)

A. Write the modern equivalents of these archaic words.

Word	Modern equivalent
1. 'twas	
2. thy	
3. hither	
4. doth	
5. hath	
6. 'tis	

Word	Modern equivalent
7. wherefore	
8. know'st	
9. oft	
10. aught	
11. e'er	
12. prithee	

B. The following words from the play have a different meaning today. Write the current meanings of these words. Then, write the meanings which they have in the play.

1. office 2. compass 3. mellow
4. constellation 5. suit 6. embassy

Grammar in Use

Direct and Indirect Speech

When we refer to the exact words of the speaker in a sentence, it is said to be in **direct speech**.

Example: Viola said to the Captain, 'What country, friends, is this?'

When we report what somebody said or thought in our own words, we use **indirect speech**.

Example: Viola asked the Captain what country that was.

Remember these points:

- In a sentence in direct speech, the words of the speaker always begin with a capital letter and are placed within inverted commas. The reporting verb is followed by a comma.
- In indirect speech, the comma following the reporting verb is replaced by **that**. The reporting verb **said** in direct speech changes to **told** in indirect speech. Inverted commas are not used. Question marks and exclamation marks are replaced by full stops (.).
- When the main verb in the sentence being reported is in the present tense, it is changed to past tense in indirect speech. When the main verb is in the simple past tense, it is changed to past perfect tense.

Example: Olivia said to Cesario, 'I **heard** you were saucy at my gates.' (simple past tense)
Olivia told Cesario that she **had heard** that he had been saucy at her gates. (past perfect tense)

- The pronouns and possessive adjectives in indirect speech change depending on the subject of the reporting verb.

For instance, in the above example, **I** has become **she**, **you** is changed to **he**, and **my** has changed to **her**.

Look at this table which shows the changes in the expressions of time and place, when we report direct speech.

Direct Speech	Indirect Speech
now	then
today	that day
tomorrow	the following day; the next day; the day after
here	there
ago	before
yesterday	the day before/the previous day
tomorrow	the next day/the day after/the following day
this/these	that/those

A. Rewrite the sentences according to the given instructions.

1. 'What an amazing sight!' (change to indirect speech)
2. 'Please don't leave me behind,' she said. (change to indirect speech)
3. 'What is Greenwich Mean Time?' (change to indirect speech)
4. He apologised for being late that evening. (change to direct speech)
5. She exclaimed with disgust that she would never travel with him again. (change to direct speech)

Look at the way a conversation can be rewritten in indirect form.

Direct speech

Olivia Yet you began rudely. What are you? What would you?

Cesario The rudeness that hath appeared in me have I learned from my entertainment. What I am, and what I would, are as secret as maidenhead; to your ears,divinity, to any other's, profanation.

Indirect speech

Olivia argued that Cesario began talking rudely. She asked him who he was and what he wanted.

Cesario replied that the rudeness that appeared in him, had been learned in jest. Who he was and what he wanted were meant for her only. He elaborated that his message was as secret as profane words were to the ears of divinity.

The reporting verbs used here are **argued**, **replied** and **elaborated**. They indicate the speakers' feelings and the tones used by them.

B. Rewrite the following according to the instructions.

1. **Olivia** Are you a comedian?

   Viola No, my profound heart. And yet by the very fangs of malice I swear I am not that I play. Are you the lady of the house?

   Olivia If I do not usurp myself, I am.

   (change to direct speech)
2. Then Opu said to the boy, 'They are real, aren't they?' 'I got them from the top branch of a very high tree and a very risky job it was. But I can't let you have them for less than two annas.' (change to indirect speech)
3. While shaking hands with his friend Trevor, Hughie exclaimed with a whisper that the model was amazing. Trevor shouted at the top of his voice and said that he thought so as well. Trevor added that such beggars were not to be met every day. He exclaimed that Rembrandt would have made a wonderful etching of him. (change to direct speech)

Listening and Speaking

A. Listen to a few conversations on people thanking each other. Now, imagine that Viola and the ship's captain speak modern day English. In pairs, write and enact the conversation where Viola thanks the captain for all his help.

21st Century Social Skills

You have studied about stress and intonation in an earlier chapter. The meaning of a sentence can change depending on the words we lay stress on. We can say the same sentence in different ways by stressing different words.

B. Listen to these sentences being read with varying intonation. Then, in pairs, read these sentences aloud, laying stress on the underlined words.

a. Are you a comedian?
   Are you a comedian?

b. Good madam, let me see your face.
   Good madam, let me see your face.
   Good madam, let me see your face.

C. Now, read the following sentences from the play aloud, with emphasis on the underlined words. Write the meaning of the sentence in each case.

1. As it is spoke, she never will admit me.
   As it is spoke, she never will admit me.
   As it is spoke, she never will admit me.

2. And what should I do in Illyria?
   And what should I do in Illyria?
   And what should I do in Illyria?

Pen it Down

A. Imagine you are a reporter for a local newspaper. Write a report, recounting the details of the shipwreck near the coast of Illyria. Include information about the passengers and the reason for the shipwreck. Your report should contain the following points:

- how the mishap took place
- a vivid description of the shipwreck
- the survivors
- testimonies from the captain and the onlookers

B. You read in the play that Viola's brother had been missing in the shipwreck. Create a 'missing' poster to help locate him. Include the following information:

- name
- any distinguishing feature
- whom to get in touch with
- description with height and weight
- the place where he was last seen

You may also mention a reward to make your poster noticeable.

Self Assessment

Now I can

- read a play and become familiar with Shakespearean language.
- observe the determination of a young shipwrecked girl and the affection developing between the central characters.
- understand archaic words, revise direct and indirect speech and practise reading sentences with varying intonation.
- write a report and create a 'missing' poster.

Read More

As You Like It: This comedy by Shakespeare tells the story of Rosalind who flees persecution in her uncle's court, accompanied by her cousin Celia to find safety and, eventually, love, in the Forest of Arden.

A Midsummer Night's Dream: This comedy by Shakespeare is about two couples who get involved in a series of misunderstandings once they enter an enchanted forest ruled by fairies. The confusion increases when a group of bumbling actors enters the woods to rehearse their play.

Research and Write

A. 'The Human Seasons' relates Nature to human life.

Haiku is a form of Japanese poetry, usually of three lines and describing a single idea. Read the following haiku by a Japanese poet.

The first cold shower
Even the monkey seems to want
A little coat of straw.

- *Matsuo Basho*

Now, write a haiku on any one of the following topics.

1. A windy morning while you are setting out for school.
2. A day when you have to study, but you wish to go out to play.
3. You are bored and wondering what to do.

B. 'The Invisible Man' and 'Miss Smith and the Black Pearl' are set in two different periods in history. While 'The Invisible Man' is set in Victorian London, the story of James Ogori is set in the contemporary world.

Read through both the texts again and note down details about the locations they are set in, the kind of clothes people wear and the way they talk. Do some research on the two time periods and write an essay on the similarities and differences between them.

C. You have read about Olympic medal winner Mary Kom in the text 'Unbreakable'. Research and fill in this table with relevant facts for each of these sportswomen who won Olympic medals for India.

Name	Sport	Medal	Age	Other awards	State they are from
1. P. V. Sindhu					
2. Chanu Saikhom Mirabai					
3. Lovlina Borgohain					
4. Saina Nehwal					
5. Sakshi Malik					
6. Karnam Malleswari					

Which of these sportswomen inspire you the most and why?

D. 'Twelfth Night' is a play written in the Elizabethan period. Research Elizabethan theatrical practices and write an essay about it.

ART INTEGRATION

You can explore the following points:

- the type of plays that were popular
- how theatres were often closed as a preventive measure against the plague
- the trend of young boys playing women
- the audience (noblemen and 'groundlings')

Literary Genres and Terms

Literary Genres

Literary narratives can be of various kinds based on their style and form. The following are some common types of narratives:

Prose

A **fantasy** is a story or novel which has a strange or other-worldly setting or characters. It often involves magic and supernatural creatures.

An **adventure** is a type of story or novel which has a lot of action and involves danger, risk and excitement.

Humour is a type of literature whose aim is to entertain people or make them laugh. A humorous story often has fun and excitement as its main elements.

A **fable** is a story about supernatural or extraordinary creatures, with a moral lesson at the end. In fables, animals, plants and non-living things often speak as humans.

A **fairy tale** is a story involving magical events and imaginary creatures like fairies, elves and goblins.

Science fiction is a type of story or novel about events set in the future or on other planets. They often involve future scientific progress, space, time travel and changes in the environment.

A **short story** narrates imaginary events and is usually only a few pages long.

A **folktale** is a story or myth handed down by word of mouth. Folk tales form part of the culture of a people, and can be based on superstitious beliefs.

A **legend** is a popular story about a particular person or place, handed down from earlier times and often believed to be true. A legend may be based on fact but may also include imaginary elements.

Mystery is a genre of fiction that deals with the solution of a crime or the uncovering of secrets.

Mythology includes traditional stories relating to gods which were once used by people for explaining various natural occurrences.

Non-fiction is a type of prose that is based on real events rather than imaginary ones.

An **autobiography** is an account of a person's life written by that person herself/himself.

A **biography** is the story of a person's life, written by someone else.

Horror is a type of story or a piece of writing which scares or startles the reader. A horror story creates a frightening atmosphere and often has supernatural themes and characters, like ghosts, witches and vampires.

A **parable** is a short story that teaches a moral lesson. Some of the best-known parables are the ones Jesus Christ told his disciples. Unlike fables, the characters in a parable are human beings.

Wildlife literature is writing related to the way animals and birds live in their natural habitat.

A **travelogue** is an account of a place a traveller has visited. It gives a glimpse into the life and culture of people who live in other — often remote — parts of the world.

An **allegory** is a narrative with two levels of meaning. The events and characters in the plot stand for abstract ideas and principles. An allegory usually aims to teach a moral lesson.

A **novel** is a long prose narrative that deals with human experiences in an imaginative way. It has a plot which charts the journeys of its various characters, and also explores their personalities in detail.

Poetry

A **lyric poem** is a short poem whose main purpose is to express emotions or a state of mind. It does not depict actions or events, as narrative poems do.

A **narrative poem** is a type of verse which tells a story. It often has the voices of the characters in the story, along with the narrator's voice.

Light verse is humorous poetry, usually dealing with playful themes and aimed at amusing the reader. It often uses literary devices, such as puns and alliterations.

A **nonsense poem** is a light-hearted, rhyming poem, often for young people, with peculiar characters in unusual situations or an unusual way of describing everyday things.

Free verse is a type of poetry which does not have a rhyme scheme. It is often written in the way people speak in daily life.

A **ballad** is a narrative poem that tells a story through dialogue and actions and is often set to music. They were originally written for dances.

A **sonnet** is a form of poetry consisting of fourteen lines. The first stanza, called octet, has eight lines and the second stanza, called sestet, has six lines.

A **dramatic monologue** is a poem in the form of a speech by a single character. The speech reveals his/her inner thoughts and feelings. The presence of other characters is revealed only when the narrator addresses them.

Drama

Drama is a type of literature that narrates a story which is meant to be acted out for an audience. There are two main types of drama: tragedy and comedy.

A **tragedy** is a play in which the central character faces misfortune and disaster. It often ends with the death or downfall of the character.

A **comedy** is a play with a light or humorous tone where the characters overcome difficult circumstances in the end. A comedy may not always be about amusing people or incidents.

Literary Terms

Writers use various techniques to convey the meaning to their readers. These techniques are called literary devices. The following are some of the literary terms you have come across in the book:

A **simile** is a figure of speech in which someone or something is compared to a very different person or thing using 'as' or 'like'. **Example:** He is as brave as a lion.

A **metaphor** is a figure of speech in which a person or thing is compared to another, otherwise unrelated person or thing by stating that they are the same in a particular way. **Example:** She is a rose.

Personification is a way of imagining non-living things or abstract ideas as human beings with thoughts, actions and emotions. **Example:** The moon danced over the water.

Alliteration is a figure of speech in which the same consonant sound is repeated in consecutive or closely-placed words in the same sentence. **Example:** Slithering snakes slither silently through the grass.

Onomatopoeia is the use of words whose pronunciation is similar to the sounds they represent. **Example:** honk, bang, buzz.

Exclamation is a figure of speech which is used to draw attention to something in a way that a simple statement cannot. It is used to express surprise, strong emotion or pain.
Example: How tall the mountain is!

Irony is a figure of speech in which the real meaning is exactly the opposite of what is said. **Example:** Oh, what a lovely day! (said when it is cold and raining).

A **pun** is a literary device which plays on the different meanings of the same word, or the similar sound of different words, to produce a humorous effect. **Example:** Without geometry, life is pointless.

A **rhetorical question** is a question to which no answer is expected. It is asked in order to encourage the listener to consider a message or a viewpoint. **Example:** 'Aren't you ashamed of yourself?'

Hyperbole is a figure of speech in which the writer makes something sound bigger or more impressive than it really is. **Example:** 'I told you a thousand times!'

Euphemism is a literary device in which an unpleasant thing or sensitive topic is described in a way that makes it more acceptable. **Example:** 'He passed away.' is a euphemistic way of saying 'He died.'

A **run-on line** is a literary device used in poems in which a sentence continues on to the next line. The full meaning of the sentence can be understood only by reading the two lines together. **Example:** Lord, please give some sense of direction to this beetle/Who keeps blundering through the open window/And falling into the goldfish bowl.

Imagery is a literary device in which descriptive language is used to help the reader imagine the world described in the narrative. It appeals to the five senses. **Example:** A burning forehead, and a parching tongue.

Repetition is a literary device where the same word or phrase is repeated at intervals to give stress on a particular idea. **Example:** But I have promises to keep, / And miles to go before I sleep, / And miles to go before I sleep.